THE CONVERSATIONS

THE CONVERS

Walter Murch and th

ALFRED A. KNOPF NEW YORK 2002

IONS

rt of Editing Film

Michael Ondaatje

This is a Borzoi Book Published by Alfred A. Knopf

Material on page xviii is from a conversation between Walter Murch and Michael Ondaatje,
hosted by Muriel Murch, on the art of editing in film and literature. The conversation was
recorded at KPFA Radio 94.1 FM in Berkeley, California, with recording engineer Jim Ben-
nett. This programme was first aired on KPFA on March 26, 1997. An edited version can be
read in *Projections 8,* published by Faber and Faber, London, 1998.

Library of Congress Cataloging-in-Publication Data
Ondaatje, Michael.
    The conversations: Walter Murch and the art of editing film/Michael Ondaatje.—1st ed.
p.cm.
ISBN 0-375-41386-3
1. Murch, Walter, 1943—Interviews. 2. Motion picture editors—United States—Interviews.
3. Motion pictures—Editing. I. Murch, Walter, date II. Title.
TR849.M86 O53 2002
778.5'35—dc21
                                                                2002021526

Manufactured in the United States of America

First American Edition

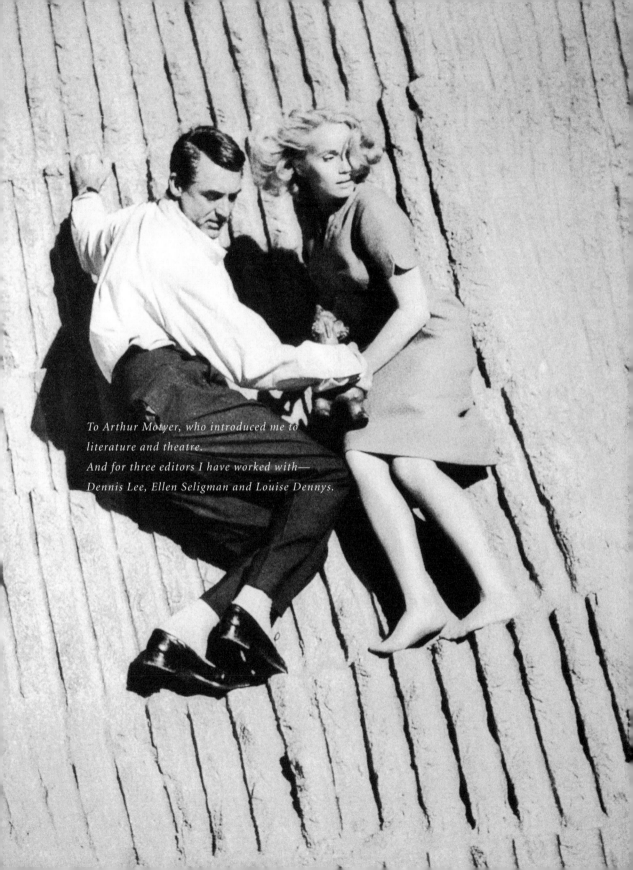

*To Arthur Motyer, who introduced me to
literature and theatre.
And for three editors I have worked with—
Dennis Lee, Ellen Seligman and Louise Dennys.*

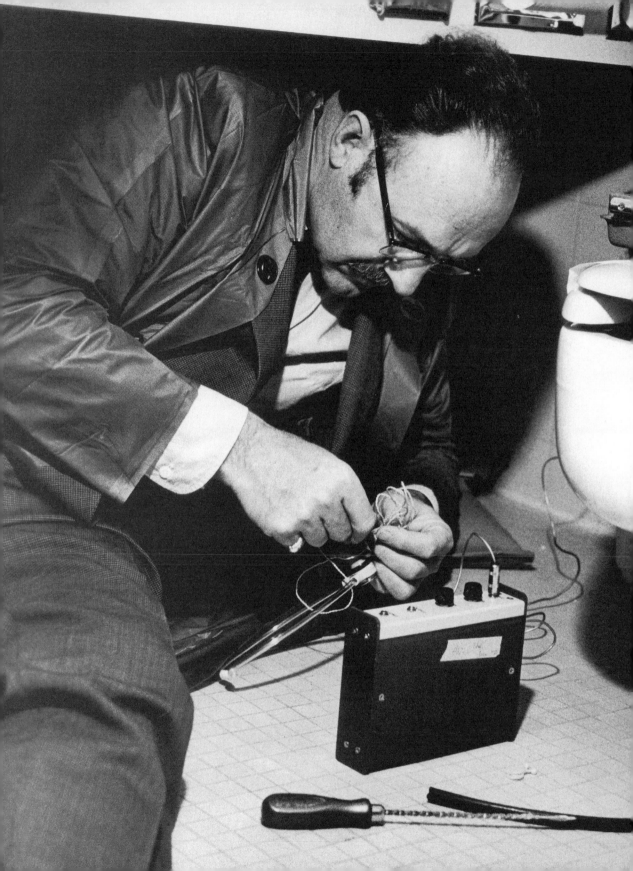

"Harry, tell him about the time you put the bug in the parakeet."

—*The Conversation*

"Film editing is a wonderful arcane art, like mosaics. I love to watch it being done, but they of course hate to be watched."

—Donald E. Westlake

CONTENTS

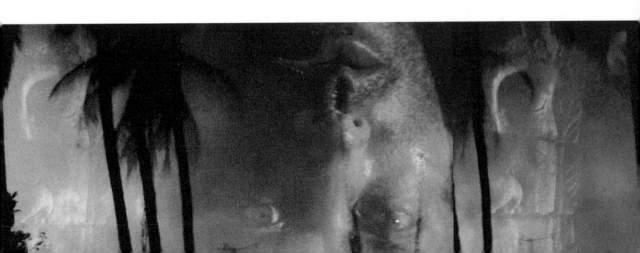

THIRD CONVERSATION   151

Editing *The Conversation* • The Invisible Partner • The Minor Key •
What's Under the Hands? • "Night Was Night": Re-editing *Touch of
Evil* • "As if Orson was sending us notes" by Rick Schmidlin • The
Wrong Echo • The Most Characteristic Angle

FOURTH CONVERSATION   201

Influences • Negative Twenty Questions • Enforced Idleness • Two
Kinds of Filmmaking • Why Did He Like It Better? • Family Life • The
Unanticipated Collisions of Things • A Pebble, A Cricket, A Wrench •
"The Blue Looked Dead" • A Wrong Reading • Divergent/Convergent •
The Disappearing Brother • Preludes • A Grease Pencil and Real Time •
"Waiting for Provocation" by Anthony Minghella

LAST CONVERSATION   279

Blessed Unrest • Writing *Return to Oz* • Just Below the Surface •
A Wonderful Line from Rilke • Dreams

MISCELLANY

Murch and the Movies   314   •   *Acknowledgements*   319
Photo Credits   321   •   *Index*   325

INTRODUCTION

It is hard for any person who has been on the set of a movie to believe that only one man or woman makes a film. At times a film set resembles a beehive, or daily life in Louis XIV's court—every kind of society is witnessed in action, and it seems every trade is busy at work. But as far as the public is concerned, there is always just one Sun-King who is sweepingly credited with responsibility for story, style, design, dramatic tension, taste, and even weather in connection with the finished project. When, of course, there are many hard-won professions at work.

The Conversations focusses on the art and the act of filmmaking through the lens that belongs to one of the essential talents on a film—the editor. For such a crucial craft, the editor's art has been mostly unimagined and certainly overlooked. Those within the profession know its central value, but outside that world it remains an unknown, mysterious skill—some smoke and mirrors, some touching up, some old black magic. So great names such as Dede Allen, Cécile Decugis, William Chang, Thelma Schoonmaker, Gerry Hambling, and Margaret Booth have never been a part of the public vocabulary.

Recently a friend gave me a book written some twenty years ago by Dai Vaughan on Stewart McAllister, a brilliant documentary film editor in England during World War II. It was aptly titled *Portrait of an Invisible Man,* and it makes a point that is still apt at the start of the twenty-first century:

> McAllister's absence from the record was not entirely a consequence of indifference, carelessness or ill-will. Even those who wished to discuss the editor found themselves somehow unable to do so. There was no

A scene with Juliette Binoche as Hana, cut from the final version of *The English Patient.*

tradition to draw upon, no corpus of received wisdom: simply no way of talking about films which would enable the editor's work to be mentioned.

The reasons for this state are legion. But Vaughan I think pinpoints the essential cause: "Underlying all debate on the subject, whether in critical journals, in Union meetings, in gossip columns or in the pub, is one master image which, even when it is not made explicit and even when it is explicitly repudiated, bends all argument by its density: the image of the Artist as solitary Creator."

So if the emphasis in *The Conversations* seems at times obsessive or one-sided, it is because there is still a need to realign the balance. Walter Murch would never suggest less significance to the role of a director, but even Napoleon needed his marshals.

This book began, as all my books do, with sheer curiosity. I had met Walter Murch during the filming of *The English Patient.* I saw a lot of him during the months of his editing of the film, and we became friends. Walter was simply always interesting to listen to. The first time I actually sat down and talked to him about film was when his wife Muriel, aka Aggie, asked me to appear on her radio show on KPFA in Berkeley, California. I said I would be happy to, but could we make it a three-way conversation that included Walter. We talked with Aggie about our mutual crafts, and it made me want to have more conversations. Maybe at some time in the future, I thought. I had always been interested, perhaps obsessed, in that seemingly uncrossable gulf between an early draft of a book or film and a finished product. How *does* one make that journey from there to here? And I remembered the moment I became fascinated in the actual craft of filmmaking—as opposed to the sheer entertainment of it—when watching Dede Allen's editing in *The Hustler* in Lennoxville, Quebec in 1962. After *The English Patient* was released, Walter and I would meet up now and then, and we had lunch when I was in San Francisco on a book tour for my novel *Anil's Ghost.* After the meal he suggested I come back to the editing room to see what he was doing. It turned out he was beginning to recut *Apocalypse Now* and also assembling a seventeen-second film by Thomas Edison and William K. L. Dickson that happens to be the oldest evidence of a film married to sound. I spent two hours with him and then went back on the road. A few days later I was in Minneapolis. My novel had taken seven years to write, and I now realized that what I really wanted to do next was sit down and talk with Walter in detail about his work, and his views about the art and the making of films, and specifically about his craft of editing. I contacted him that night, proposed the idea, he agreed, and we began a couple of months later.

The Conversations is made up of talks that took place during our meetings over the next year, starting in July 2000. We met whenever and wherever we could. Walter always surprised me with his ideas. George Lucas says he was originally drawn to Walter because he was "strange like me." My favourite lines in this book come where Walter remembers an incident that led to a technical solution for a film he was working on: "For some reason I had put the recorder at one end of the African Hall, and stood at the other end and just shouted incomprehensible, guttural speech. It echoed in a beautiful way and it was recorded." But there is nothing in the words of his recall of the incident to suggest this might be slightly abnormal behaviour, especially as he admits it took place very late at night.

The other quality that made me lucky in this project is that Walter has simply been in interesting places. He has worked on projects that have become central to the culture of our time. And speaking of these works, he describes the precise techniques used to solve a problem or to improve a moment, as opposed to discussing abstract theories and themes. Most of all, Walter is a filmmaker whose interests are in no way limited to film. There are very few in Hollywood who could speak of Beethoven and bees and Rupert Sheldrake and astronomy and Guido d'Arezzo with such knowledge. In fact it soon became clear that the one weak link in Walter's knowledge was film history. "I don't know enough about film history" is not a modest remark but a truthful one.

On one of my first visits, Walter and I were driving the curving road towards San Francisco when he glanced down at the odometer and said, "This car has almost reached the moon." *What?* "The distance to the moon is 238,713 miles, this car has gone 238,127. And most of it has been on this winding road."

Walter is a man whose brain is always peering over the wall into the worlds of scientific knowledge and metaphysical speculation. The book on his table is likely to be *Our Place in the Cosmos* by Hoyle and Wickramasinghe. For years he has campaigned to revive the discredited theories of the eighteenth-century astronomer Johannes Bode. I first heard of Bode during the making of *The English Patient.* Half of Walter's computer held all the information he had collected on *The English Patient,* peculiar data that provided an X ray of the movie in progress: at the push of a button he could show that Hana had seventy-six minutes on film, the Patient fifty-four, Kip thirteen. But the other half was filled with notes and planetary maps about Bode's theories.

He is a true oddity in the world of film. A genuine Renaissance man who appears wise and private at the centre of various temporary storms to do with filmmaking and his whole generation of filmmakers. He has worked on the sound and/or picture editing of such films as *American Graffiti, The Conversation, The Godfather* (*Parts I, II,* and *III*), *Julia, Apocalypse Now, The Unbearable Lightness of Being, Ghost,* and *The English Patient.* Four years ago he recut *Touch of Evil,* following Orson Welles's ignored fifty-eight-page memo to Universal. He has written and directed *Return to Oz,* an ambitious sequel to *The Wizard of Oz.* He has written *In the Blink of an Eye,* a sort of "Zen and the Art of Editing," as pertinent for writers and readers as it is for filmmakers and audiences.

But he is a man who also lives outside the world of film, the son of an artist whose theories and attitudes on art have deeply influenced him. He can sit at the piano and play "the music of the spheres," based on the distance of the planets from one another, translated by him into musical chords. And in recent years he has been translating the writings of Curzio Malaparte. He doesn't like to watch other movies when he is working on one himself, as he is ninety percent of the year. And he doesn't watch television, ever.

He is a low-key, gliding presence in a crowded and noisy room. He has a pair of ears that can pick up the hint of hum on a soundtrack, hiding within a twenty-track scene made up of gunfire, burning napalm, shouted orders, and helicopters. In the editing rooms of Francis Coppola's Zoetrope Studio, or the Saul Zaentz Film Center, he stands in front of an Avid editing machine, fine-tuning a cut that will eventually *seem* fluid but which is in reality a radical jump cut. He will turn to the self-invented coded charts on his wall and read the dramatic bones of the film he is working on. Yellow for this character's presence, blue for a certain location—"Venice" or "desert" or "Italian restaurant"—now and then a diagonal card for a scene that is a turning point in the story: the "mirror" scene in *Ripley,* the "first dance" in *The English Patient.* In this way, as editor, he can gaze down along the path of the narrative as if it were an easily understood steeplechase or the Tour de France. And from this perspective he deals with the crucial questions and possibilities an editor has to ask at some time or another: Can we eliminate that detour to the oasis scene completely? Can we leap the next three minutes and nestle this moment with that moment, thereby bonding two scenes that are strangers?

The more important considerations come with the subtler problems. How to eliminate that slightly superior tone that has emerged in the central character, how to avoid a series of plot bottlenecks later, how to influence or "save" a scene in the fifty-third minute of the film by doing something very small in the seventh, how to double the tension by doubling the sense of silence or not cutting away to that knife at all. How, even, to disguise the fact that an essential scene was never shot. To watch Murch at work is to see him delve into almost invisible specifics, where he harnesses and moves the bones or arteries of a scene, relocating them so they will alter the look of the features above the skin. Most of the work he does is going to affect us subliminally. There is no showing off here. We tend not to discover how his devices are working on us. I remember seeing the film of *The English Patient* for the first time after he had mixed it. I told him that I had heard a distant bell at the moment the Patient ate a plum. Aha, he said, quite pleased at my picking this up. Yes, we had put in the sound of a bell some distance away, about half a mile. It was to hint at a memory opening up. The Patient as he eats his plum begins to remember (in fact his first flashback comes a minute later). The bell we now hear signals the past for him; it takes over from the plum's taste as the catalyst of that memory. Walter then also pointed out that the bell, hardly even heard by audiences, is the first positive sound of human civilization up to that point fifteen minutes into the film. Till then the only man-made sounds are of bombs and machine guns and crashing planes and trains. It is in this way that much of the real editorial influence on the audience in a film such as *The English Patient* is subliminal. I would also notice that after the mix many of the visual cuts from location to location were slightly foreshadowed by a sound cut: we could now hear the noise of sandpaper on stone, for instance, before we cut visually to the archaeologists in the desert, or there would be the soft clang of the metal spile Hana throws as a hopscotch token, evolving into the sound of Berber music, thus preparing us for a leap back in memory.

This is, of course, the kind of craft that any careful writer uses as he or she edits a novel, or the craft a record producer counts on to shape an album with a hundred small details in the last stages. It is not just the editing of the individual scene that Murch is dealing with, but the more crucial larger structure: the issue of a film's pace, of the film's moral tone, which are influenced by a thousand fragments that have to do with speed, background noise, even how the antagonist may turn away from a conversation, or even, more deviously, how quickly the editor makes us cut away from that character's remark. This is from *In the Blink of an Eye*:

> For instance, by cutting away from a certain character before he finishes speaking, I might encourage the audience to think only about the face value of what he said. On the other hand, if I linger on the character after he finishes speaking, I allow the audience to see, from the expression in his eyes, that he is probably not telling the truth, and they will think differently about him and what he said. But since it takes a certain amount of time to make that observation, I cannot cut away from the character too early. . . . I hold until the audience realizes he is lying.

Watching Murch edit a scene between Willem Dafoe and Juliette Binoche—the summer after *The English Patient* shoot—I saw how he would remove one-fifth of the information and "bank" it, so extending the hook of this scene's unspoken knowledge to a later point in the film. When I saw *Washington Square*—a film Murch had nothing to do with—I understood what he was up to. In that film the edit was so competent, the scenes so articulate and so fully expressed, that every episode was complete in itself. The film progressed in a series of well-made, self-sufficient moments, and so it felt as if there was a wall between every perfectly articulated scene.

At some stage Walter might take a scene and turn it upside down and shake it to see how essential it is. Sometimes he becomes perversely obsessed with the rightness of removal. The director Anthony Minghella talks of how he was away from the editing room for a few days and came back to find Walter had removed the key dance scene between Almásy and Katharine Clifton, now convinced it was not at all necessary. But while the scene was eventually re-installed, the shock of discussion and threat of edit tightened it and made it even stronger later on.

There were times when Walter would show us a scene that appeared perfectly edited and crafted—the love scene between Almásy and Katharine during the Christmas party—and then return a few days later with a magical addition. In that case it was the use of a remade soundtrack that capsized the sounds of the good-natured Christmas spirit outside their room; he had added the noise of jostled furniture, the hint of bridles, and other sounds that made the scene dangerous. He had made the soundtrack a debate between a passionate private music and the carol-singing, social world close by. Murch and Minghella have a tremendous knowledge of music that helped govern the rhythm and shape of their film. And both were remarkably articulate, both able to argue their way out of suitcases. (Compared with them, the producer Saul Zaentz and I were the kind of people who would upset the Monopoly board in fury and stalk off, refusing to play by the rules of conversation anymore.)

Henry Green has called prose "a long intimacy," and it is a phrase that aptly describes the work of an editor, who might spend hours studying and aligning a small gesture in an actor; who knows actors—though they often do not know him—in such detail and intricacy that he even knows how to use their bad moments to benefit a performance. In our conversation with Aggie, Walter had talked about the editor's recognition of these subliminal signs: "For instance, some actors might turn their head to the left before they say the word 'but' or blink seven times a minute when they're thinking hard. . . . You learn all these things, and they're important. They're as important to you as signs in the forest are important to a hunter. Where were the deer? Is this a trail? What does this bent twig mean? All these things become tremendously significant. You have to find things that are good that work with the film. . . . By the same token, you begin to realize that if you put something weak in the right place, it can actually be very compelling. There are a number of times that I've used shots of actors trying to remember their lines. It's a very honest emotion. They are embarrassed, they're confused, they hope they remember the line, and you can see all of this on their face. In a certain context, that's absolutely the wrong thing to use. But placed in a different context, it can be wonderful and magical."

As a writer I have found that the last two years of any book I work on are given over to its editing. I may have spent four or five years writing in the dark, but now I have to discover the shape of the object I have been struggling to make, its true organic shape, that figure in the carpet. I have made two documentary films, and my fictional works tend to follow this structural process: shooting or writing everything for a number of months or years, then shaping the content into a new form, till it is almost a newly discovered story. I move things around till they become sharp and clear, till they are in the right location. And it is at this stage that I discover the work's true voice and structure. When I edited my first film documentary I knew that *this* was where the art came in. When I watched Walter Murch at work during my peripheral involvement with the film of *The English Patient,* I knew that *this* was the stage of filmmaking that was closest to the art of writing.

Murch likes to quote Robert Bresson to the effect that a film is born three times—in the writing of the script, in the shooting, and in the editing. With *The English Patient* there were, in fact, four births, because there was also a book as the source. It is interesting to chart how variable those births were in terms of just one scene. In the novel there is a moment when Caravaggio, whose hands are bandaged, watches a dog drink from a bowl of water and remembers how he was tortured three years earlier. Something about the table he is sitting at begins this quick flood of memory. The scene is about two paragraphs long, and the dog beside him in the present and the torture scene from the past merge. Caravaggio doesn't want to face that traumatic memory, so it is vaguely, and intentionally vaguely, remembered. It is dreamlike, not at all realistic.

When Anthony Minghella wrote the script, the scene went on for about four pages of sharp and frightening dialogue. It was now a scene where the German interrogator (not Italian, as in the book) tries to break down the defenses of the caught spy Caravaggio. In order to link Caravaggio to the crimes of the "English patient," it is clear in Minghella's version that Almásy is the cause of Caravaggio's capture which results in his torture. We are therefore already a long way from the scene in my book: in the novel the past haunts Caravaggio at certain moments, but none of his torture is described in detail, just suggested— only the way he is handcuffed to the table is remembered. Minghella's scene of the interrogation is full of tension, the phrases of dialogue repeated again and again, with the interrogator casually circling around to catch Caravaggio by surprise.

The next "birth" was the shooting of the scene. As Willem Dafoe, who played Caravaggio, said, "We shot the hell out of the scene." And they did, at least fifteen takes and then the close-ups—a razor opening, the typist recording the interrogation, a fly (stunned by being shaken in a bottle) crawling over Caravaggio's hand and buzzing off as the razor enters the frame. I remember one astonishing take where the camera remained on Dafoe's face all through the scene and stayed with him while he pulled the table to which he was handcuffed all the way to the back of the room to avoid that razor. When I saw the dailies, this was the moment that I thought most remarkable: Minghella had taken another step forwards from the written screenplay with the shooting of the scene. Now he gave it to Walter.

And what did Walter Murch do with this scene?

Well, he had been reading the Italian writer Curzio Malaparte on the "Nazi character," and he plucked from his reading the fact that the Nazis hated any demonstration of weakness. This idea was certainly not in my original paragraph, not in Minghella's script, nor in any of the hundred minutes of footage that had been shot and that somehow had to be cut down to a nerve-racking three or four minutes. Every scene, every film, for Murch, needs to have a larger science of patterns at work within it, and this would be the idea or concept that governed how he cut the scene.

At one point Caravaggio/Dafoe says, before he even sees the razor, "Don't cut me." He says it once. Walter has the interrogator pause in his questioning when he hears this, extending the time of his response. He has threatened the spy with the idea of cutting off his thumbs, but only in a casual, not serious, way. When Caravaggio says, "Don't cut me," the German pauses for a second, a flicker of disgust on his face. The interrogation continues. Walter found *another* take of Dafoe's line, this one with more quaver in the voice, and decided to put it in again, a few seconds later. So Dafoe *repeats* his fear. And now time stops.

We see the look on the German. And now we know he has to *do* what he was previously just thinking about. To emphasize this, Murch, at that very moment, pulls all the sound out of the scene, so there is complete silence. And we, even if we don't realize it as we sit in the theatre, are shocked and the reason is that quietness. Something terrible has been revealed by the spy, about his own nature, and now something terrible is going to happen. To this point, Murch has built numerous layers of sound to give us the feeling of being within that cavelike room; he even provides sounds taking place *outside* the room (a favourite device of his—listen to the street sounds when Michael Corleone commits his first murder in *The Godfather*). In this scene there is the sound of a firing squad somewhere outside, soldiers yelling, while inside there is that continual typing, the fly buzzing, the telephone that keeps ringing, all this behind the tense conversation between the two men. Then, when Dafoe repeats the line—which in reality he did not repeat, which was not even there in the script—Murch makes the response to the line a total and dangerous silence.

Walter has said that the use of silence in movies did not come in until the invention of synchronous sound in 1927. Until then there was the continuous accompaniment of music: live orchestra, organ, or piano. Murch always tries to find a moment in his films when that shock of silence will fill the theatre. And in *The English Patient* it happens now. It feels as if it lasts five minutes but it really lasts only about five seconds, and during that time everything is decided. After that moment all hell breaks loose. This is when members of the audience begin to close their eyes and when some faint. In fact, they faint probably because they close their eyes. We see nothing violent on the screen. But we *hear* the suggestions of it. And the ones with closed eyes are now under the control of this master editor and so they must imagine it all.

THE CONVERSATIONS

FIRST

CONVERSATION

SAN FRANCISCO

In the spring of 2000, Walter Murch, at the suggestion of Francis Ford Coppola, began to re-edit *Apocalypse Now,* a film he had worked on back in 1977–1979 both as sound designer and as one of the four picture editors. Twenty-two years later, all the takes and discards and "lost" scenes and sound elements (carefully preserved in climate-controlled limestone caves in Pennsylvania) were brought out of vaults to be reconsidered. *Apocalypse Now* is a part of the American sub-conscious. And in some way this was the problem. Having dinner with the novelist Alfredo Véa in San Francisco, after spending my first day with Walter at Zoetrope, I mentioned what was happening with the re-editing of *Apocalypse Now,* and Véa immediately launched into Marlon Brando's monologue about the snail on a razor blade. This was followed, during dinner, by Véa's precise imitation of Dennis Hopper's whine: "What are they gonna say about him? What are they gonna say? That he was a kind man? That he was a *wise* man? . . ." For Véa, who fought in Vietnam, *Apocalypse Now* was *the* movie about the war. It was the work of art that caught it for him, that gave him a mythological structure he could refer to, that showed him what he had gone through and would later write about himself in books such as *Gods Go Begging.*

Mark Berger, Francis Ford Coppola and Walter Murch mixing *Godfather II,* 1974.

So those working on the new *Apocalypse Now* were aware that there would be problems connected with their dismantling and restructuring a "classic." It was now public property.

"It *has* become part of the culture," said Murch. "And that's not a one-way street, as you know from your writing. As much as a work affects the culture, the culture mysteriously affects the work. *Apocalypse Now* in the year 2000 is a very different thing from the physically exact-same *Apocalypse Now* in the second before it was released in 1979."

The idea for a new version grew out of Coppola's desire to produce a DVD of *Apocalypse Now* with a number of major scenes that were—for reasons of length—eliminated from the 1979 version. Also, 2000 was the twenty-fifth anniversary of the fall of Saigon, so it seemed appropriate to re-evaluate editorial decisions that had originally been made while the war was still a vividly painful bruise on the nation's psyche. But rather than have the restored scenes appear in isolation, appended in their own chapter, why not integrate them into the body of the film as originally intended? The problem was that the editing and sound work on the excised material had never been finished, and one scene in particular was eliminated before it was completely shot. Fortunately, the negative and original sound for all this material were perfectly preserved in original laboratory rolls, and could be retrieved, two decades later, as if the film had been shot a few weeks earlier.

And so Walter Murch was now working in San Francisco, in the old Zoetrope building. Mostly he had to collect and reconsider the material for three large sequences that were cut from the film in 1978—a medevac scene involving Playboy Bunnies; further scenes with Brando in the Kurtz compound; and a ghostly, funereal dinner and love scene at a French rubber plantation. In Eleanor Coppola's book about the making of the film, she writes of this scene:

> I heard the French plantation scene is definitely out of the picture. It never seemed to fit right. I am one of the people who liked it, but it did stop the flow of Willard's journey. Today I was thinking about all the days of agony Francis went through during the shooting of that scene.

The hundreds of thousands of dollars spent on the set and the cast flown in from France. Now the whole thing will end up as a roll of celluloid in a vault somewhere.

"The film acquired a body in the absence of these limbs," said Murch, speaking of those missing scenes. "Now we're trying to sew them back on, and who knows? Whether the body will accept or reject or find the addition difficult is something we're struggling with right now. I have a sense of it and it's actually been going quite well, but until we finally step back and look at the work as a whole, we won't be able to say whether this will be artistically successful or whether it's simply going to be a curiosity piece for those who were already interested in the film."

The three scenes are the major additions in the new version of the film, but there are many other small changes that Murch and his colleagues were making—additions that give a different tone to much of the film. There is more humour, and with the addition of bridges between episodes that had been cut because of time concerns the film has also become less fragmentary. Those previously missing elements, said Murch, "were casualties of the hallmark struggle in every editing room: How short can the film be and still work? Even though Francis had final cut, he was as acutely aware as anybody of the strictures of getting a film into the theatres as lean as it could be. With the new version, that particular drive—for compression above all—is not as compelling."

Much of our first conversation took place during four days in July 2000, while Walter worked on the new version of the film. Our talk during those days dealt with the "new" scenes but also with the differences and similarities between writing and editing, music, and his feelings about other editors. We talked as Walter worked on the Avid in his editing room at Zoetrope and later continued over lunch at a Chinese restaurant on Columbus Avenue. The new version of *Apocalypse Now Redux* would not open in theatres for almost a year, and Walter was still uncertain about several changes.

We began, however, by talking about the early days and how he became involved with the world of sound and eventually film.

HUMBLE SOUNDS

O: You're an editor who works in sound as well as picture. You created "sound-scapes" for films such as *Apocalypse Now.* When did you first become interested in this landscape of sound?

M: It was with me from as early as I can remember. Maybe I heard things differently because my ears stuck out, or maybe because my ears stuck out people thought I would hear things differently, so I obliged them. It's hard to say. What's true is that if words failed me I would switch to sound effects, I would imitate the sound of something if I didn't know its name. Back then there was an animated cartoon character, a boy named Gerald McBoing-Boing, who spoke in sound effects instead of words, and he was able to communicate with his parents this way. That was my nickname: Walter McBoing-Boing.

Around that time the tape recorder was becoming available as a consumer item. The father of a friend of mine bought one, so I wound up going over to his house endlessly to play with it. And that passion, which was a kind of delirious drunkenness with what the tape recorder could do, completely possessed me. I eventually convinced my parents that it would be a good idea if our family had one, because we could then record music off the radio and wouldn't have to buy records. In fact, I rarely used it for that, but I would hold the microphone out the window, recording sounds of New York. I would construct little arrangements of metal, and tape the microphone to them, striking and rubbing the metal in different places. It was fascinating.

And then I discovered the concept of physically editing tape—that you could rearrange it by cutting out sections and putting those sections in a different order. You could record two things at different times and juxtapose them, getting rid of the middle, or you could turn the tape upside down and play it backwards, or flip it over and play it back muffled, or any combination of these things.

O: So did European movements such as *musique concrète* in the fifties inspire you?

M: Definitely. I came home from school one day and turned on the classical radio station, WQXR, in the middle of a program. Sounds were coming out of the speaker that raised the hair on the back of my neck. I turned the tape recorder on and listened for the next twenty minutes or so, riveted by what I was hearing. It turned out to be a record by Pierre Schaeffer and Pierre Henry—two of the early practitioners of *musique concrète.* I could hear a real similarity with what I had been doing—taking ordinary sounds and arranging them rhythmically, creating a kind of music on tape. In France at that time, people would go to concerts and a big speaker would be wheeled out onstage. Somebody would come out and turn the tape recorder on with a flourish, and the audience would sit there patiently listening to this composition being played back. Then at the end they'd all applaud. This was the future!

O: You were how old when this hit you?

George Noble provides sound effects, and his brother, Joe Noble, receives a knockout in the first lip-sync animated cartoon for British Talking Pictures, 1928.

Pierre Schaeffer, the celebrated French *musique concrète* composer who inspired Murch when he was making his own recordings at age 10.

M: Ten or eleven, something like that. It was intoxicating to realize that somebody else was doing the same things I was. Up to that point I'd thought that this was just my strange little hobby. But here was validation. There were adults in the world who took it seriously. I felt like Robinson Crusoe finding Friday's footprint in the sand.

O: And these were essentially documentary recordings with an artistic structure?

M: It was an early, technically primitive form of sampling. What's strange—only in retrospect—is that I didn't follow through with it. By the time I was fifteen or sixteen, I had relegated all of this passion to my pre-adolescence—I thought I now had to get serious. Maybe I was going to be an architect. Or an oceanographer. Was I going to be . . . what? It was only in my early twenties that I discovered those early interests all came together in film.

O: Did someone like John Cage interest you, were you interested in what he was doing?

M: My father was a painter and tangentially involved in Cage's world. We would go to some of his concerts. I appreciated them, but I was moved more by the *idea* of what he was doing—that by taking humble sounds out of their normal context you could make people pay attention and discover the musical elements in them. It was very close to what my father was doing in his paintings: taking discarded objects and arranging them in ways to make you see them with new eyes.

O: Was the interest in editing film something that existed at the same time? Or did it come much later?

M: When I was a student at Johns Hopkins, a group of us made some short silent films, and I discovered then that editing images had emotionally the same impact for me as editing sound. It was intoxicating. You write eloquently about that in *Anil's Ghost,* about the state of mind of a doctor in the middle of surgery: You get to a place where time is not an issue at all, and you're oddly at the centre of things but also you are not. You're the person doing it, yet the feeling is that you're *not* the origin of it, that somehow "it" is happening around you, that you are being used by this thing to help bring it into the world. I felt that way when I was eleven, playing with my tapes. I didn't know how to interpret it then, but I discovered, when I was twenty, that editing images gave me the same feeling. Then when I got to the University of Southern California as a graduate student, both of those things—sound and picture—came together.

As I've gone through life, I've found that your chances for happiness are increased if you wind up doing something that is a reflection of what you loved most when you were somewhere between nine and eleven years old.

O: Yes—something that had and still has the feeling of a hobby, a curiosity.

M: At that age, you know enough of the world to have opinions about things, but you're not old enough yet to be overly influenced by the crowd or by what other people are doing or what you think you "should" be doing. If what you do later on ties into that reservoir in some way, then you are nurturing some essential part of yourself. It's certainly been true in my case. I'm doing now, at fifty-eight, almost exactly what most excited me when I was eleven.

But I went through a whole late-adolescent phase when I thought: Splicing sounds together can't be a real occupation, maybe I should be a geologist or teach art history.

O: Did you think of going into the sciences at all?

M: No. Although I was interested in them—and interested in math—as revelations of hidden patterns. What you do as an editor is search for patterns, at both the superficial and ever deeper levels—as deep as you can go.

The fact is that there is always much more film shot than can ever be included in the finished product: on average, about twenty-five times too much—which would mean fifty hours of material for a two-hour film. Sometimes the ratio is as high as a hundred to one, as it was on *Apocalypse Now*. And films are almost always shot out of sequence, which means that on the same day the crew could find themselves filming scenes from the beginning, the end, and the middle of the script. This is done to make the schedule more efficient, but it means that someone—the editor—must take on the responsibility for finding the best material out of that great surplus and putting it in the correct order. Although there is a universe of complexity hidden in those short words "best" and "correct."

When it works, film editing—which could just as easily be called "film construction"—identifies and exploits underlying patterns of sound and image that are not obvious on the surface. Putting a film together is, in an ideal sense, the orchestrating of all those patterns, just like different musical themes are orchestrated in a symphony. It is all pretty mysterious. It's right at the heart of the whole exercise.

Walter Murch was nicknamed Walter McBoing-Boing after the fifties cartoon character who talked in sounds.

HIGH SCHOOL CONFIDENTIAL

Q: How did you go from being that boy in New York to someone working in film in California?

M: I was studying art history and Romance languages in Italy and Paris, in '63–'64, the height of the French New Wave. I came back to the States buzzing with the idea of film, and then I realized that there were actually schools where you could study it, which I found incredible, delicious, almost absurd. I applied to a number of them, and miraculously won a scholarship to the graduate program at USC. Strangely enough, I only discovered that films needed sound when I got there: it was a revelation to me that the sound had to be recorded separately from the image and "cooked"—edited and mixed—before it was finished. But I immediately saw the connection with what I had been doing twelve years earlier, and that was exciting.

Q: You were at film school with other filmmakers you would later work with—Francis Coppola and George Lucas?

M: Francis was across town at UCLA, but George was a fellow student at USC. UCLA and USC were naturally rivals, but we all knew each other. UCLA accused us of being soulless sellouts to technology, and we accused them of being drug-crazed narcissists incapable of telling a story or wielding a camera. But it was a fraternal kind of jealousy, and underneath it all we were the same. Our general feeling in the mid-sixties was that American cinema was having a hard time. It was the tail end of the old Hollywood studio system and there had been a corresponding revitalization of European cinema, starting with Italy and Japan in the late forties, then the New Wave in France in the early sixties.

So when I graduated from USC in 1967, I found that the job opportunities for a film student were very poor in Hollywood. But one of the advantages of going to film school, on a practical level, is that you form friendships with people of like minds and interests. And those friendships created a kind of informal old-boys' network. If you have fifteen people in a group, the chance that one of them will get a job is pretty high. That's sometimes enough to lead to something else. My good friend Matthew Robbins had landed a job at Encyclopaedia Britannica Educational Films doing odd jobs and set construction, and when some other opportunity came up for him, he asked me, Do you want my job? I applied and was hired. Three or four months later one of the filmmakers there, who was preparing a film on the function of the eye, asked me if I wanted to edit the film. I said, Fantastic!

After Britannica I freelanced for a while, working briefly at Dove Films—a commercial production house owned by two cameramen, Cal Bernstein and Haskell Wexler—where I

James Caan and Shirley Knight in *The Rain People*, 1969, *right*. George Lucas and Francis Ford Coppola, *opposite*, on the set of *THX 1138*, which Lucas directed from a screenplay he wrote with Murch, 1970.

FIRST CONVERSATION

edited commercials for Foremost Milk and a documentary on modern art for the U.S. Information Agency. Then in December of 1968, about a year and a half after I'd left film school, I got a call from George Lucas. He and Francis Coppola had met. It turned out they had rented Cal Bernstein's equipment to shoot a film, *The Rain People*. Francis needed somebody to do the final sound, and asked me if I wanted to move to San Francisco and do that. He was thinking of basing American Zoetrope up there.

O: How well did you know George Lucas at film school?

M: We'd known each other since 1965, and I'd worked on a couple of his student films. We were the two finalists for a six-month Warner Bros. scholarship. As we were going in for our final interview, we realized, naturally, that one of us was going to get it—and the other one wasn't. So we made a pact that whoever did get it would turn around and help the other if something good came along.

Well, George got it. And when the chance came, he called me. He had met Francis at Warner Bros., where he was directing *Finian's Rainbow.* They bonded, for many reasons—not the least of which was that they were the only two people at the studio with beards. Francis subsequently wrote *The Rain People,* financed by Warner Bros., and hired George to shoot a documentary about the making of the film.

Walter Murch, *above,* and his Ducati 200 Elite in the Appenines during a trip from Perugia to Paris with Matthew Robbins, late summer 1963. *Overleaf:* The celebration of the opening of American Zoetrope and the completion of its first film, *THX 1138.* The group includes John Milius, Caroll Ballard, Jim McBride, Walter with cap; on extreme right, George Lucas and Francis Ford Coppola, 1971, on the roof of the Zoetrope offices, a former warehouse.

O: So you were asked to join them in San Francisco.

M: Right. Specifically to create the sound effects for, and mix, *The Rain People,* but also to be part of Zoetrope, which was a professional extension of the film school ideal. You know, when you're at that stage as a young person, the world is big and wide and open, and the idea of settling down in Los Angeles permanently was not on my mind. Aggie and I had gotten married in 1965, after I graduated from Johns Hopkins, and for our honeymoon we had driven cross-country on a motorcycle. Our son, Walter, was born in 1968, so I was now a dad. It was all extremely exciting and Zoetrope seemed a natural thing to do.

O: This was a new, independent company starting up—did it seem a great risk to all of you?

M: Well, for Francis there was a big risk, as it turned out. But not for us, other than the normal risk of plunging into the unknown, uprooting your family and not knowing what would happen. I remember George saying, Well, we may all be back in a year with our tails between our legs, but at least it'll be fun while we're doing it. Who knows what'll happen!

Most people in Hollywood thought what we were doing was crazy. But it was the late sixties, it was San Francisco, it was all part of what we saw then as the beginnings of the technical democratization of the filmmaking process—with comparatively little money you could actually go on the road and shoot a feature film, you could locate wherever you wanted.

Also, the mood in Hollywood at that time was down. Some of the old studio bosses were holding on—Sam Goldwyn, Jack Warner—but the old paradigm was no longer functioning. In retrospect you can see that something new was emerging, but it hadn't really happened yet. On a practical level, the unions were still quite restrictive. Without connections—and that went for all of us, none of us came from film backgrounds—the chance of getting employment in film was low. In fact, being a film student then was a strike against you. So, we thought, If it's going to be low, why not make it low in an interesting place? Which is what we found San Francisco to be.

(Zoe gk. LIFE + Trope

CARROLL BALLARD   TIM HUNTLEY   JOHN MILIUS   GEORGE LU

HN KORTY

BARRY BECKERMAN

LAWRENCE STURHA

SAN FRANCISCO, DECEMBER 12TH: A CELEBRATION of the opening of the AMERICAN ZOETROPE

nt, Turn, REVOLUTION)

ROBERT DALVA

AL LOCATELLI   FRANCIS COPPOLA

NIS JAKOB

STEVE WAX   WALTER MURCH

JIM McBRIDE

e completion of photography of its first production, THX 1138, and the beginning of A NEW DECADE.

"STRANGE LIKE ME"
by George Lucas

I met Walter in the darkroom at the University of Southern California. He never talked very much, so we got along very well. I think my first impression was that he was very tall.

I'm not sure what it was about USC in those years in the sound department . . . just the fact that there was a group of us who grew up with popular music. We were really focussed on sound. That department was designed architecturally so that the screening room backed into the patio where everybody hung out. If you had a good soundtrack in a movie, it would pull all the students into the screening room to see what was going on. It was there I realized that sound is really half the experience of this medium, and that the visual and sound combine to make the experience work.

What we were doing was pretty much trying to reinvent film, without knowing too much about the medium. We were sort of making things up as we went along. We were studying film in an academic way, but our relationship with the industry was fairly tenuous in those days.

Walter, even then, was quite superior at sound. Francis and I were travelling across the country, doing *The Rain People,* with about fourteen people altogether—a very, very small crew. We were talking about moving to San Francisco, and he was going to go to Germany which had a new mixing system he was going to buy. He said, Do you know anybody who knows anything about sound? I said, I know just the guy, he's a genius. There was only one person I thought could do that job. And that was Walter.

In school, I was very much an anti-story, anti-character kind of guy. I was of the San Francisco avant-garde film school and cinéma vérité, that sort of thing. I got the chance from Francis to do a feature, and he said, What are you going to do? I said, I can't write a script. He said, You'll have to learn to write if you're going to become a director. And I said, Oh, God! I went off and dutifully wrote a script and brought it back to Francis. He said, Well, you're right—you can't write a script! So we hired a writer—a very good writer, actually, a novelist and a playwright—and he wrote a script. He tried very hard to make it into something, but it wasn't at all what I wanted to do with the movie. That was extremely frustrating and Francis said, Let's go and spend a week on the boat. After a week, he said, This is not working—is there anybody else who can help you with it? I said, Maybe Walter—he's strange like me, and probably we could work this out together. So Walter and I got together and started writing. It was very collaborative, we had the same sensibility in a lot of ways. You can see that *THX 1138,* while an attempt to do something normal, is at the same time strange, in a youthful, collegiate way, and also has the wild sense of humour that Walter and I share. We had a great time making that movie. It was a lot of fun. The film got a rather confused reception, but it has become a cult classic.

Sound was very important to us. In *THX 1138* we decided we would create a soundtrack that was primarily sound effects–based—the music would operate like sound effects and the sound effects would operate like music. We carried that idea on to *American Graffiti,* where we took all the music and made it so that it would bounce around the environment and be part of it, as a sound effect rather than as music. Then we took sound effects and used them in the places where we really needed tension and drama—in two or three scenes where there's real drama going on. We pulled the music out and just used sound effects. . . .

O: When you began to work on the sound edit of *The Rain People,* had the picture been edited?

M: When I started work, the editor—Barry Malkin—was going back to New York. He said, It's done, I'm going home. Francis is in Europe, he'll be back in a month or so. So there I was, in a cabin up Benedict Canyon, all alone with the film, a Nagra tape recorder, a Moviola, and a transfer machine, recording and adding the sound effects. I became a little paranoid—I was nonunion and an ex–film student working on a studio feature film—and I felt I couldn't go to any of the film libraries and get prerecorded sound. I was afraid they would ask, Who are you? What are you working on?

Plus I had never used libraries when I was at film school. I'd gone out and recorded everything myself. So that's what I did for *The Rain People.* I recorded all the sound effects—*all* the sound, except for the dialogue and music—and then organized it across a number of different tracks. We mixed *The Rain People* up in San Francisco in May of 1969 on the new KEM equipment from Germany that Francis had bought.

After that, I worked with George on the screenplay of *THX 1138.* The basis of *THX* was a treatment that Matthew Robbins and I had written as students. George, who was by his own definition not a writer, needed a script for a class he was taking, and had asked us, Aren't you going to do that underground thing? When we said no, he took it, renamed it *THX 1138,* and made it much more wonderful than our two-page outline.

So, as the wheel turned, George and I found ourselves in San Francisco in the summer of '69, collaborating on this feature-length version of *THX.* He started shooting in September. Quite fast, when you think about it. It didn't seem fast at the time, but now I see that it was.

Once they were shooting, I began to record the sound effects. George, after directing, also edited the film himself. We were working out of a little house in Mill Valley, where George and Marcia Lucas lived. There were three of us doing postproduction: George doing the editing, Marcia as George's assistant, and me doing the sound. I would arrive on my motorcycle at nine o'clock, start working, and at the end of the day go back to the houseboat, in Sausalito, where Aggie and I and Walter were living.

When the executives at Warner Bros. saw the director's cut of *THX* in June of 1970, they were so distraught they cancelled the development deal they had with Zoetrope. All the projects that were slated—*Apocalypse Now, American Graffiti, The Black Stallion, The Conversation,* and others—were abandoned. Not only that, they demanded all the development money back. It was out of this crisis that Francis considered directing *The Godfather,* as a way of making ends meet.

We were still finishing up *THX 1138* as Francis was beginning to shoot *The Godfather.* Eventually we took *THX* to Cannes in May '71, but it was not a financial success when it was released in the States. That summer I started working on the sound of *The Godfather.* The movie really set Zoetrope up as a professionally recognized production company, a platform for films like *American Graffiti, The Godfather Part II, The Conversation, The Black Stallion, Apocalypse Now.* All those classic films from the 1970s were produced as a result of the success of *The Godfather.* Ironically, *The Godfather* was not the kind of film Francis wanted to make. Initially it was exactly the kind of big Hollywood film he wanted to get away from. But as he worked on it, he saw that he could infiltrate it, make it resonate with his interests, include personal details about Italian-

Murch holding *THX 1138* which he had been editing with Lucas and his wife, Marcia, in the attic of Lucas's house in Mill Valley.

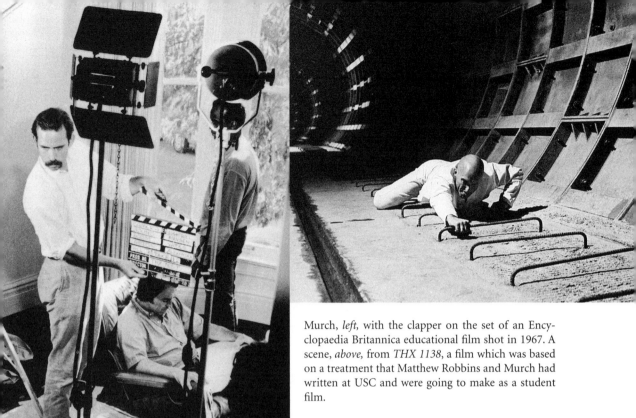

Murch, *left,* with the clapper on the set of an Encyclopaedia Britannica educational film shot in 1967. A scene, *above,* from *THX 1138,* a film which was based on a treatment that Matthew Robbins and Murch had written at USC and were going to make as a student film.

American life, and draw on his own style of filmmaking to turn it into a more European kind of American film. To that end, he specifically hired Nino Rota, Fellini's composer, to write the music for it.

INFLUENCES

O: Was European filmmaking important to all of you? Who were significant role models for you?

M: Godard, Kurosawa, Bergman. Fellini—definitely. Kubrick's *Dr. Strangelove.* But Kubrick was already an exile from the Hollywood system. I didn't gravitate towards the Americans. It was the Europeans and the Japanese.

O: And Truffaut?

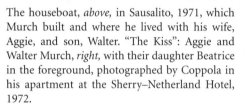
The houseboat, *above,* in Sausalito, 1971, which Murch built and where he lived with his wife, Aggie, and son, Walter. "The Kiss": Aggie and Walter Murch, *right,* with their daughter Beatrice in the foreground, photographed by Coppola in his apartment at the Sherry–Netherland Hotel, 1972.

M: I remember viscerally the effect of the freeze-frame at the end of his *The 400 Blows.* It was electrifying, both dramatically and as a possibility of what you could do technically with cinema. It was the first time I'd seen anything like it.

O: Are there other moments that have affected you like that?

M: The use of slow motion in *The Seven Samurai.* There's a thief who holds a little girl hostage in a house. The head samurai goes in to talk to him. You aren't shown what's happening in the house, but the film cuts to the doorway, and in slow motion the thief, with a bewildered expression on his face, comes out clawing at the air. He tumbles and falls to the ground, dead, and you realize that he's been sliced by Takashi Shimura, who plays the head samurai.

The moment the whole idea of filmmaking hit me was when I was fifteen and went to see *The Seventh Seal* by Ingmar Bergman. I'd seen lots of movies

before that, of course—the average number of films a kid growing up in New York City would see. But *The Seventh Seal* was the film where I suddenly understood the concept that *somebody made this film,* and that there was a series of decisions that could have been different if someone else had made the film. I got a sense of a single person's interest and passions through watching that film. It was astonishing—this was Ingmar Bergman, after all!

I remember I saw it at the Plaza Theater, Fifty-eighth Street off Madison Avenue, and walked all the way home to 119th Street, thinking about what I'd seen. As I said, I must have been about fifteen. When you're younger than that, movies just kind of happen to you. You look at them the way you look at a landscape. When you ask a ten-year-old, "What did you think of that movie?" it's a little like asking, "What did you think of that forest," or "that mountain range?" He may like it, or not, or it may give him a funny feeling. But he doesn't readily imagine that it could be any way other than it is.

Of course, buried in the realization that *somebody made this film* is the corollary that *I could make a film.* Godard's *Breathless* and Truffaut's *Shoot the*

Toshiro Mifune, *left,* in *The Seven Samurai,* 1954. Jean-Pierre Leaud in the freeze frame at the end of Truffaut's *400 Blows, right,* that Murch found "electrifying."

Piano Player reinforced the idea for me. But it was all still unconscious.

O: And here was Truffaut using David Goodis's American novel, and transplanting it to France. It's interesting what the French have learned from American B novels, which they then send back to America. . . . What about a film like Robert Rossen's *The Hustler,* based on Walter Tevis's book? It's a great film, beautifully edited, unlike many American films of its time, but also pure Americana—in a way less sentimental than the French versions of America.

M: Definitely. If I had to think of one American film that had a big impact on me from that period, it would be *The Hustler.* But it was not a typical Hollywood production in any sense, even though it starred Paul Newman.

O: The editing of the pool games is stunning.

M: Dede Allen was the editor.

O: She worked mostly with Arthur Penn, didn't she?

M: Yes, they did five films together: *Little Big Man, Bonnie and Clyde,* et cetera. . . . Also, before you leave the Zoetrope building you should go down to the second floor and say hello to Anne Coates, who's working there. She's roughly the same age as Dede, both in their mid-seventies. Anne was the editor of *Lawrence of Arabia.* A real dynamo. She's edited a film a year since 1952.

O: Really? And still working!

M: The most recent was *Erin Brockovich.* Anne has been a hero of mine for a long time.

O: Why do you think women like Dede Allen and Anne Coates end up as editors? It seems to be the profession where women have more power.

M: In fact, many of the editors of early films—back in the silent days—were women. It was a woman's craft, seen as something like sewing. You knitted the pieces of film together. And editing has aspects of being a librarian, which used to be perceived as a woman's job.

O: And the man is the hunter-gatherer, coming back with stuff for her to cook!

M: The men could bring it home, but they didn't quite know what to do with it. But there was a big shift when sound came along in 1927. Sound was somehow a "man" thing—it was electric. It was complicated in a different way, an engineering way. A lot of men started coming into editing at that point, and women left.

But if you made a list of the ten best editors ever, Anne Coates and Dede Allen would be in there. They've been an inspiration to a whole generation. Dede got her start in New York. I never ran into her there, because I had moved out here to the West Coast, but Richie Marks, Barry Malkin, Steve Rotter, and many other New York editors my age grew up under her guidance. Margaret Booth, who is still alive at 102, was the preeminent editor at MGM during its glory days. Her films included *The Barretts of Wimpole Street, Mutiny on the Bounty,* and *Camille.* . . .

O: So who are the other ones, your top editors?

M: The director David Lean, who started out as an editor and continued to edit the films he directed, though he never took credit. Gerry Hambling, who works mostly for Alan Parker. Thelma Schoonmaker, who cuts for Scorsese.

O: *Raging Bull* is certainly one of the great works in terms of editing.

M: I agree.

O: Are there films you've seen, say in the last ten years, where the editing style has startled or impressed you so much that you will possibly alter your own techniques or rules?

M: Hmmm . . . You know, I see so few films. My film background is selective and intense. . . .

O: A film like *The Battle of Algiers,* for instance, did it suggest a possible way to edit?

M: Yes, that was one of a number of films, along with the works of Godard, Truffaut, Kurosawa, and Bergman, that influenced me early on, as a student. I guess I'm sort of like the queen bee who gets impregnated once and can lay millions of eggs afterwards. The influence of those films is still with me.

Here's our bill. . . .

O: My fortune cookie says: "Executive ability is prominent in your makeup."

M: Mine is: "You have a quiet and unobtrusive nature. . . ."

DIRECTORS AND EDITORS

O: What's the distinction of roles between editor and director—in the way a scene is finally cut or the way a plot is possibly altered from a script? We know the editor has a very intimate relationship to the material. Does this give him or her a finer sense than the director of subliminal details and hidden structures in the film?

Film editor Dede Allen with the director Jim Bridges, *above*, at the old David O. Selznick studio, Los Angeles; David Lean, *center*, in the white shirt, directing *Great Expectations*. Lean started out as an editor and continued to edit the films he directed; Thelma Schoonmaker, *far right*, working on *Woodstock*, 1969.

For instance, for me, in Coppola's *The Conversation* there are some wonderful framings of scenes, or a peculiar emphasis on, say, an abstract shot of the back of Gene Hackman's head, or of the grey-green wall, or the scenery behind him—and I wonder if these were "recognized" by you, plucked out of a secondary shot and perhaps made more significant than Coppola originally conceived them. Two random shots of a character's feet in a film suddenly can become potent, symbolic. It's interesting to me how fragments in a corner of the screen can become important. In courtroom scenes I'm always drawn to the court stenographer typing silently, I'm always watching her hands.

M: A talented director lays out opportunities that can be seized by other people—by other heads of departments, and by the actors, who are in effect heads of their own departments. This is the real function of a director, I believe. And then to protect that communal vision by accepting or rejecting certain contributions. The director is ultimately the immune system of the film.

Those images you were talking about from *The Conversation* are images that Francis shot. He chose to shoot them, and in ninety-nine percent of the

cases I chose to use them deliberately—I recognized their power and put them in the order you see in the finished film. Francis would then of course see my work and accept or reject the approach I was taking.

There were many other possible alternatives: the structure of a film is created out of finding those harmonies we were talking about earlier—visual harmonies, thematic harmonies—and finding them at deeper and deeper levels as you work on the film.

Sometimes it happens in purely accidental ways, but I don't think an editor—except in certain kinds of documentaries—can impose on a film a vision that wasn't there to begin with. All the things you talk about were in Francis's head, in some form. I may have found things that worked along with his vision in a unique way, orchestrated it more fully in certain areas perhaps, but I doubt whether that would have happened had Francis not already written the melody, so to speak.

I become tuned to see things in a certain way when I'm working on a film. One of your obligations as an editor is to drench yourself in the sensibility of

the film, to the point where you're alive to the smallest details and also the most important themes. This also applies to the head of every department. It's very similar, I'm sure, to how a conductor relates to the performers in an orchestra.

The practical aspect of what you were talking about though is very potent. The editor is the only one who has time to deal with the whole jigsaw. The director simply doesn't. To actually look at all the film the director has shot,

A scene, *above,* from Gillo Pontecorvo's *Battle of Algiers:* "The influence of those formative films is still with me . . ." *Opposite:* Murch and Coppola. Murch, in the background, was working on *Julia* in England when Coppola flew him to the Philippines for the weekend during the shooting of *Apocalypse Now* to discuss mixing the film.

and review it and sort through it, to rebalance all of that and make very specific notes about tiny details that are sometimes extremely significant, this falls to the editor.

As it's happened, I've always done the initial assembly of the film myself. I sit with the director when we watch dailies. If he or she has something to say about a particular moment, I note it. But if I were to add up the Director's Comments column on my database, I wouldn't find a tremendous amount of information there. What's there *is* significant, though, and leads to other decisions. The smallest suggestion can help guide my eye to see the film the way the director is seeing it.

In the end, the editor of a film must try to take advantage of all the material that is given to him, and reveal it in a way that feels like a natural but exciting unfolding of the ideas of the film. It's really a question of orchestration: organizing the images and sounds in a way that is interesting, and digestible by the audience. Mysterious when it needs to be mysterious, and understandable when it needs to be understandable.

O: And not too much on the nose.

M: If you're too much on the nose, or you present too many ideas too quickly, either they are so obvious that they're uninteresting or there's so much confusion that you can't take it all in.

The editor works at both the macroscopic and the microscopic level: ranging from deciding how long precisely each shot is held, to restructuring and repositioning scenes, and sometimes to eliminating entire subplots.

EYES HALF CLOSED

0: When you began as an editor, thirty years ago, you must have discovered certain principles that worked for you. When you look at those early films, do you feel those rules and values have altered? Do you have a desire to re-edit them the way a writer might who looks at an old book?

M: I was interested to go back and look at the first two films I edited, *The Conversation* and *Julia,* which I had done "mechanically"—physically cutting the film itself. After I made the transition to "electronic," and started working on the Avid in 1995, I was curious to see if there was a difference between my mechanical and electronic styles. There wasn't—in fact I was struck by how immediate the earlier films seemed. I would make the same editorial choices today. It made me wonder: How did I know how to do all that?

0: I know you don't like to watch other people's films when you're editing—but when you *do* see other films, by your contemporaries, are you surprised by editors and what they do and how they work?

M: Sometimes. But it has to be extreme. Usually when I'm watching a film, I turn off a part of my critical thinking. But if that same film did appear on my editing machine, I would have a very different reaction to it. That's what happened with Orson Welles's *Touch of Evil* and Robert Duvall's *The Apostle.* When I saw *The Apostle* projected, I thought, Well, perhaps it could be shorter. I didn't have many specific ideas how to help: the negative had already been cut, and it had been screened a few times, to good response. But when I was given the film—to try to reduce its length by twenty or thirty minutes—and was looking at it on the Avid, I realized, Yes, absolutely, this could be shorter, that could be different, I could move these scenes around. . . . I could do this, I could do that. There's a musical equivalent to this, and I'm sure a surgical equivalent—at a certain point your fingers do things that are beyond what your conscious mind is capable of.

O: Do you feel you're essentially imposing your taste, as you do this? It's not just a mechanical thing—

M: I am always at the service of the film, and the film, by rights, belongs to the writer, the director. I'm aligned with them. Financially it belongs to whoever financed it. In the case of *The Apostle*, Robert Duvall financed it, wrote it, acted in it, and directed it. I was lending it my editorial eye, but that was just my take on Robert Duvall's vision.

O: Was *The Apostle* a difficult film to re-edit?

M: No, because the original edit was good, and it was such a linear story. Linearity does sometimes present its own problems, however, particularly regarding a film's perceived length. That was true with *The Conversation,* and *The Talented Mr. Ripley* as well. Those three films are told from the point of view of the central character: the Apostle, Harry Caul, Tom Ripley. Films with a single point of view are on borrowed time if they are more than two hours long. Since there's only one point of view, there's no relief if the audience is not one hundred percent *with* the film, and it can subsequently seem too long even if it isn't objectively so.

O: When you say point of view, in terms of film, you're talking about focussing on just one character—

M: In *The Talented Mr. Ripley,* everything the audience sees is either Tom Ripley or something Tom Ripley sees. There are no scenes where we go off with other characters—as is always happening in *The English Patient,* for instance, where you have a complex dance, different people with different attitudes to the same events. But *Ripley* is about Tom Ripley. Likewise *The Apostle*—there is only the Apostle's story.

O: And that's deadly, you think?

M: No, no, it's not deadly, it's just that the clock runs faster with that kind of film, and unless there's something wildly unusual or different about it, it's better not to have those films be more than two hours long. *The Conversation* is only one hour, fifty-two minutes. Even then, some people think it's too long. With more points of view you can sustain that juggling act for longer, just because it's richer and more complex. A symphony can be longer than a sonata.

O: In writing, especially in poetry, you are always trying to find ways to forge alliances between unlikely things, striking juxtapositions, finding the right shorthand for ideas, metaphors. You see it in the influence of Spanish poetry, what in the West we call "leaping poetry"—those sometimes surreal, sometimes subliminal connections that reveal a surprising path or link between strangers. The way a pun or even a misprint can work on a simpler level. There's the story about Auden writing the line "The poets know the names of the seas" in a poem. It came back from the typesetter as "The ports know the names of the seas," and Auden realized that the misprint was better, and kept it.

M: That's how Harry Caul got his name. Francis was reading the novel *Steppenwolf* at the time he was writing *The Conversation,* and he transformed *Steppenwolf*'s hero Harry Haller to "Harry Caller." Then he thought, No, that's too much, too literal—since Harry was a professional eavesdropper, bugging telephones, et cetera—and he shortened it to "Harry Call." Then his secretary accidentally typed "Caul." And—it was exactly as happened with Auden—he thought, This misprint is much better. "Caul" sounds like "Call," but it gave Francis a visual metaphor for the film, of a man who always wears a semi-translucent raincoat, which is a caul-like membrane, and whenever he's threatened or something bad is going to happen, he retreats behind pieces of

Gene Hackman, as Harry Caul, in *The Conversation,* wearing a caul-like raincoat that became a visual metaphor for the film.

plastic or rippled glass. In several scenes, Francis has Harry spell his name out, C-A-U-L, so we get the point.

0: And that led to—

M: It led from the costume to a way of acting, a way of being: Harry Caul is a man who has a membrane between himself and reality. The film is about the shedding of that membrane, and how painful it is for this character.

0: What's your "state" when you first start to edit the material you've been given? How strict are you? How quick to decide?

M: There's an interesting phenomenon I ran into early on in editing *The Conversation*. As you're putting something together for the first time, you have your own ideas about how it is supposed to work. You see the material that is being shot, and you are simultaneously reacting to it and gently shaping it. Of course the film has dramatic ups and downs, peaks and valleys, but the script indicates an overall shape. When you detect what *you* think is a deviation from that shape, your first impulse is, Well, I'll get to work and fix that now.

Let's say the dramatic slope seems to be going up too fast. Your tendency will be to do things editorially to compensate. Then when you think it's going too slow, you will shorten things or boost the intensity.

If you let that impulse completely loose out of its cage, what you'll find is that you may have pushed down a bulge at point A, but unbeknownst to you, later, at point C, there's going to be a compensating lift that you don't know about yet—no one may know about it since films are usually shot out of sequence. So by pushing down on A you will have an overreaction at C.

It's a stage in the process I call "editing with eyes half closed." You can't open your eyes completely, which is to say, you can't express your opinion unreservedly. You don't know enough yet. And you're only the editor. You have to give everything the benefit of the doubt. On the other hand, you can't be completely without opinion, otherwise nothing would ever get done. Putting a film together is all about having opinions: this not that, now not later, in or out. But exactly what the balance should be between neutrality and opinion is a very tricky question. The point is, if you squash *this* down, then you push the whole curve of the film down, whereas it might have righted itself by its own mysterious means. If you try to correct the film while putting it together, you end up chasing your own tail.

What you really want to do when first assembling a film is to put it together, right from the beginning, without second-guessing anything. Don't try to be too smart too early. When you've finally gotten it all assembled, you can see how far the film has strayed from its intended trajectory. There may have been lots of deviations, but in the end let's say they've mostly cancelled one another out and the film is only ten percent off. Now you can stand back from the whole thing and begin to reshape it judiciously, with some objectivity. Is it the same thing when writing something for the first time?

O: I never have a strict controlling governor present during the first draft of a book. I write as if it were a rehearsal, I attempt or try out everything, though of course a subliminal editing is taking place. But I'm not thinking of that. And I find I am always surprised later. A scene I might think is too casual when I am writing it will later, in context, have just the right tightness. I remember when I was writing the first draft of *Anil's Ghost,* there was a somewhat wild and lack-adaisical chapter where the exhausted doctor, Gamini, hires a car and goes north for some rest, and has a few drunken adventures . . . I was winging it, thinking, well, I will go along with it right now but I suspect I will have to lose it. But when I came back to the section much later, it had just the right energy and change of pace for that moment in the book.

M: Exactly. But the thing about film editing, as opposed to writing, is that there's this huge machine, grinding on inexorably, whether you do anything or not. There are all these deadlines. You have to exercise certain opinions, but it's all a matter of your intuition and judgement about how deep those opinions are on the first round. . . .

Let me ask you a question. As the author of a book, you're in some sense more like our imagined filmmaker of the year 2100, who has a digital power-house in his hands, who can create an entire film by thinking it—someone who can go into a room and come out with a finished film. Within the limits of their craft, that's what writers have always done. There's rarely collaboration in writing a novel as there is in making a film. How do you cope with the authority you therefore have? As you can tell, I'm always trying to break up the authority of the film to allow other voices to be heard—chance voices.

O: There are some writers who have a plan before they sit down for those years of writing a book—they have a concept or plot that's very certain. These are good writers, who know exactly how the story will end. I seem to have none of those assurances. I'm much more uncertain, insecure almost in the way that I'm continually being fed and diverted by the possibilities from the world around me—chance anecdotes overheard, the texture within a rumour—as much as by what my research reveals. For those four or five years, I collect such things, and they fall into a form or a shape or a situation I have established . . . the final stages of the war in Italy, the preparation for death by a gunfighter. . . . As I said, I don't have too much of a governor at work. So it's similar to what you say about the first pass at editing a film. When writing I reject nothing. I am much looser about that, much more accepting at that early stage.

I do this till I have a complete but rough first draft, by which time I've essentially discovered the story. I then put on a different hat—I put on *your* hat—and I start eliminating the wrong notes, the repetitions, the trails that go nowhere. I start merging and tightening the work . . . at this stage three scenes can become one. I take this process as far as I can. There are numerous drafts. . . . Eventually I try it out on my peers and my editor, and I try not to be too defensive about the work. I don't always agree with them, but their responses and notes are an essential stage for me. The only way I can get that democratic, communal sense is to be not so sure about what I have done. But it is also important that I *don't* show them the work until that stage is reached, until I've taken it as far as I can go. I don't want their influence to come too early in the process after my discovery of the story and the form.

And until the last days I always know that this isn't the final draft. The whole tone can be changed or a problem solved by a small structural shift. This is why I love working in theatre. I love the energy of that communal opinion and participation. And especially the influence of that practical side of an art. I've always been more interested in the blocking and the gestures and the lighting and the pacing than whether my words are correct. And I like the radically different chancelike situations. Unlike Beckett, who insisted that the play could be done only one way, and always to his unbending rules.

But all writers have a different set of habits and rules. Apparently Anthony Burgess, who began as a composer, couldn't afford music sheets, so he perfected each page before he copied it onto a sheet. And when he became a novelist he would write the first page, then rewrite it ten times, and only then go on to the second page. Which I personally think would be a deadly limitation to a natural pacing—re-editing yourself, reevaluating yourself every moment and then stepping forwards again.

M: It's all a question somehow of metering out the right amount of generative impulse and modulating that with the right amount of critical impulse, and knowing when to say, I'm not going to touch that right now, I'll wait until I know more.

O: I remember when I was writing *Anil's Ghost,* I had a sequence where Anil was working at a grave site. I wasn't certain, during the first draft, where it was taking place. Guatemala perhaps? Or somewhere in Sri Lanka? The scene appeared about two-thirds of the way through the story. It wasn't working, so I dropped it. Much later, during the final stages of the book—when I sought reactions to it—some people felt Anil was too tough verbally on those around her in the beginning (I had seen that as a defensive quality, but it wasn't coming across). One editor felt that the book hit the ground running—Anil landed by plane in Sri Lanka and the story took off before we knew much about her. I then remembered that scene at the grave site and tried it at the very start as a prologue, now clearly set in Guatemala, where she had been working before going to Sri Lanka. It gave Anil a history, clarified her profession as a forensic anthropologist, showed the reader that her profession was nomadic, and that the job in Sri Lanka began as just another assignment, though she had been

Serolle dropped his arm down into the hollow and struck a match against the rock, so it was not given down there. Light spluttered up and she smeck-bid sunce. Well, when she slammed the door in Boureg he was a dead man to her.

~~An insect chirped like~~ a ~~scratch~~. One of the ~~inhabitants~~ inhabitants ~~this field~~ of the lover of ascetics ~~the~~ ~~min~~ slipped, slid to alongside the ~~actining~~

~~such thing~~

An insect ~~chip~~ chirped like someone ~~winding~~ a watch, one of the inhabitants by the lover of ascetics the mind *kept being* ~~to~~ interrupted by, *kept shid* alongside, the activity ~~such~~ thing. "There has always been slaughter and passion," heard Perone say.

(next 2 pages with one line in both does not ~~mean~~ (~~other~~ this).

_____

Serolle ~~dropped his arm down into the~~ ~~hollow~~ struck a match against the rocky. So it was not a ~~given~~ down there. Light *flickered* ~~spluttered~~ up and she smelled ~~the~~ bid. *beside the ambulance* when she slammed the door in Bourego he was a dead ~~man to her~~.

~~An~~ insect chirped like ~~someone winding a watch~~, *the sound of a watch being wound* one of the inhabitants ~~by~~ the lover of ascetics. [~~Kept being interrupted by, kept shid alongside, the activity of two ascetics~~] "There has always been slaughter and passion," she heard Perone say.
Petipena

born there. But more valuable, the scene also showed her unspoken compassion and empathy for the woman waiting beside the grave site as she worked. I had rejected that moment too quickly. But when I found the right place for it, it solved a lot of problems. And in the right place the scene suggested a lot about her character.

M: We hope we become better editors with experience! Yet you have to have an intuition about the craft to begin with: for me, it begins with, Where is the audience looking? What are they thinking? As much as possible, you try to *be* the audience. At the point of transition from one shot to another, you have to be pretty sure where the audience's eye is looking, where the focus of attention is. That will either make the cut work or not.

O: So before you make the cut, if you feel the audience is looking towards point X, then you cut to another angle where the focus of attention is somewhere around that point X.

M: Yes. If you think of the audience's focus of attention as a dot moving around the screen, the editor's job is to carry that dot around in an interesting way. If the dot is moving from left to right and then up to the right-hand corner of the frame, when there's a cut, make sure there's something to look at in the right-hand corner of the next shot to receive that focus of interest.

O: Or else the film's movement stops and starts again.

M: Right. After each cut it takes a few milliseconds for the audience to discover where they should now be looking. If you don't carry their focus of interest across the cut points, if you make them search at every cut, they become disoriented and annoyed, without knowing why. Now, if you are cutting a fight scene, you actually want an element of disorientation—that's what makes it exciting. So you put the focus of interest somewhere else, jarringly, and you cut at unexpected moments. You make a tossed salad of it, you abuse the audience's attention. That creates the impression of chaos. Or, if you want to hide some-

A manuscript page from *Anil's Ghost.*

thing, by misdirecting the audience's attention you can make them unaware of the thing you would rather they not see. Like an actor's hand in a different position, or a scene where the stage line is crossed, or a mismatched piece of costume or something. . . . These are all the traditional techniques of magic, which is to make the audience look to the right while you secretly do something over here to the left. . . .

And then there is the issue of composition, which is deeper and more mysterious. You can have the man looking at the woman and facing the woman, and saying, "I love you." If the framing is off, it can imply, he really doesn't. *She* thinks he does because he just said so. But the filmmakers can frame the shot in a way that says: He doesn't, really.

Framing a shot in an "off" way to convey another meaning than what is being spoken: in *The Godfather*, Michael Corleone telling Kay it's better if she doesn't come with him.

There's a fascinating example of that, in the first *Godfather,* when Michael is saying good-bye to Kay. She's saying, "Maybe I could come with you." He replies, "No, Kay, it's family, there will be detectives, you just can't." And suddenly the framing has shifted, suggesting that something is wrong. Even though he's still facing her, and being nice to her, the framing says the opposite. He's being pulled by something behind him, something that is going to take him away from her. It's easy for him, in this new composition, to move away from her, into the empty space that's on the right side of the frame....

THERE IS ONLY ONE FIRST TIME

O: When you work now with directors like Francis Coppola or Anthony Minghella, do you go over the scripts with them before they begin shooting? Do you have meetings with them? And if so, what's discussed at such meetings? I would think your influence would be much greater than simply editing a film after it was shot.

M: When I'm considering a project, I read the script, take notes, type them up, and give them to the director. I would include both what I think is good about the script—what attracted me to it—and where I think there may be room for improvement. Perhaps I don't know what I'm supposed to feel at a certain moment. The director may have a very good idea in mind, but I'm just reporting that I don't get exactly what is intended from what's on the page. Or there may be something too long or repetitive, or maybe the script gave me some idea about transposing two scenes. Already, I'm kind of editing.

Writing out these notes helps me see into the project, get under its skin, and the notes give the director some idea of my thoughts and approaches to the material. If he doesn't agree with them, it's good to learn that early. Maybe something can be changed—or maybe I'm just not the right person to edit the film. Either way, the notes serve a purpose.

O: I remember when I first saw you in Rome at Cinecittà, watching rushes of

The English Patient that had been shot the day before, sitting in the dark with your laptop, writing as you watched each take. . . .

M: I write down whatever occurs to me about what I see on the screen. And that text appears in the left-hand column of my database. These are the *emotional* responses: How does the shot make me feel when I see it for the first time? Are there any associations? If, say, the image of a banana occurs to me for some reason, I write "banana," even if I have no idea why. Maybe later I'll find out the reason—but at the moment I don't question any of these things. I try to remain completely open to whatever is going through my mind.

O: That's your response to your very first viewing?

M: Yes, and because the film has come straight from the lab, it's being projected in the order it was shot, so there's usually a degree of chaos. You might suddenly find yourself looking at material from the middle of another scene, which just happened to be shot as a pick-up.

Murch's editing notes from *The English Patient:* the interrogation of Caravaggio.

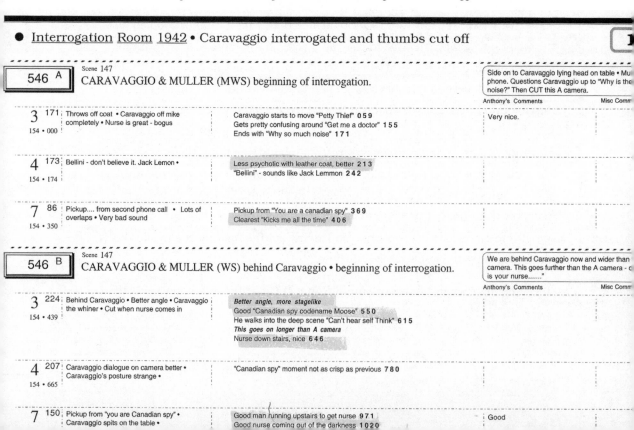

● <u>Interrogation Room 1942</u> • Caravaggio interrogated and thumbs cut off

---

546 A — Scene 147
CARAVAGGIO & MULLER (MWS) beginning of interrogation.

Side on to Caravaggio lying head on table • Mu phone. Questions Caravaggio up to "Why is the noise?" Then CUT this A camera.

		Anthony's Comments	Misc Comm

3 171
154 • 000

Throws off coat • Caravaggio off mike completely • Nurse is great - bogus

Caravaggio starts to move "Petty Thief" 0 5 9
Gets pretty confusing around "Get me a doctor" 1 5 5
Ends with "Why so much noise" 1 7 1

Very nice.

4 173
154 • 174

Bellini - don't believe it. Jack Lemon •

Less psychotic with leather coat, better 2 1 3
"Bellini" - sounds like Jack Lemmon 2 4 2

7 86
154 • 350

Pickup.... from second phone call • Lots of overlaps • Very bad sound

Pickup from "You are a canadian spy" 3 6 9
Clearest "Kicks me all the time" 4 0 6

---

546 B — Scene 147
CARAVAGGIO & MULLER (WS) behind Caravaggio • beginning of interrogation.

We are behind Caravaggio now and wider than camera. This goes further than the A camera - c is your nurse......."

		Anthony's Comments	Misc Comm

3 224
154 • 439

Behind Caravaggio • Better angle • Caravaggio the whiner • Cut when nurse comes in

Better angle, more stagelike
Good "Canadian spy codename Moose" 5 5 0
He walks into the deep scene "Can't hear self Think" 6 1 5
This goes on longer than A camera
Nurse down stairs, nice 6 4 6

4 207
154 • 665

Caravaggio dialogue on camera better • Caravaggio's posture strange •

"Canadian spy" moment not as crisp as previous 7 8 0

7 150

Pickup from "you are Canadian spy" •
Caravaggio spits on the table •

Good man running upstairs to get nurse 9 7 1
Good nurse coming out of the darkness 1 0 2 0

Good

These "emotional" notes are as close as I will ever get to the reactions of the audience seeing the film. There is only one "first time."

Later, when I'm getting ready to put the scene together, I take a second series of notes: these are less emotional and more surgical, and appear in the centre column of the database. I'm no longer the lover beholding the beloved, I'm the surgeon looking at the patient, analyzing her joints and ligaments, writing down the exact footage number at each comment. The free-associative emotional notes give me insights about primary reactions; the surgical notes give me insights about how best to take things apart and connect them again.

Both columns of notes are always in front of me when I'm assembling the film for the first time, but afterwards, in re-editing, I use them less. If I want to completely change the premise of a scene then I'll go back to them, but ordinarily I don't. When I started creating this database, in 1986, I thought I would be referring to my notes all the time. But it turned out differently. At a certain point, I've internalized them.

O: When researching my memoir *Running in the Family,* I interviewed a large number of people, on tape. But in fact I never listened to the tapes again. It's as if I was learning how they spoke, and that allowed me to discover *how* they would tell their stories.

I suppose a writer, unlike a film editor, has to research *and* compose *and* assemble simultaneously during a first draft. When I began the memoir I had no plan for it and certainly had no structure or series of sequences in my head. However, the book was taking me in a hundred directions. I realized I needed some frame or limit, even if it was minimal. I knew it had to do with the persona of the narrator, who had returned temporarily to his birthplace in Sri Lanka, and because of the state of his life at the time was being drawn to certain stories. So that became the point of view—though the subject matter and the content could come from anywhere. I also realized that the story's events could take place only in Sri Lanka, on the island which I left at the age of eleven. They couldn't continue in England or North America. The values and behaviour of that culture were bound to be different elsewhere. The book would lose the magic and the rules of this semi-invented landscape, that sense of fairy tale that comes with a reinterpretation of childhood. As a result, the portrait of my father, whom I knew only in Sri Lanka, is much larger than that of my mother, whom I really got to know in England and Canada. But those were the boundaries I gave to the structure as I wrote.

The thing is, the structure in a book allows the reader a more meditative participation than film. Because we are not bound by time. The experience of a book is not finite. The reader can "investigate" the given story and look back and pause and qualify the material. But I suspect you see the viewer of a film participating in a different way?

M: In film, there's a dance between the words and images and the sounds. As rich as films appear, they are limited to two of the five senses—hearing and sight—and they are limited in time—the film lasts only as long as it takes to project it. It's not like a book. If you don't understand a paragraph in a book, you can read it again, at your own pace. With a film, you have to consume it in one go, at a set speed.

But if a film can provoke the audience's participation—*if* the film gives a certain amount of information but requires the audience to complete the ideas, then it engages each member of the audience as a creative participant in the work. How each moment gets completed depends on each individual person. So the film, although it's materially the same series of images and sounds, should, ideally, provoke slightly different reactions from each person who sees it.

Even though it's a mass medium, it's those individual reactions that make each person feel the film is speaking to him or her. The fantastic thing about the process is that they actually see their own version on the screen. They would swear that they saw it, but in fact it wasn't there. *Enough* was there so that they completed it in their own way, but as it's happening they don't stop to think: That's just me completing it. They *really see* something that appears as authentic to them as anything else that's actually physically in the film.

How does this happen? It can only be because the film is ambiguous in the right places and draws something out of you that comes from your own experience. And then you see it on screen and think: Only I know that, so the film must be made for me.

O: I remember receiving very moving letters from people who had read *The English Patient* to a parent or friend who was dying. And then when the film came out, they found it heartbreaking to see a young woman reading to a dying man in a bed. . . . What seems odd with film is that this private experience takes place in a public space. With the book, you're alone in your living room reading it, but to have that sense in the Colosseum—

M: It's a kind of mass intimacy. A paradoxical state, because you're in a group and benefitting in some strange way from the group experience—yet if the film is any good, you also feel that it's speaking directly to you. Even though it's touching all these other people as well. The ambiguity comes from the fact that it's flowing through, like a river. You don't have a chance to say—

O: Wait a minute—

M: As you do with a book.

O: One of the things about watching a video is that it never feels private. I'm always conscious of it as a group thing. But it never feels that way in a cinema— even at a comedy with people laughing around me. Watching a video at home, I'm always conscious of others in the room—or even if you're alone, there's still the situation of the room. So you can become self-conscious during an erotic scene. . . .

M: The first step in the cinematic state of mind, which is what I think you're talking about, is the urge to leave the familiar surroundings of the house and be drawn outside to a particular film. You are in some way dissatisfied with where you are. You need to get out, to be part of something larger than yourself, yet you're drawn to this particular film in the hope that it will speak to you directly. So again it's this same paradox: Film is a mass medium—you go to the cinema *because* of the massness of it—but you feel good only if the film speaks inti-

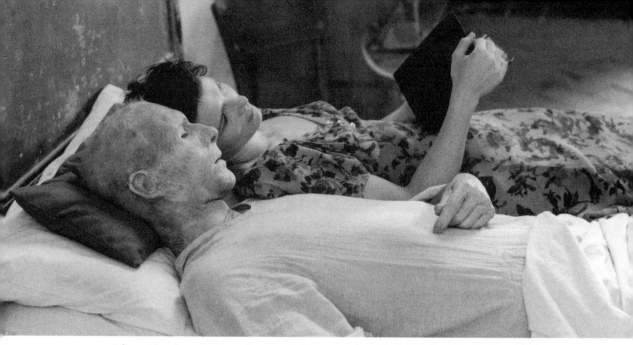

Juliette Binoche as Hana reading to Ralph Fiennes as Almásy in a shot not used in *The English Patient.*

mately to you. Whereas video is something you've brought into your house. It's there at and for your pleasure.

O: Strangely, if you watch a DVD on a computer, with headphones, you get back to that true intimacy that film has.

M: I hadn't thought of that, but you're right. That gets back to the very origins of film, with Edison, who didn't like the idea of projection. He thought film should be seen by individual people looking into their own Kinetoscopes. He thought he would make more money that way.

O: Marcel Duchamp insisted his last artwork, *Étant donnés* . . . , could only be seen by going up to an old door in a gallery wall in which there were tiny holes the viewer had to peek through to see the work that was constructed behind the wall. He wanted his last piece of art to reawaken an original private and child-like curiosity. So it's this shared secret, between two. . . .

THE DARK AGES

O: Dai Vaughan's book *Portrait of an Invisible Man,* on the World War II documentary film editor, Stewart McAllister, has a beautiful epigraph by Ernst Toller: "What we call form is love." And there's a lot in the book about McAllister's interest in mathematics and music and science and patterns—things central to your interests and work too. Perhaps all editors have this pattern-recognition ability.

M: There are underlying mathematical influences that determine how a film gets put together, which are amazingly consistent, seemingly independent of the films themselves. Over the years, I've come to rely on these influences—navigation points—as I work on each film. For instance: 2.5—an audience can process only two and a half thematic elements at any moment; 14—a sustained action scene averages out to fourteen new camera positions a minute; 30—an assembly should be no more than thirty percent over the ideal running length of the film. But these are perhaps just islands above a larger submerged continent of theory that we have yet to discover.

Actually, when you stop to think about it, it is amazing that film editing works at all. One moment we're at the top of Mauna Kea and—*cut!*—the next we're at the bottom of the Mariana Trench. The instantaneous transition of the cut is nothing like what we experience as normal life, which seems to be one continuous shot from the moment we wake until we close our eyes at night. It wouldn't have been surprising if film editing had been tried and then abandoned when it was found to induce a kind of seasickness. But it doesn't: we happily endure, in fact even enjoy, these sudden transitions for which nothing in our evolutionary history seems to have prepared us.

O: What do you think is going on?

M: Well, many things—not least of which are the visual dislocations that happen all the time when we dream. I believe that one of the secret engines that allows cinema to work, and have the marvellous power over us that it does, is the fact that for thousands of years we have spent eight hours every night in a "cinematic" dream-state, and so are familiar with this version of reality.

On the other hand, here's a wonderfully simple experiment which clearly shows that our visual cortex is also routinely editing our perceptions—while we are wide awake—without our ever being aware of it. Stand about eight to ten inches from a mirror and look at your left eye. Now look at your right eye, and then back at your left eye. Do this five or six times in quick succession. You will not notice any movement—your eyes will seem to be completely still. But this is in fact *not* the case, as an observant friend will immediately tell you: your eyes move quite a lot with each shift of focus.

The blurred swish during the movement of the eye is somehow snipped from our conscious awareness, and we are left with just the significant images before and after the movement. Not only do we *not see* the blurred movement, we are *unaware that anything has been removed.* And this is happening all the time: with every movement of our eyes, an invisible editor is at work, cutting out the bad bits before we can ever see them.

. . . I think cinema is perhaps now where music was before musical notation—writing music as a sequence of marks on paper—was invented. Music had been a crucial part of human culture for thousands of years, but there had been no way to write it down. Its perpetuation depended on an oral culture, the way literature's did in Homeric days. But when modern musical notation was invented, in the eleventh century, it opened up the underlying mathematics of music, and made that mathematics emotionally accessible. You could easily manipulate the musical structure on parchment and it would produce startlingly sophisticated emotional effects when it was played. And this in turn opened up the concept of polyphony—multiple musical lines playing at the same time. Then, with the general acceptance of the mathematically determined even-tempered scale in the mid–eighteenth century, music really took off. Complex and emotional changes of key became possible across the tonal spectrum. And that unleashed all the music of the late eighteenth and the nineteenth centuries: Mozart, Beethoven, Mendelssohn, Berlioz, Brahms, Mahler!

I like to think cinema is stumbling around in the "pre-notation" phase of its history. We're still doing it all by the seat of our pants. Not that we haven't made wonderful things. But if you compare music in the twelfth century with music in the eighteenth century, you can clearly sense a difference of several orders of magnitude in technical and emotional development, and this was all made possible by the ability to write music on paper. Whether we will ever be able to write anything like cinematic notation, I don't know. But it's interesting to think about.

One of those great ear-opening experiences happened to me when I was nineteen and working at a radio station, cataloguing its classical record collection. I thought this would be a good opportunity for me to teach myself music history, so I started with the oldest music first, listening to what I was cataloguing as I went. It was a summerlong project, and after three weeks I'd only reached the fifteenth century. I should mention that this was a lonely, one-person occupation—I didn't have much contact with anyone else at the station. But one day I had to go upstairs to the control booth for some reason, and the moment I opened the door my ears were assaulted with a cacophony of rhythmic and dissonant weirdness. This was a staid classical station, and I thought: We don't play this kind of music! What is this?

Holding my ears, I asked the engineer, and he picked up the record jacket and showed me: J. S. Bach's *Saint Matthew Passion.* Suddenly this "chaotic" music began to transform itself, and in only a few seconds, my ears navigated the three-hundred-year distance between the fifteenth century, where I had been, and the eighteenth century, where I was now. I learned, viscerally, that what we think of as normal is largely a question of what we are most often exposed to.

The rules of fifteenth-century music had been almost burned into my head after three weeks, so I could hear that Bach, whom we think of today as very "classical" and "formal," was in fact radically advanced. The *Saint Matthew Passion* is one of the miracles. . . .

"I'm *not* going to mix the picture upside down!"
by Francis Ford Coppola

I met Walter when he was in his twenties. He had come from New York. He was very likeable, obviously extremely intelligent, kind of like the film world's one intellectual, in a way—he had concerns and interests on many levels. At first I thought of him only as a sound artist. Then, as I got to know him, I realized his interests were deeper. We'd have conversations about all kinds of strange things that he was interested in, and my respect for him as a fully dimensional thinker and person only increased. And he had his own impish, quixotic style.

At that time Zoetrope was really more of a lifestyle than it was a film company. We were a group of friends, we had kids, and the kids would come around and play amongst us. We'd gone across the country and made *The Rain People* as a sort of self-contained movie studio—we had all our equipment in a special truck that George Lucas and I had figured out and built.

In Europe I had seen all these young people making films. They had everything—all sorts of sound-mixing equipment—and I told George: we can have that too!

And I spent all the money for the sound mix for *The Rain People* on equipment I bought in Germany! So we had no money left. I said to Walter, Look, we have this wonderful machine and you can do the mix! Of course, all the instructions were in German. . . . I thought it was something that you just plug in and use—but this was all very new, way beyond just plugging it in the wall.

Meanwhile we'd gained entry for *The Rain People* in the San Sebastiän festival, so now we had to deliver it. Walter looked at the equipment and scratched his head. Fortunately we had a teletype machine, and we'd send questions to Germany: What do we do? How do we do this? The answers would come back in German and somebody would translate them. We were all sleeping in the place because we only had a week and a half to do it. Then the whole thing almost came to an abrupt, horrible end, when it turned out that we had to do the sound mix by watching the film on a television. And it turned out that this high-tech specially machined German video camera unit wouldn't work, so we couldn't see the picture.

Everyone was discouraged. What were we going to do? We had no money. I couldn't take it to a studio to do it, so I had a brilliant idea—I went out and bought an amateur Sony camera. This is now getting late and Walter is ready to go—he's like a great pianist—he's ready to mix this picture. So I jam the television in and there's the film on the monitor, but the picture is upside down!

Walter said, That's it! I'll work with this German equipment, but I'm *not* going to mix the picture upside down!

We were really stuck. . . . Then I took the television set and turned it upside down. So Walter then started mixing *The Rain People,* in this room, and he mixed the film in three days and three nights. We got it to the festival. Walter saved us.

. . . We wanted very much to credit Walter for his incredible contribution—not only for *The Rain People,* but for all the films he was doing. But because he wasn't in the union, the union forbade him getting the credit as sound editor—so Walter said, Well, since they won't give me that, will they let me be called "sound designer"? We said, We'll try it—you can be the sound designer . . . I always thought it was ironic that "Sound Designer" became this Tiffany title, yet it was created for that reason. We did it to dodge the union constriction.

Later on, when I realized that my film *The Conversation* was going to be a sound composition, I thought of working with Walter again. Although the film was about privacy, sound would be the core element in it. So I suggested that he edit the picture as well, which he hadn't really done before and didn't think of as his specialty. He agreed. And that was when I got to know Walter as a filmmaker, because of his editing both the picture and the sound.

Walter is a fabulous theorist about many things, and certainly about structure. I think he's one of the few film artists who really thinks in a broader context—in terms of literature or philosophy—rather than just zeroing in on the film. His approach is tempered by his interests in these other areas. In working with Walter, discussing things with Walter, he has his own slow style to arrive at things. It's because he thinks it out—for him structure is an aspect of plot or presentation—whereas I'm very haphazard and jump to this or that. He's like the slow gears that grind very carefully and arrive at a conclusion. I remember talking to him at great length about the structure of *Apocalypse Now,* when I came back for three weeks during a break in the shooting. He suggested I add a sequence, sort of a My Lai massacre scene. The sampan ambush at the beginning of the first act wasn't in the original script. That was his idea.

. . . Normally an editor focusses on the immediate details of his craft— how to match the cutting so it seems smooth—but Walter's perspective starts more with the whole theme of the piece or the narrative goals of the work—rather than with specific dramatic moments.

All editors vary. You consider whether you'll feel comfortable relying on them for the big overall narrative dramatic issues. Or do you just work with them on textural things, things more focussed on editing as a craft? It's like you're working with a tailor. There might be a tailor who can really cut cloth and sew it beautifully! Then another one who will also have an overall design concept. Walter is interested in the overall design concept, but is also a craftsman of the specifics. Whatever he does—even if it's sound—he always offers incredible perspective. He's sort of what a producer is like, or a collaborator who's helping you on the whole project.

A post-production meeting at Francis Coppola's house, during the editing and mixing of *Godfather II*, October 1974. Murch is partially visible at the right edge of the frame.

O: You've been working on re-editing *Apocalypse Now* for the last few months, and you're still in the midst of it. It seems to me to be changing in important ways. For instance, the gunboat crew is more linked to the people they meet in the landscape they go through, and they now react more to the situations they find themselves in: they don't just witness Kilgore's speeches, they talk back, mock him, and even steal his sacred surfboard. Looking back on the original version, I feel that though it had a powerful dramatic plot line—find Kurtz and kill him—the story seemed to insist on its episodic quality.

M: It *is* episodic. It's the nature of this particular beast. But counterbalancing that, there's the river—the liquid track that keeps this story moving forwards despite those episodic interludes.

O: Maybe its episodic feel is also the nature of the quest genre, where the central character—Willard, sent on a secret mission to kill an American colonel

Albert Finney, *right,* as Lawrence of Arabia; he left the film after four days, replaced by Peter O'Toole. Martin Sheen replaced Harvey Keitel in the role of Willard after a month of filming. Coppola, *far right,* directing a river scene in *Apocalypse Now.*

who has seemingly gone insane—simply responds to the events he travels through. . . . He's not an overtly dramatic central character!

M: It's true, Willard—Martin Sheen—is almost entirely inactive until he kills Kurtz—Marlon Brando—at the end of the film. The one nonreactive thing he does is kill a wounded woman in the aftermath of a massacre. Otherwise, he's the eyes and ears through which the audience sees and hears this war. Incidentally, I think Willard's passivity was one of the reasons Francis, who started out with Harvey Keitel in the role of Willard, switched to Martin Sheen after a month of filming.

O: Keitel tends to play extreme characters, he is certainly not Everyman.

M: Marty has an openness to his face, a depth to his eyes, that allowed the audience to accept him as the lens through which they were able to watch this incredible war. Keitel is perhaps more believable as an assassin, but you tend to watch *him* rather than watch things *through* him. And if he doesn't do anything, it's a frustrating experience.

O: Did you ever see the footage with Keitel as Willard?

M: About five months into the editing of the original *Apocalypse Now*, I found myself stuck on some story point, so I got up and walked around, down a hallway . . . and there I found an entire rack of film!—hours of material!—that I had never been told about. I thought: Maybe there's something in here that can solve my problem. I asked my assistant, Steve Semel, but he shook his head and muttered, You don't want to see that! And of course that made me want to see it all the more. I said, Why? What is it? He finally confessed that it was all the original Harvey Keitel footage.

I was now burning with curiosity. I grabbed a roll of film at random and threaded it up on my machine, hit the Play button, and within ten seconds knew Steve was absolutely right. I felt as if my mind was warping in some time-space experiment. There was nothing wrong with the material in itself, it was just profoundly different. Yet the same.

After more than a year of production and many months of editing, the Marty Sheen *Apocalypse* had acquired its own unique immune system—its own blood type and genetic structure. And looking at this material I was suddenly confronted with that difference. It was like meeting a brother you never knew you had.

If Francis had continued in that original Harvey Keitel direction, the film would have been very different. But he soon realized he had to make some very big changes. Not only did Keitel leave the film, but so did many other people associated with the production. It was a big change of regime. I forget how long the interruption was—a couple of weeks maybe—and then they started up again, with a new approach.

O: Albert Finney was supposed to play the lead in *Lawrence of Arabia*, but left after four days. You also wonder what might have happened there. Did Keitel's leaving alter the script?

M: Not so much the script as the attitude towards the material. At the end of *Godfather II*—a big, intense production on all levels—I was talking to Francis about the experience, and he said words to the effect, "I know there are other ways to make films than what we've just gone through. It was like I was hauling my guts out and hacking away at them in full view of the public, and then stuffing them into the film. Why do I have to be so personally involved, and have all these resonances between my life and my films? Just once I'd like to experience what it's like to have a healthy distance from the material. I want my next film to be full of action and three or four bankable stars who will guarantee the financing. And then I can sit in a chair and raise my megaphone and say, 'Action!' and these wonderful things will unroll in front of me. I'd like to do that—just once!"

Lo and behold, a couple of weeks later Francis announced he was going to do *Apocalypse Now*. What was that line from the film? "I wanted a mission, and for my sins they gave me one."

It seems strange now, in hindsight, but the spark of Francis's desire to do *Apocalypse* was an understandable attraction for a big, formulaic action film with bankable stars. So *Apocalypse* rumbled down that unlikely road for about a month, until Francis, to his regret but also his credit, must have realized: I can't pull off this distanced, formulaic kind of filmmaking, I have to get intimately involved in it.

You can see that the dramatic dilemmas of the *Godfather* films, or even *The Conversation,* were close enough to his own life and family and work that whenever he got into a quandary about what to do next he could simply reach into his own experience: he could make such-and-such a character like his uncle Mike. Harry Caul's electronic eavesdropping in *The Conversation* was similar enough to making motion pictures that metaphors were readily at hand from a world he was completely familiar with. However, other than going to military school for a year, Francis had no combat experience—other than making motion pictures!

BURNING CELLULOID

O: The remarkable opening sequence of *Apocalypse Now,* where we see Willard drunk in a Saigon hotel room, seems to cradle all aspects and moments of the film, as well as introducing us to Willard, who will eventually be sent out to kill Kurtz. How was that scene conceived and built?

M: After Francis hired Martin Sheen, he began to feel there were Willard-like character traits in Marty that Marty was not able to fully utilize because they were too dangerous: a certain kind of anger and vulnerability, linked to Marty's problems with alcohol at the time. So Francis set up the scene in the hotel as an acting exercise, but he shot it with two cameras, at right angles to each other, almost as a laboratory experiment. It's a technique Francis had used before: to do a rehearsal but with the cameras turning—to burn celluloid almost as a kind of incense. Because it's a natural human reaction to take things to a deeper level when film is being exposed. It raises the spectre that the scene might wind up in the film. If the conditions are right and if you're lucky, this technique can brand certain things into the psyche of the actor that ordinary improvisation doesn't quite achieve. The original intention was not to use that material in the film, but there were aspects to it, once it was projected, that were provocative: Marty spontaneously smashing his reflection in the mirror, for instance.

Right around this time, Francis set off the biggest gasoline explosion in film history. This was for the napalm drop in the Kilgore—Robert Duvall—section of the film. It was a risky, once-only event, so there were eight cameras running, positioned at different locations. One of the cameras had a telephoto lens, and was running at high speed, producing a slow-motion effect. The material from this camera was not used in the Kilgore sequence, but the shot itself, in slow motion with the telephoto lens flattening the jungle, and the sen-

The scene with Martin Sheen as a drunk Willard in the Saigon hotel room was shot with two cameras at right angles to each other as a rehearsal, with no idea that it would end up in the finished film.

suously licking flames, and the helicopters like metallic dragonflies drifting through the frame at odd angles, was so compelling that it seemed to Francis to capture some essence of what *Apocalypse* was about.

So the opening scene of the film is the collision of those two ideas: of Willard in his hotel room, and that slow-motion napalm explosion, knit together with additional material that Francis shot to help everything coalesce. These concepts were already in place when I joined the crew in August of 1977. But exactly how all of it was going to come together hadn't been worked out— and that became my job: to create an abstract, dramatic, multilayered, visually arresting scene out of this raw material.

O: You worked on the soundscape of the film and were also one of the original editors. How many editors worked on the film?

M: When I started there were already three, so the film was divided into four sections. I had responsibility from the beginning of the film till the end of the sampan massacre, with the notable exceptions of the whole helicopter/ Valkyries attack, which was being edited by Jerry Greenberg, and the Playboy concert, which was edited by Lisa Fruchtman. Richie Marks, who was the supervising editor, had responsibility for everything after the sampan massacre. Jerry left the film in the spring of 1978, and then I took over the helicopter sequence. I worked on that and everything else in the first half of the film for another six months. All told, I was editing picture for a year and then working on sound for another year. Two years—kind of like enlisting in the military!

O: How did all those editors work together, in terms of linking the film stylistically? Did you attempt to combine your styles?

M: We were in and out of each other's rooms all the time, and there were screenings of the film about every month. The work was so complicated, there

were so many decisions that had to happen, both consciously and unconsciously, that you couldn't depend on all the goals being articulated. At a certain point, though, we began to have intuitions about how each of us was approaching the material. That's how it happens. You pick up the good things that the other editors are doing and you metabolize those approaches into what you're doing, and vice versa. It's kind of like women who live together eventually having their periods at the same time.

The most intense discussions happened once Michael Herr joined us to write the narration: ideas would be tossed around as to where Michael's material would go in the film.

O: How much was Michael Herr around during the editing?

M: I believe he started in the spring of 1978—a year after the postproduction began—and was involved right through to the end.

Coppola, *above,* directing Robert Duvall in a helicopter during *Apocalypse Now.*

O: Was the narration in the film script there from the start, or was it added?

M: The original shooting script had voice-over narration—Willard spoke to us. By August of 1977, however, the decision had been made to jettison the narration. And yet, we were supposed to have the film finished in December of 1977. So we had four months to lock the film and create the soundtrack! In retrospect, it wasn't realistic, given the state of the film at the time.

But I was new to the project and I thought that if we were even remotely going to consider a December release, the only way to do it was to reinstate the narration. This seemed perfectly natural to me because I had just finished editing Fred Zinnemann's *Julia,* which had narration. And in the circumstances it seemed necessary—because Willard is such a relatively inactive, inarticulate character. So I took the old narration that was written for the original script, recorded myself reading it, and then put it into the film, both to help get information across—there didn't seem to be any other way to get it in the time available—and also to help structure the events. And just to see how all this might work.

O: Was the narration you recorded at that early stage written by Michael Herr?

M: No, by John Milius and Francis.

O: And then Herr was brought in, I suppose, because of *Dispatches,* his great book on Vietnam.

M: And because, I believe, Milius had adapted some of Michael's articles in writing the screenplay of *Apocalypse Now.*

O: There's something very much like the Do Lung Bridge scene in Herr's book.

M: Milius had read the articles when they were originally published in *Esquire,* and had adapted them—I'm guessing without Michael's approval. So it was also a way of bringing Michael into the fold as a collaborator on the film, and not having him on the outside, saying, Wait a minute! That's my stuff up there!

O: Did Herr do a lot of the rewriting of the narration?

M: Yes, he rewrote all of it. The narration went through maybe a year of evolution. The film would get to a certain stage, Michael would write something new, Marty would come in and read it, and then we would integrate that into the film. The film would change as a result, and then maybe six weeks later we'd go through the whole process again. I think there were seven different recordings of the narration.

O: Did Michael Herr respond specifically to your editing? Did he see it in raw footage and say—

M: He saw the version which had me reading the old narration. I'm sure he thought, I can do better than that!

O: I love the narration. Not just for what it's saying, but also the way we are made to hear it. What was done to create that very intimate, inner voice?

M: There's a direct line from the narration in John Huston's *Moby Dick* through Zinnemann's *Julia* into *Apocalypse Now*. Les Hodgson, whom I met when I was working on *Julia* and who cut sound effects on *Apocalypse Now*, also worked on the sound effects for *Moby Dick*. Fred Zinnemann wanted the narration for *Julia* to have a sonically intimate quality, as if we were somehow overhearing someone's private thoughts, but how do you achieve that? Les told us that when they were recording narration for *Moby Dick* with, I think, Richard Basehart, Huston was dissatisfied with how it was sounding because he thought it had a declamatory quality. Huston was in the studio downstairs and Basehart was up in the booth. Basehart leaned forward close to the microphone and asked: "John, what should I do next?" The microphone was right against his mouth. And Huston said, "That's it! That's what you should do! I want all the narration to sound just like that." "But I'm much too close." "No, you're not!" So the narration in *Moby Dick* was the first to be recorded with the microphone right *here*, with somebody talking just the way I'm talking now, very low and close.

If you position the microphone perfectly, you can get that intimacy without too many unwanted side effects: distorted *b*'s, *p*'s, and *s*'s. I asked Marty to imagine that the microphone was somebody's head on the pillow next to him, and that he was just talking to her with that kind of intimacy.

O: Was it mixed and re-recorded in any special way?

M: In the final mix we took the single soundtrack of his voice and spread it across all three speakers behind the screen, so there's just a soft wall of this intimate sound enveloping the audience. The normal dialogue between characters in the film comes only out of the centre speaker. So aside from the intimacy of the original voice recording itself, there's a distinct shape to the sound as it hits the screen, and it's very different from the rest of the dialogue in the film.

O: When Russell Banks was asked about the narrative voice he used in his novel *Rule of the Bone,* he said he imagined two young boys lying in their bunks, in the summertime, almost asleep. One is looking up at the ceiling and talking. Russell wanted the narrative voice to have a similarly open confessional tone, as if saying: "It's dark and I trust you, and you're lying next to me and we're near sleep, and I'm going to risk telling the truth."

BRANDO

They were common everyday words—the familiar, vague sounds exchanged on every waking day of life. But . . . they had behind them, to my mind, the terrific suggestiveness of words heard in dreams, of phrases spoken in nightmares. Soul! If anybody had ever struggled with a soul, I am the man. And I wasn't arguing with a lunatic either. . . . No eloquence could have been so withering to one's belief in mankind as his final burst of sincerity. He struggled with himself, too. . . . I saw the inconceivable mystery of a soul that knew no restraint, no faith, and no fear, yet struggling blindly with itself.

Heart of Darkness

O: In Conrad's *Heart of Darkness* the moral debate between Marlow and Kurtz when they finally meet is never actually spelled out—there are just chilling paragraphs of Marlow talking about fighting to save Kurtz's soul, and Marlow gives up in the end. My memory of the film's last sequences in Kurtz's compound is of constant smoke and shadow, with Brando half seen. For me the finale didn't have the danger and clarity that was there in the rest of the film. There was a "religious" or "mythical" pitch I didn't fully believe. I wonder if there is other material you found in the process of re-editing that makes the climax clearer, less hidden?

M: Well, we're adding one scene in the Kurtz compound after Willard has been mentally and physically broken down. He's in a metal shipping box—a Conex container—which has been left out to bake in the sun. The door opens and there is Brando/Kurtz. He sits down, surrounded by Cambodian children, like a happy Buddha, and reads Willard three short paragraphs from *Time* circa 1967, about how well the war is supposedly going. As he leaves he tosses the articles to Willard, and says, "We'll talk about these things later." Willard tries to stand up, collapses, and then is brought into the temple.

This addition allows you to see Kurtz in full figure in daylight, which is significant: he's coherent, ironic, and authoritative. And it forecasts the next sec-

A scene added to *Redux:* Kurtz reading an article from *Time* about how the war is going to Willard and the Cambodian children after Willard has been let out of the Conex container used to break him down.

tion of the film, Kurtz's "pile of little arms" monologue: his realization that there is no clean path to victory—you have to fight a war like this on the ground, and ultimately you have to become as savage as the people you are fighting, in order to defeat them. But do you? And at what cost? For an intellectual like Kurtz, ready to go all the way upriver, he arguably becomes more savage than his opponents because he has more resources. In any event, the cost to Kurtz, personally, is his sanity: he cannot act with savagery and remain the human being that he was. It's going to be fascinating to see how including this scene will shift the chemical balance of the film!

O: Perhaps it will locate us more in that place and that time, more than abstract visions of Kurtz in the half-lit darkness did.

M: I hope so. It will certainly amplify the earlier discussions at the French plantation, where the French were arguing about their version of the same problems in Vietnam fifteen years earlier: What is it like for a soldier out in the field to feel he's being sabotaged by protesters back home, who don't know anything about the predicament he's in? And yet why has he been placed in that predicament? The French were in Vietnam because they had been a colonial power in that part of the world. . . . It's very much like what's happening in Zimbabwe now. The white farmers think the land is theirs. By their own logic, this is home: they have been there for four generations, enough to convince them that the land is theirs and they have no other. But their ancestors displaced people who had been on the same land for hundreds, thousands of years.

The Americans had none of that history in Vietnam. Southeast Asia, other than the Philippines, was never part of the American orbit, so the persistent questions are: What are we doing here, and what do we think we're accomplishing? The French had very definite, personal answers to those questions, and even they failed.

O: Were Brando's monologues improvised?

M: Yes. In the sense that Brando hadn't memorized any text. But he and Francis had worked out what he was going to talk about.

O: Brando came on the set quite late in the filming, didn't he? How closely attached was he to the role of Kurtz?

M: He arrived in the Philippines in September of 1976 and claimed to be dissatisfied with the script. The discussions that followed were exacerbated by the fact that he was heavier than he said he would be, and therefore couldn't reasonably do what his part called for. When they reached an impasse in these discussions, Francis would say, Well, just read *Heart of Darkness.* That is where you can see what I'm talking about. And Brando would answer, I've read *Heart of Darkness* and I hate it! And Francis would think, Oh my God.

The production shut down for a week or so while Marlon and Francis battled it out. Finally, by chance or design, a copy of *Heart of Darkness* was left in Brando's houseboat. The next morning he appeared with his head shaved and said, It's all perfectly clear to me now. All along, he had thought John Milius's original script was *Heart of Darkness.*

O: So he'd never read Conrad's novel before. . . .

M: And it had a tremendous impact on him. And now he was bald like the novel's main character, Kurtz. After that turning point, everything went as well as it could. The problem was they'd eaten up so much time arguing and Brando would not back down from his original deal. Whatever he got—his millions of dollars—was for a certain inflexible amount of time. They'd lost the first week in discussions, and everything with Brando now had to be done in half the time.

He even wanted to adopt the name Kurtz, which he had previously resisted. Prior to that, when he'd read the script, he'd said something to the effect that, "American generals don't have those kinds of names. They have flowery names, from the South. I want to be 'Colonel Leighley.' " So Francis had agreed. Suddenly, after reading Conrad, Brando wanted to be Kurtz. But many scenes had already been shot, and his character was being referred to as Colonel Leighley. In the scene where Willard is given his mission, Brando is spoken of as Colonel Leighley.

O: So what happened to that scene?

M: We had to re-record the dialogue. The actors' mouths are saying "Colonel Leighley," but in fact we hear them saying "Colonel Kurtz." It's very carefully done. Listen and watch this scene. . . .

O: Here's Harrison Ford, in a small role as an officer, saying "Colonel Kurtz"— but I guess mouthing "Leighley." It *is* a strangely shot scene.

M: The Italian camera operator on *Apocalypse* didn't speak English. And in this scene, Francis instructed him: "Whenever you're bored, just pan the camera." His rationale being that Willard is very badly hungover, and this camera position is his point of view. It was the most complicated thing to edit, however. I could never tell when anyone was going to be on camera: just in the middle of a big speech, the camera would drift off to the left. The actors weren't sure when the camera was going to be pointing at them, which gave an extraordinary, unsettled feel to the performances. Here you've got Harrison Ford, checking out where the lens is. But it has this wonderful quality. . . . He seems to be watching Willard conspiratorially, as if to say: This is really crazy what's going on here.

O: Did John Milius and Coppola continue to work on the script throughout the production, or was Milius's original script just a starting point?

M: I think John did go to the Philippines. There's a very amusing section in *Hearts of Darkness,* Eleanor Coppola's documentary about the making of *Apoc-*

alypse Now, where, as I remember, John flies out to the Philippines to set Francis straight on some things. But by virtue of Francis's personality and his powers of persuasion, John comes back completely turned around, ready to follow Francis into the volcano if necessary.

O: Was *Apocalypse Now* a project the two of them thought up?

M: No. Originally George Lucas was going to direct, so it was a project that George and John developed for Zoetrope. That was back in 1969. Then when Warner Bros. cancelled the financing for Zoetrope, the project was abandoned for a while. After the success of *American Graffiti* in 1973, George wanted to revive it, but it was still too hot a topic, the war was still on, and nobody wanted to finance something like that. So George considered his options: What did he really want to say in *Apocalypse Now*? The message boiled down to the ability of a small group of people to defeat a gigantic power simply by the force of their convictions. And he decided, All right, if it's politically too hot as a contemporary subject, I'll put the essence of the story in outer space and make it happen in a galaxy long ago and far away. The rebel group were the North Vietnamese, and the Empire was the United States. And if you have *the force,* no matter how small you are, you can defeat the overwhelmingly big power. *Star Wars* is George's transubstantiated version of *Apocalypse Now.*

WILLARD'S GAZE

O: I'm very aware, watching *Apocalypse Now,* how much the characters seem to look directly at us—directly into the camera. In the scene where Willard receives his order from the general to search out Kurtz and kill him, for instance, all the other characters—the general, the CIA agent, the aide-decamp—look directly into the camera.

M: It's a rule, of course, that normally you never allow anyone to look into the camera unless you want to "break the frame" and have the characters directly address the audience, usually for laughs.

Yet in *Apocalypse Now,* you're right, actors look into the camera quite often and it seems to integrate effortlessly into the flow of the film. The curious thing is that I've never read or heard anyone talk about it—it's never referred to in any studies about the film, even though it breaks one of the cardinal rules of filmmaking. In that briefing scene where Willard gets his mission, the characters are looking straight at the camera when they talk to Willard. If they are doing that, the mathematically correct thing would be to have Willard looking at the camera too. Instead he's looking to the left side of the lens, which is correct according to conventional film grammar. Yet you never feel the general is looking at the audience: you believe he's looking at Willard. But when Willard finally *does* look at the camera, at the end of the scene, you feel *he's* looking at *us*—at the audience—and thinking: *Can you believe this?*

I guess it has to do with the intense subjectivity of the film: the fact that Willard is the eyes and ears through which we comprehend this war, and  through whose sensibilities the war is going to be filtered. It's logical, all of that, but it's still amazing that it works as effortlessly as it does.

O: How conscious were you of that, when you were cutting the film? Obviously you *were* conscious of it, but was it something that Coppola had worked out before shooting? Was that something the two of you discussed?

M: It's funny, it was never discussed.

O: Even during the editing process?

M: No. That was the material. There was no alternative.

O: That scene was shot in only that way?

M: They didn't do alternate takes, looking to one side or the other. When the actors talked to Willard, they looked right into the camera.

On Editing Actors
by Walter Murch

The editor has a unique relationship with the actors. I try never to go on to the set to see the actors out of costume or out of character—and also just not to see the set. I only want to see what there is on the screen. Ultimately, that's all the audience is ever going to see. Everyone else working on the film at that stage is party to everything going on around the filmed scene: how cold it was when that scene was shot; who was mad at whom; who is in love with whom; how quickly something was done; what was standing just to the left of the frame. A director particularly has to be careful that those things don't exert a hidden influence on the construction of the film. But the editor, who also has an influence on the way the film is constructed, can (and should, in my view) remain ignorant of all that stuff—in order to find value where others might not see value, and on the other hand to diminish the value of certain things that other people see as too important. It's one of the crucial functions of the editor. To take, as far as it is possible to take, the view of the audience, who is seeing the film without any knowledge of all the things that went into its construction.

In the course of editing, you look at all the material for the scene, over and over again. Your decisions about timing, about where to cut a certain shot and what shot to go to next, all those things, are dependent on an intuitive understanding of the actors. You have to have, and you do acquire, a deep, deep knowledge of the actors. On a very limited bandwidth, you know certain things about them better than they do, and probably better than anyone else on earth does. You see them forwards, backwards, at twenty-four frames per second, at forty-eight frames a second, over and over and over again. You are studying them the way a sculptor studies a piece of marble before deciding to chisel it—here. So I have to know all the hidden veins and strengths and weaknesses of the rock that I'm working with, in order to know where best to put the chisel.

It's disconcerting for me to actually meet an actor in the flesh. For the most part, they have no idea who I am—I'm just a person who worked on the film. There's a vague kind of distraction that I detect in their gaze. On the other hand, I know them better than anyone! But it's only a very narrow spectrum; there are whole areas of their personality that I have absolutely no knowledge of. But, nonetheless, when I meet an actor, the current is flowing in one direction only. It's interesting up to a point, but it's so tricky for me after a while that I excuse myself. . . .

From a conversation between Walter Murch and Michael Ondaatje, hosted by Muriel (Aggie) Murch, on the art of editing in film and literature broadcast on KPFA, Berkeley, California, 1997.

THE NEW SCENES

O: In re-editing the film, you're not just adding new sequences but moving some really well-known scenes to different locations in the plot. And from what I've seen, this is changing the emotional colouring in surprising ways. The water-skiing scene, for example, happened much earlier in the 1979 version. By moving it later, there's now an *earned* delirium and joy, so it's more powerful. It's earned R&R!

M: Yes, it used to come before the Kilgore—Robert Duvall—sequences. Now we've moved it to where it was in the script, which is much later, after the Playboy Bunny show. In its original placement the scene said, in effect, "This boat, this crew is, already and always, kind of wild and crazy." The audience is led to believe this sort of thing must happen all the time with these guys. In this new version you've survived the Kilgore madness, you've been through the Tiger in the Jungle, through the Playboy show and Hau Phat supply depot—where Clean buys the radio that plays "Satisfaction" and Chef buys his *Playboy* magazine with Miss December on the cover. And although we don't see it, somehow Kilgore's surfboard gets exchanged for the water skis. In this new version you see the progression of the crew from order to chaos. There's a smoother arc, which helps reduce the episodic feel of the film.

O: What most alters everything for me, perhaps, is the scene we now have where Willard steals Kilgore's surfboard and gets into the boat, laughing like a kid. He's a teenager. It's his happiest moment in this story. So, suddenly, everything else in our portrait of him gets altered.

M: How did they promote *Ninotchka*? "Garbo Laughs!" We could do the same thing here: "Willard Laughs!"

■

O: What you're recutting on the Avid now is just before the new medevac scene . . . right?

M: Yes. In this sequence Willard is on the boat reading Kurtz's letter to his son, while the boat passes a burning helicopter and trees with bodies hanging from them. And you hear Chief saying, very low, "Alpha Tango . . . Request dust-off. Three, maybe four KIAs [killed in action]. Over." He wants somebody to come in and get the bodies out.

What we're going to do now is add some extra dialogue, Chief repeating, "Alpha—do you read me? Over," to give the idea that he's not getting through. Something's wrong upriver.

We will dissolve from the burning helicopter to this new scene of the boat arriving at the medevac station in the rain. And in addition to the dialogue that was originally shot, there will be some extra lines referring to Chief's earlier request for a dust-off. But the soldiers he's talking to don't seem to give a damn. All this extra dialogue will have to be recorded, so we're going to have to find Albert Hall, the actor who played Chief, and bring him into the studio twenty-four years after he originally played the scene.

The burning helicopter—which before was just a passing event—is now the thing that causes the boat to stop at the medevac station, where we discover

In a new scene from *Redux:* in the Playboy helicopter, Fred Forrest as Chef gets to meet his dream centerfold, Colleen Camp.

Used in *Redux:* the typhoon beginning to hit the set of the medevac camp. Coppola filmed in the rain, creating a sense of dismal hopelessness that also affected the sex scene that follows.

that the impresario Bill Graham—played by himself—and the three Playboy Bunnies are also stranded. Willard negotiates with Graham, who needs fuel for his own helicopter. The problem was that the negotiation was never filmed—a typhoon hit with full strength on that day and they had to abandon filming for a month or so.

O: That missing scene with Bill Graham that was never shot, how do you deal with that?

M: We're treating the moment elliptically. You see Willard wandering through the desolate camp, and we intercut his wandering with a fight that's beginning among the crew of the boat. Then Willard is beckoned into one of the tents by Bill Graham. The fight escalates, Willard returns, stops the fight, and tells them about the deal he's made: the crew can spend a couple of hours with the girls in exchange for fuel.

O: That'll solve it?

M: I hope so! The audience will see the results of the missing scene rather than the scene itself. Francis has just viewed this section and thinks it's worthwhile trying to put it in.

THE DEAD FRENCH

O: I find the addition of the French plantation scene in the new version the most remarkable. The audience is left wondering whether the characters there are real, or whether the gunboat is meeting ghosts. Why wasn't the scene included in the original film?

M: Probably the trickiest thing in this version of *Apocalypse Now* has been the French plantation sequence and how to get into it—even trickier, how do we get out of it? It was something that completely foxed us back in 1978. Structurally, the scene always happened too late in the film: once the boat passed beyond the nightmare of the sampan massacre and Do Lung Bridge, it seemed to enter another world, and there wasn't the physical, temporal, or even psychic space for a dinner-table discussion about the French involvement in Vietnam in the early 1950s. The viewer needed to arrive at the Kurtz compound as quickly as possible.

We tried many different approaches—shortening the scene, putting it earlier in the film—but nothing worked. An important element of the French plantation is the burial of Clean—Larry Fishburne—who has just been killed in a firefight, the first crew member to die. If the scene came earlier, the burial would have to be eliminated. But burying Clean is one of the reasons for the boat to come to shore. It was a dilemma.

At any rate, the scene lingered in the film like an invalid, getting shorter and shorter, until finally we cut it out completely. The unavoidable side effect of this decision was that Clean's body just disappears. In the original version of the film you never know what happened to him, which is a little strange, and out of keeping with Chief's obvious grief at losing someone who was like a son to him.

Frames of the French plantation from the original and later shoot; only the later, ghostly dock was used in *Redux*.

Back in 1978, I had never seen any of the raw material for the French plantation since my responsibilities ended halfway through the film, with the sampan massacre. When I started looking at it, I discovered that Francis had shot the approach to the plantation in two different ways. In the original shoot, the French were very proper, and they came down to the dock, which was in immaculate condition, and formally introduced themselves to Willard and the crew.

Later, Francis restaged the boat's approach with the dock in ruins, and with the French soldiers materializing, bedraggled, out of a swirling mist, as if they were ghosts. I believe Francis was responding, even at that stage of shooting, to the awkward problem that the French can't quite be real people, so far upriver, so late in the film. Where do they get supplies, how do they get in and out, how do they sell their rubber?

All this was a revelation to me.

So I screened the material for both versions of the approach, and it seemed that the ruined, ghostly version was probably the best path to take.

But there was a problem waiting for me: the *departure* from the French plantation had been shot only once and showed the dock in its pre-ruined state. There was no departure with a ruined dock. You couldn't arrive in ruins and depart with the dock all fixed up! So if we used the ruined-dock material to get into the sequence, I couldn't get out.

Then, in combing through the raw material, I found a shot with Martin Sheen—Willard—and Aurore Clément where she gets out of bed, undresses, and closes the mosquito netting all around the bed. There was something beautifully evocative about seeing her silhouetted against the mosquito netting, and I thought, She looks like a ghost, and the mosquito netting looks like fog.

It was *then* that I made the connection. If we began the French plantation later, if we let Chief's grief for Clean's death take us into the fog that overwhelms the boat, when the fog begins to lift, there are the ruins of the plantation, as if Willard and the crew had gone back in time. Then the film could get

In *Redux* at the plantation, Aurore Clément gets out of bed with Willard, closes the mosquito netting, and becomes a disembodied silhouette.

into what Francis described as the Buñuel-like ghostliness of the dinner discussion, people stuck forever in the political passions of the early 1950s, which were a mirror image of the American involvement in Vietnam fifteen years later.

0: And ghostliness is created at the end of the sequence by the simple physical barrier of that mosquito net between Aurore Clément's character and Willard. A startling moment.

M: What originally happened next is that Willard grabbed her and pulled her through the mosquito netting, they made love, and—as in the script—you found them the next morning. But in this version the image of Aurore dissolves away and you're left with the disembodied silhouette of this woman, hovering against a milky-white background. Then you realize you're back on the boat, where you started.

When I discovered that transition, which was not intended in the script, something unlocked for me. I felt that I was beginning to grasp the language of this new version.

O: At what stage will you be able to tell if all these additions blend into an organic whole?

M: What I haven't done yet is look at all the additional scenes within the framework of the complete film, although I've done it in thirty-minute sections. But Francis and I haven't run the film from the beginning to the end to see what effect all this has. And to get a greater sense of how the themes of the film have been building up. When I watch a scene in the context of the whole work, it may appear just the opposite of how it seemed when I saw it in isolation. But it's already clear that this is the funny, sexy, political version of *Apocalypse Now*. Willard has a romantic interlude at the French plantation. Lance and Chef have theirs at the medevac station. There are political arguments about the French involvement in Vietnam, so similar to ours. And Kurtz questions the accuracy of how the war is being reported back home.

With *Apocalypse Now Redux,* we're grafting these branches onto a tree that already had an organic, balanced structure. Knowing that we're changing the organism, we're trying not to do anything toxic to it, and to keep everything in some kind of balance. At this point, I don't know what the result will be. I have some intuitions, but my mind is completely open.

O: What happens next?

M: Once we have the sequence of scenes in something like the final order, we can begin to get the soundtrack prepared for the final mix. This alone is terrifying enough: we have to go back to the original masters and find a way to reweave the fabric of the sound—so not only will the transitions into and out of the new material be perfectly undetectable but also the quality of the sound of the new sections will coexist on friendly terms, both artistically and technically, with the work that we did twenty-one years ago, which is not being changed.

Luckily, some of the crew who worked on the film back then are constructing the new soundtrack: Michael Kirchberger and George Berndt—and of course me—so there's enough of what you might call "tribal knowledge" to get us through some of the potentially difficult rapids.

One peculiarity that we confronted almost immediately was that none of the original sound synced up with the image. This was a problem back in 1977, and the "fix-it" solution then was to remove one frame every thirty seconds to keep the sound from drifting slowly ahead of the picture. On short takes, less than a minute, it would hardly be noticeable, but Francis shot many ten-minute takes. Fortunately, what we have now that we didn't have then is a digital toolkit for such problems: we can dial in the amount of drift and compensate for it automatically. I don't know why the problem was never rectified—I think it had something to do with the humidity and the Technovision cameras that Vittorio Storaro had brought with him from Italy.

We are also going to have to ask Marty Sheen, Robert Duvall, Albert Hall, and Sam Bottoms—who played Lance—to come back into the studio and re-record some of the dialogue from the scenes they shot back in 1976, twenty-four years ago. I don't think that's ever happened on a film before.

O: How will the original footage and newly added footage live together?

M: Vittorio Storaro hopes to print the new version using the Technicolor "three-strip" process. This is how all Technicolor films were made until the mid-1970s, when the process was abandoned because it was too labour-intensive. Now the old technology has been revived in a computer-controlled version. So the printing of the final film will actually be a dye-transfer process, somewhat similar to the way pictures are printed in magazines. Even though it's film, it's not a photographic process.

The sound team, *top right,* accepting Academy Awards for *Apocalypse Now. Left to right:* Richard Beggs, Mark Berger, and Walter Murch, 1979. Rod Steiger looks on. Leaving the Palais de Festivals after presenting *Apocalypse Now Redux* out of competition for the 54th Cannes Film Festival, May 11, 2001. *Left to right:* production designer Dean Tavoularis, Aurore Clément, Francis Ford Coppola, Walter Murch, and Sam Bottoms.

54ᵉᵐᵉ FESTIVAL INTERNATIONAL DU FILM

CANNES 2001

The advantages of this system are that there is less photographic grain, and Vittorio will have greater control over the individual colours and densities—plus it will never degrade. A normal film colour negative, even if it's stored very carefully at the correct temperature and humidity, is slowly eating itself alive, chemically speaking. You can only slow that process down, you can't stop it from happening.

The hair-raising thing, though, is that to go with this three-strip process we have to recut the old negative and integrate it with the negative of the added material, and once we do that, we can never go back to the original. But Vittorio feels that the only way to make the new version work is with the three-strip process, which gives him the ability to counteract the fading that's apparent in the negative of the original film.

There's a very good fine-grain master copy of the 1979 negative, so it won't be completely destroyed, but it's a big, irrevocable step to take.

O: Ingmar Bergman talks somewhere about how making a film, with a large group of people, is akin to a medieval community building a cathedral.

M: We were talking earlier about having multiple editors on a film like *Apocalypse Now*. But it seems to happen throughout the filmmaking process. How do you get 150 temperamental artistic types to work together on the same project, and make something that not only comes in on schedule, on budget, but that has an artistic coherence. It's simply beyond the ability of a single person, a director or a producer, to cause that to happen by any series of direct commands. It's so complicated that it just can't be done. The question is: How does it happen?

If you've ever remodelled a house, you'll know how difficult it is even to get four or five carpenters to agree on anything: billions of people have been building houses, for thousands of years—"houseness" should almost be encoded in our DNA. And yet when you remodel, it's very common to go double over budget and schedule.

By comparison, we've only been making films for a hundred years, and a film crew is made up of sometimes hundreds of people, yet somehow, miraculously, at the end of "only" a year, there is, one hopes, a wonderful, mysterious, powerful, coherent, two-hour-long vision that has no precedent—and the more original the vision, the more the process is amazing. And yet studios are furious with us if we go ten percent over budget and schedule!

We tend to accept this miracle because we're right in the middle of it—it seems somehow normal—but I think in the future, hundreds of years from now, people will look back on our period a bit the way we look back at Gothic cathedrals. How did they build those cathedrals, when they didn't have computers, when they didn't have the engineering knowledge and tools that we have? How did they know exactly how to build those gigantic creations, each more marvellous than the last? It would be a challenge for us today, despite all our power and knowledge, to duplicate Chartres cathedral. And yet it was done with human muscle and, literally, horsepower. How did they dare to dream and then accomplish such a thing? These fantastic buildings seemingly came out of nowhere. Suddenly Gothic architecture was happening all over Europe at the same time. It's phenomenal what went on, and it's mysterious to us today how it was actually accomplished. It's the same with the Egyptian pyramids. I think future generations with powers we can't even imagine will look back on filmmaking in the twentieth century and say, How did they do all that, back then, with their ridiculously limited resources?

SECOND

CONVERSATION

L O S   A N G E L E S

Walter and I met up again in October 2000 in Los Angeles on the day when he was to be fêted by the Academy of Motion Picture Arts and Sciences for his work as an editor and sound designer. Various friends and colleagues were to speak that night about his work, including Francis Coppola, Saul Zaentz, George Lucas, and Rick Schmidlin.

The theatre was packed, and the mood was affectionate. The film community was celebrating a talent that was a secret to most of the public, but not to them. Film editors and sound editors, such as Randy Thom, who had worked with and learned from him in the past, were there, as well as many old friends like writer-director Matthew Robbins.

Our second conversation once again ranged across large areas and included many subjects—from the influence of Beethoven and Flaubert on film; to the editing techniques handed down to the West by Eisenstein as well as Kurosawa and other Asians, to the essential quality of ambiguity in any art. For two long mornings we sat huddled over coffee in the empty café of an L.A. hotel after a breakfast with Walter's wife, Aggie, wandering into discussions of

Walter recording the perfect wind to have for future projects during a sandstorm in Egypt, near Saqqara, 1980.

opera or Jim Morrison, lost scenes in films, early "metaphorical sound" in *King Kong* and in the work of Renoir and Welles and Hitchcock, the difficult art of translating novels to film, and finally, Walter's new passion—translating Curzio Malaparte's work into poetry, which he has been doing in his spare time.

THE RIGHT TIME FOR THE INVENTION OF THE WHEEL

O: We talked once about the people you thought had influenced the direction and the form of cinema. I think among these were Edison, naturally, but also other more unlikely names.

M: Yes, the three fathers of film: Edison, Beethoven, Flaubert! It's an attempt to answer a tantalizing question: Why did film develop as a storytelling medium so quickly after its invention? It seems natural to us today, but there were many people a century ago, including even the inventors of film—Edison and the Lumière brothers—who didn't foresee this development. Auguste Lumière went so far as to say that cinema was "an invention without a future."

He could have been right—there *are* frequently "inventions without a future," inventions that are ahead of their time, or outside their appropriate culture. The Aztecs invented the wheel, but didn't know how to use it except as a children's toy. Even though they built roads that to us scream out to have a wheel put on them, nonetheless they continued to drag things around. The society itself was blind to the possibilities. The Greeks did the same with the steam engine. So you have to look not only at the invention itself, but the social and cultural context that surrounds it. They all have to mesh.

O: So what would have happened if somehow film had been invented in 1789 rather than 1889? Would we have known what to do with it? Or would this imaginary eighteenth-century cinema have remained a kind of "Aztec wheel"?

M: I rather suspect the latter. Because there were cultural movements that matured in the nineteenth century—the ideas of realism (from literature and painting) and dynamics (from music)—that are actually as much a part of cinema as the technical nature of film itself. And in 1789, realism and dynamics had not yet been born.

This is where my idea of the Three Fathers comes in. I'm using Edison to stand for all the technical geniuses of early film—people who invented the physical side of film, its mechanical, chemical nature. But almost fifty years earlier, writers like Flaubert—using him in the same shorthand way—had invented the idea of realism.

There were many people in France writing realistic novels in the nineteenth century—Balzac comes to mind—but Flaubert was the most conscious of what he was doing, and agonized about it the most. Closely observed reality, for its own sake, had not really been a part of the tradition of literature in the eighteenth century. Flaubert will spend a whole page evoking tiny sounds and motes of dust in an empty room because he's getting at something. He's saying there's meaning to be got out of the very closely observed events of ordinary reality. In literary, scientific and photographic terms—the invention of photography happened when he was in his teens—the nineteenth century, to a much greater degree than the eighteenth, was concerned with the close observation of reality. All of science in the nineteenth century was about very close observation of small things. . . . The nineteenth century focussed and greatly expanded these concepts. It made them central to the novel, to the symphony, to painting.

As often happens with revolutionary ideas, they were not easily accepted at first. To some readers realism must have seemed too ordinary to be literature: if the writer was just describing what the reader could see with his own eyes, why write at all? It probably seemed very drab.

And thirty years before Flaubert, composers like Beethoven exploited the idea of dynamics—that by aggressively expanding, contracting, and transforming the rhythmic and orchestral structure of music you could extract great emotional resonance and power.

Composers before Beethoven had, as a rule, composed in separate movements, but every movement both defined and then explored a unified musical space. If you listen to ten seconds of the first movement of any Haydn symphony and then to another ten seconds halfway through and another ten seconds later in the same movement, they resemble one another. When you listen to the whole piece, it's as if you were moving through different rooms of a palace, going in one room, looking around, and then, closing the door and, with the next movement, going into the next room.

Beethoven—I think because he was so enormously influenced by nature rather than architecture—threw that away. The space of each movement has tremendous variety. He will take a huge sound, one that involves all the instruments of the orchestra, and suddenly reduce it to a single instrument. Everything will come down to a single flute for a while, and then a rhythm you haven't heard before will creep up in the background, and then you go off on another tangent again—all within one movement.

Beethoven set the agenda for the entire nineteenth century, musically. By and large, the revolution he instigated was accepted quite quickly. He was deemed a genius of music in his own time. Young people got really excited about this, and old folks thought the world was coming to an end. Carl Maria von Weber said after listening to the Seventh Symphony, "If Beethoven wants his passport to the lunatic asylum, he's just written it!"

If you're used to the old form, this new form sounds like somebody who can't stick to a topic. It's as if a very excited person comes to sit by you while you're having a nice conversation, and then starts talking about ten different things one after another. But music for the rest of the nineteenth century followed that form, and it's a form that film is naturally suited to.

0: So even if Beethoven and film are separated by a century, the line of influence is there.

M: When you listen to Beethoven's music now, and hear those sudden shifts in tonality, rhythm, and musical focus, it's as though you can hear the grammar of film—cuts, dissolves, fades, superimposures, long shots, close shots—being worked out in musical terms. His music didn't stick to the previous century's more ordered architectural model of composition: it substituted an organic, wild, natural—sometimes supernatural—model.

In any case, by the end of the nineteenth century there had been almost a hundred years of Beethoven—this dynamic representation of form—and not quite a hundred years of Flaubert's closely observed reality. And the reason film blossomed into the form we know today—we didn't experiment very long with film, it evolved rapidly—is that it happened to be the right place for these two movements—realism and dynamism—to come together and find some sort of resolution. Given its photographic nature, film is very good at closely observing reality. Because you can move the camera and move the people—and because you can edit—it's very good at the dynamic representation of "reality." Much better than theatre, for instance, which is not very good at, say, fight scenes: when you have a big fight, you're looking at relatively small people onstage fighting each other, whereas a fight scene in a film can be simply overwhelming.

By the end of the nineteenth century these once revolutionary ideas of realism and dynamism had been thoroughly accepted into European culture. Generations of artists, writers, and composers—as well as society at large—had by 1889 completely internalized these ways of looking, thinking, listening. The whole nineteenth century was steeped in realism and dynamism!

And then along came film: a medium ideally suited to the dynamic representation of closely observed reality. And so these two great rivers of nineteenth-century culture—realism from literature and painting, and dynamism from music—surged together within the physical framework of film to emerge, within a few decades, in the new artistic form of cinema.

Within fourteen years of its invention, film grammar is being determined in *The Great Train Robbery*—the cut, the close-up, parallel action—even while social and economic changes are helping integrate cinema into the pattern of people's daily lives, and making the whole thing pay for itself. Within another dozen years, the feature film was almost as we know it today, thanks to D. W. Griffith and *The Birth of a Nation*. And then synchronous sound was added twelve years later virtually completing the revolution.

O: And we also had the influence of nineteenth-century painters. We were essentially handed the concept of those large screenlike canvasses.

M: When Manet exhibited his painting *Olympia,* there was an outcry because she was just an ordinary woman, not a mythical creature. Mythical creatures could be painted in the nude, but not ordinary women you could see walking down the street.

O: Do you remember John Berger's essay about Géricault and the portraits he did of people in mental hospitals? He talks about how these were the first portraits done of people who were not a part of high society. Film wasn't just the shock of an art form that dramatically thrilled you—it also recorded reality graphically. And also could be socially conscious, depicting real, unhistorical people.

M: You sometimes get a situation in chemistry, where a solution is supersaturated: a vessel full of water and salt, and the salt is unable to crystallize. An unbalanced situation, where it's ready to react but not quite yet, because the vessel is so polished and perfect. But if you tap the vessel, you can shock the solution into crystallizing suddenly. I think film is one of those shocks, an invention that was unanticipated, in all its glory. And the shock of it caused certain things to crystallize within the supersaturated solution of nineteenth-century culture.

O: Even the fast-changing demographics at the end of the nineteenth century, as people moved to the cities, helped create the audience for film.

M: Exactly! The industrialization of Europe and North America concentrated people in cities and provided an audience that didn't exist at the end of the eighteenth century. Particularly in North America, there was a large immigrant urban audience from many different countries who had no common language: cinema provided that language. That providence is a cornerstone of American cinema. It's one of the reasons American cinema proved and is still proving to be so strong all over the world: the roots of American filmmaking were in finding the common denominator that unified people from different cultural backgrounds. This was not true in other countries.

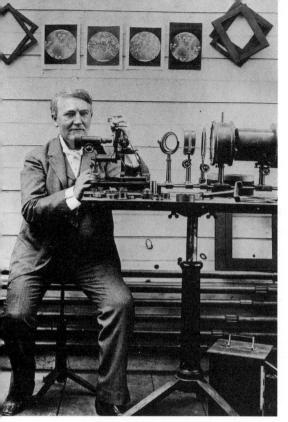

Thomas A. Edison with his micrograph, photographed by Edward M. Dickson, 1893.

O: And then there's the technical influence—the other filmic influence you mentioned—of the inventor Thomas Edison.

M: What's fascinating about Edison is that he was much more interested in the sound than the picture. Towards the end of his life, when he was asked what his favourite invention was, he unhesitatingly said, "Sound recording."

O: This from the man who invented the lightbulb and motion pictures and thousands of other things. . . .

M: I think it was because sound recording was completely unanticipated. It seemed doubly miraculous. People had been toying with the idea of motion pictures, in some form, all during the nineteenth century. Electric light as well. Sound, almost by definition, was uncapturable: sound imagery was used in many poems as the epitome of the evanescent—the flower that fades as soon as it blossoms. So it was a fantastic surprise to people that Edison could record this most ephemeral thing.

William Dickson, on the other hand, was a young man who had emigrated from England to the United States on an almost holy quest to invent motion pictures. He had seen the implications of Muybridge's experiments in England in the late 1870s.

Dickson badgered Edison—you can imagine the number of people who wanted to work for the great inventor in those days—until Edison finally hired him and tested his mettle by putting him to work for five years on an ore-smelting idea. So Dickson, who was about twenty-six, went through a five-year

sorcerer's apprenticeship, finally devising a way to economically extract bismuth from raw ore.

Eventually Edison relented, and they started to work on motion pictures—Edison's rationale was that people might be interested to see the faces of the people who sang on his records. Cinema began as a music video! That was about the extent of its appeal, as far as he was concerned. Whereas Dickson was clairvoyant about the potential of motion pictures. He wrote a book in 1895, which has been reprinted by the Museum of Modern Art in New York, and it's astonishing how many of his predictions have come to pass.

O: When I first saw you working on *Apocalypse Now Redux,* you were also working on an old piece of film by Edison and Dickson. The project reminded me of an archaeological dig, because I think you were reconstructing one of the earliest pieces of film that was married to sound.

M: Yes, it was a real detective story, involving a forgotten, broken sound cylinder found at Edison's lab in Menlo Park. It started when Patrick Loughney, the head of film and television at the Library of Congress, developed an intuition that this cylinder, which first appeared mislabelled in a 1960s inventory, might actually be the soundtrack for a seventeen-second Kinetoscope that Edison made in 1894. The film is of Dickson playing a violin into a huge recording horn, and it's clear from looking at the image that they must have been recording the sound as they were filming. But the accompanying soundtrack had been lost—some wondered if it had ever even existed. That is, until a few years ago, when Patrick located this particular broken cylinder and had it repaired.

The first known recording of film with sound: frames from a seventeen-second Kinetoscope made by Edison in 1894 showing William Dickson playing a violin into a large recording horn. Murch was able to put the film and sound track in sync.

And it turned out in fact to be a recording of someone playing the violin, with many stops and starts, and fragments of muffled conversation. But the Library of Congress had no means to put the image and the sound in sync: the film was shot at forty frames a second (rather than our standard today of twenty-four) and lasted seventeen seconds, whereas the sound on the cylinder was two and a half minutes long. So the question was: Which seventeen seconds of sound went with the film? And then, once you decide that, how do you put it in sync with the film, which is playing at a nonstandard frame rate?

O: How did you get involved in all this?

M: I was put in touch with Patrick through Rick Schmidlin, who had produced the restoration of Orson Welles's *Touch of Evil,* and Patrick asked if I could help. I had my assistant, Sean Cullen, digitize both the sound and the picture, and consequently was able to render the film at normal speed and then find various sync points with the music. I tried dozens and dozens over a period of a couple of hours, until I found the one that worked. The soundtrack and the picture were finally in sync with each other for the first time in 106 years!

O: So this is the first known recording of film with sound?

M: Yes. It pushes back the threshold of film sound by a couple of decades. There's anecdotal evidence of something done a few years earlier, in 1891, but neither the film nor the image for that has turned up yet.

As for this fragment from 1894, I'm anxious to use some new technology that's just been developed to see if we can eliminate the surface noise and reveal what might be an off-the-cuff conversation between Edison and Dickson. This would be doubly fascinating! Not only would it be Edison and Dickson, pioneers of

cinema, but it would be the first recording ever of a natural conversation between people unaware that they were being recorded.

There's a formality to all recordings of the human voice we have from that period, very much like the photographs of people sitting in their Sunday best, looking right at the camera with blank expressions on their faces. Photography for most people was a once-in-a-lifetime experience: when they looked into the lens of the camera, they were looking at eternity—this is how they would be seen by future generations. It was the same with sound: the experience of having your voice recorded was a magical thing. So you spoke in your Sunday-best voice, very clearly, into the recording horn.

But on parts of this particular cylinder—the violin test from 1894—people were simply talking, naturally. I hope we can decipher it: not only for what they say, but how they are saying it.

0: I hope we don't hear them saying, "He'd kill us if he got the chance."

M: They probably were. . . .

0: I remember seeing the first filmed interview, done in a mining town in England. One of the first documentaries made, produced, I think, by John Grierson, of a couple whose house is full of rats. The wife is speaking to the camera and the husband is also—like this—looking at the camera, kind of caught in the glare. For the first minute he's just staring at the camera, and then slowly we begin to witness him listening to what his wife is saying, and his head turns and he watches and listens to her in amazement as she tells a story of how she caught three rats. He's completely forgotten the camera . . . for the first time.

Opposite: From *Housing Problems,* 1935, a documentary produced by John Grierson about working-class housing problems, in this case, one large rat. Small and big films: Coppola, *above left,* rehearsing a scene from his second film, *You're a Big Boy Now,* with Elizabeth Hartman, Peter Kastner, and other actors; and, in striped sweater, *above right,* under the dolly, checking a shot in *Godfather II.*

MURDER MUSIC

O: You and Francis Coppola and George Lucas were originally only involved with low-budget/independent films. Did you feel you'd stepped into another kind of realm when you worked on the sound for the first *Godfather* film for a large studio?

M: Absolutely. It was terrifying! We were in our twenties, remember. It was still us ex–film students, but suddenly there was now the added element of the studio. For a while we were allowed to continue to work in San Francisco. But in October of 1971, Bob Evans—who was head of Paramount—ordered that the film come down to Los Angeles. For the first time I was going to be working in Los Angeles, on a feature film, at a studio, with access to their sound library, but also with all the other things that go along with studio productions, both good and bad.

I learned a lot, not least how much I, even with my lack of experience, could push the studio system to produce unusual results. So rather than simply saying, This is a studio film, this is the way they do it, I kept trying to push the soundtrack in the direction of the films we had already made.

In order to get the right sound atmosphere for the wedding scene in *The Godfather*, Murch used the "music guide track," usually thrown away, and mixed it with the original music. He also did this the next year with *American Graffiti*.

For instance, I was already fascinated with the ability to shift perspective in sound, particularly in something like the wedding scene in *The Godfather*—the shift from the noise of the wedding outside to the noise of it inside the room, and even when you're outside, to hear different perspectives. I wound up using the music guide track—something that's shot at the time of filming, and usually thrown away—that Francis was playing during the shoot to get people to be in the mood of a happy Italian wedding.

I thought, This sounds great, why throw it away? It sounds like a real wedding. In fact, you could see the loudspeakers in the film. So I painfully reconstructed, out of bits and pieces, a master track of this atmosphere—which had voices in it but mainly that loudspeakery music—then found the original recording of the music and put those two things in sync with each other, so that in the mix we could blend from one to the other and have lots of reverberation and rackety voices, or have it be more up front, with a fuller sound. This was something I also did the next year, on an even more developed level, with *American Graffiti*. But there are actually little fragments of this technique, in embryonic form, in *THX 1138* and *The Rain People*.

O: This was not the usual way of doing this on a studio film at the time?

M: Don't make me laugh! However, many years later, I learned this was exactly what Orson Welles had done on *Touch of Evil*, in 1958. He had the idea to use the "bad" sound of recorded music coming over loudspeakers to give a sense of place and as a way of scoring the film using source music.

My twist on the idea was having a track of the good sound too and then being able to fade between both, to have different proportions of one and the other, depending on where you wanted to be. If you were close to the band, you featured the live sound.

Explaining what I wanted to do, and getting that through the machine of the studio, was a challenge. But the mixers actually got excited by it. They thought it was a good idea.

O: Did you have control during the mix of *The Godfather*?

M: To a certain extent, I did. Francis was directing *Private Lives* for American Conservatory Theater, up here in San Francisco, so I was his "man in Havana"—I was the person representing the intentions of the director, which, because Francis trusted me, were frequently my own intentions.

O: Were there any scenes that created problems for the studio?

M: There was an intense crisis with the music. When Bob Evans heard Nino Rota's music, he felt it would sink the film, that it was too lugubrious and didn't have enough energy. He wanted Henry Mancini to rescue the film and to make it more hard-boiled. He didn't like these rather soft-edged ideas that Francis and Nino had come up with—he wanted it to be more American and punchy. So there was a big struggle between Francis and Evans, during which Francis at one point said he would quit the film and take his name off it if that happened.

O: You mean the main theme music?

M: Yes . . . well, *all* the music.

O: My God, it's a trademark!

M: Well, nobody knew that at the time. Remember, someone at MGM wanted to cut "Over the Rainbow" from *The Wizard of Oz.* Frequently what happens in film is that people, especially distracted executives, will say, I hate—pick one—the music, camerawork, art direction, acting in your film. But if you actually get under the skin of that prejudice, you can discover the particular thing they really hate—the pea under the mattress. It often comes down to one or two small things that spoil everything else. When I talked to Bob Evans, it turned out he hated the music for the horse's-head scene, where Woltz pulls the sheet back and the severed head of his half-million-dollar horse is revealed in the bed. Maybe because Woltz is the head of a studio and Evans was the head of a studio and it's a particularly striking, grisly scene—the first violence in the film—he felt the music should be appropriate to that.

I tried to listen to what Nino had written with Bob Evans's ears, and I thought he had a point. The music, as it was originally written, was a waltz and it played against the horror of the event. It was sweet carousel music. You were seeing those horrible images, but the music was counterpointing the horror of the visuals. Perhaps it needed to be crazier a little earlier.

So I tried something I had done on *THX 1138*—layering the music, playing records backwards, turning them upside down, slowing them down—a version of what I'd done when I was eleven years old.

Nino's music for the horse's-head scene had an A, B, A musical structure. That is to say, it had an opening statement, then a variation, and then a return

Murch mixing *The Godfather II*, 1974.

to the opening statement. This structure allowed me to make a duplicate of the music, slip the sync of the second copy one whole musical statement, and then superimpose them together. The music started off A, as it was written, but then became A + B, simultaneously, and then B + A. You now heard, superimposed on each other, things that were supposed to be separate in time. So it starts off as the same piece of music, but then begins—just as Woltz realizes that *something* is wrong—to grate against itself. There is now a disorienting madness to the music that builds and builds to the moment when Woltz finally pulls the sheet back.

O: This happened in the shot where we're coming into the bedroom at night, or first thing at dawn?

M: Early morning. All is normal until he starts to stir and realizes that something is in bed with him—that's when this madness, this second element, comes in. Really a replay of the opening statement but harmonically interweaving with the second . . . You know the way you feel when you're woken by something, and something is wrong, and you wonder, *Is* something wrong? What is wrong? Oh my God! No, it can't be! It's even worse than I thought! *Aaarghhh!*

We played this version for Evans, and he thought it was fantastic. He asked us to rewind it as he phoned up Charlie Bluhdorn, who was head of Gulf + Western, in New York. He took the telephone all the way up to the screen and said, "Listen to this, Charlie! Roll it!" holding the phone up to the screen as the music played. I can't imagine what it must have sounded like at the other end of the line, or what Bluhdorn thought, but Evans was very happy: he felt some corner had been turned.

I was sitting at the mixing desk, with Dick Portman, who was the lead mixer, and the whole thing had made Dick very nervous. To do something like this with the music was . . . well, people didn't do this. It was certainly very risky if it hadn't worked out. So we were both sitting there, looking at this wonderful scene—a big projection in black-and-white of the head of this fictional studio boss discovering a horse's head in his bed as the real head of Paramount stood holding the telephone receiver up against the screen, his shadow cast across it as the scene unwinds. It was one of those iconic moments that you can't believe as it's happening.

The result was that some of the heat was taken off the music. There were still struggles, but they were within the context of Nino's music, not about hiring somebody else to come in and rewrite everything.

O: Was that kind of dissonance used elsewhere in the film?

M: No, that was the only example. It's a very particular scene. The general tendency in *The Godfather* is to play big scenes in silence and then to bring the music in afterwards. For instance, the killing of Carlo, Michael's brother-in-law, at the end of the film has no accompanying music. In a so-called normal film you would have dramatic murder music, but we had only that sound of Carlo's feet squeaking on the windshield as he's being choked to death. Then his foot smashes the glass and you're left with the image of his foot sticking through the windshield and the sound of the gravel crunching as Michael walks back to the house. Then the music comes in.

Also the killing of Luca Brasi and even the killing of Michael's first wife in Italy—all these things happen with just sound effects. Music only comes in after the fact.

O: The murder in the car, the shoes on the windshield . . . I remember talking to someone after I'd seen it about how unpornographic it was, there was no suggestive manipulation, no thrill to it. . . .

M: A fixed camera. The camera is on the hood of the car and it doesn't cut away. You see everything, all through the whole process. Not having music also gives the emotional effect of not cutting away.

When music makes an entrance in a film there's the emotional equivalent of a cutaway. Music functions as an emulsifier that allows you to dissolve a certain emotion and take it in a certain direction. When there's no music, the filmmakers are standing back saying, simply, Look at this. Without appearing to comment.

O: Do you know of examples in, say, early gangster films, where the same kind of thing happens—a restraint in the music—or was there always a traditional musical stamp?

M: I don't know enough about film history. . . .

FIVE TYPES OF AMBIGUITY

O: It seems the sound mix is the crucial stage in a film, where everything jells and in some way the film almost doubles in power? Has the process of doing a sound mix changed much since the early days when you worked on *The Godfather*?

M: The mix is still really the final stage at which any last opportunity can be seized or any last insoluble problem solved. If you're lucky, and if you have the right approach, a certain blend of music and sound can sometimes solve problems that could not be solved in any other way. That's part of the filmmaking process. Every stage leaves a residue of unsolved problems for the next stage—partly because the particular dilemma you're facing cannot be solved in terms of the medium that you're working in right then. For instance, at the script stage there may be issues that have to be left undecided, so the actors can have a fruitful ambiguity to work with. It would be deadly if you *did* solve all the problems in the script—you do not *want* to be asking for the gods' help at every stage—because then everything subsequent would be a mechanical working out of an already established form.

The acting, the shooting, the editing, and the sound may all blend into one another, but in fact there are five stages in a film's life: the script stage; the preproduction stage, where you cast and choose locations; the shooting; the editing; and then the sound and music stage. Each is fateful in its own way.

But because the sound mix is the very final stage—and because it's very flexible—there's a tremendous amount of variety you can call upon during the mix, by both eliminating things you thought were absolutely essential or, at the last minute, bringing some new element in.

To answer your original question: I guess the thing that's changed since the days of *The Godfather* is that we now do much more preliminary mixing, what's called temp mixing. This is so we can preview the film earlier than we ever would have thought of doing before. Something Fred Zinnemann, for example, would have abhorred.

The result is that there are generally fewer surprises in the final mix. This can be both good and bad.

O: It's an odd thing: I've heard you talk before about the importance of ambiguity in film, and the need to save that ambiguous quality which exists in a book or painting, and which you think a film does not often have. And at the same time in a mix you are trying to "perfect" that ambiguity.

M: I know. It's a paradox. And one of the most fruitful paradoxes, I think, is that even when the film is finished, there should be unsolved problems. Because there's another stage, beyond the finished film: when the audience views it. You want the audience to be co-conspirators in the creation of this work, just as much as the editor or the mixers or the cameraman or the actors are. If by some chemistry you actually did remove all ambiguity in the final mix—even though it had been ambiguous up to that point—I think you would do the film a disservice. But the paradox is that you have to approach every problem as if it's desperately important to solve it. You can't say, I don't want to solve this because it's got to be ambiguous. If you do that, then there's a sort of haemorrhaging of the organism.

O: And more of a confusion.

M: Yes. I keep thinking about it, and it's a wonderful dilemma: you have to acknowledge that there must be unsolved problems at each stage. As hard as you work, you must have this secret, unspoken hope that one very significant problem will remain unsolved. But you never know what that is until the film is done. You can almost define a film by the problem it poses, that it can't answer itself, that it then asks the audience to solve.

For instance, in *Return to Oz,* the identity of Ozma: Who is this ambiguous character you see at the beginning of the film, and who then presumably dies and goes to the heaven that is Oz? Is she a real person? Or is she an abstract Oz creature, who projected herself into the dimension of the real, in order to influence certain events?

Well, right at the beginning of writing the script, my notes say, *Who is Ozma?* How am I going to seize on to that character? Because a lot of things depended on that: the casting and how I would choose to shoot it, the directing, everything. Years later, I was talking to David Shire, who was composing the music, about the themes—what about the theme for Ozma? And he said, Who is she? I felt myself stuck. Even though I'd answered the question in many guises, I hadn't answered it in musical terms. So here was the problem restating itself.

Princess Ozma of Oz, a key figure in the later books of L. Frank Baum, whom Dorothy restores as ruler of the Emerald City.

I went back to my notebooks, and sure enough, the very first note was: *Who is Ozma?* I felt my heart sink, thinking, Oh my God! I've gone through this whole process, and the very first question I asked, I can't answer! But then I read the next paragraph, which was a laying out of the issues that were present in the book, in which Ozma was not a girl but a boy who turned into a girl, which was something I'd decided not to follow. I suddenly realized how far I had come. In fact, I had solved, had answered, the persistent question at each stage. But it was restating itself.

So probably, for that film, that question—Who is Ozma?—is given to the audience to answer. The film doesn't answer it. It doesn't say she is a real person who died and went to heaven; nor does it say she's a person from another dimension, who came into this dimension in order to bring Dorothy back with her to save Oz. The music perhaps suggests the latter, because Ozma's theme is a sort of musical inversion on Dorothy's theme. The music says maybe she's a projection of some aspect of Dorothy. But maybe it's the opposite.

O: Some years ago I was reading an article by Donald Richie, about the difference between Eastern and Western film, or art. He was distinguishing between Eisenstein and, say, Kurosawa, and how they work, and how when Eisenstein edits he builds the scene, while Kurosawa erases and removes. The scene is *revealed* in a Kurosawa film, whereas in Eisenstein or in the Western tradition you're *building* a scene. Richie points out that the master shot—the shot that shows us the choreography of the whole scene—is traditionally the essential Western setup, the base, whereas in Japanese film, you can pick a small fragment of the corner of a table and that particular fragment can be used to suggest the whole scene. . . . As an editor, do you feel this is a real distinction? Do we, in the West, tend to work only with the Eisenstein method?

M: First of all, remember that film is just over one hundred years old. The discovery of editing was in 1903. It has not yet reached its century mark. And this early on in the development of a new art form you would expect national or regional characteristics to influence the grammar of film, especially in Russia. There was a huge dialectical influence, from Kant to Hegel and Marx, and then Eisenstein and others found a way to show Marxian dialectics—opposition and synthesis—in cinema. In the Soviet Union, cinema was seen to be the art that most clearly showed the superiority of Marxian dialectics in its very essence. The Communists naturally pushed that aspect of it, the editing, very hard.

We who are not Marxian always worked with those elements but didn't push them so hard. Yet as time has gone on, over the last three or four generations of filmmakers, there's inevitably been a coming together of regional characteristics. We are hungry to find out whatever works.

I think Richie's idea about Eastern and Western film is true. Maybe in the West—because we have a long tradition of the master scene, ever since the invention of three-dimensional perspective at the beginning of the Renaissance—we do tend to think the idea of figures in three-dimensional space is tremendously important. So it's natural that in cinema we would go in that

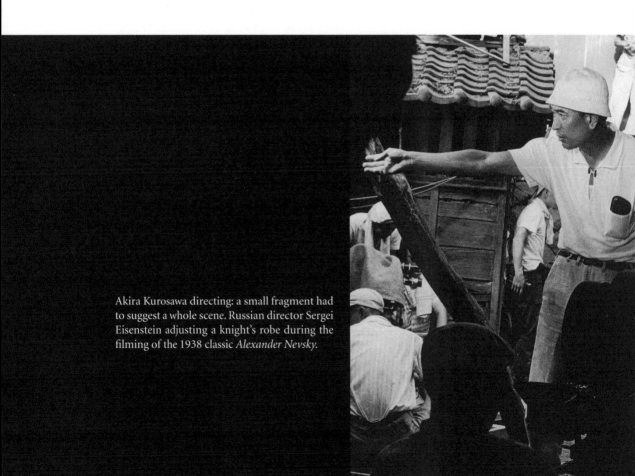

Akira Kurosawa directing: a small fragment had to suggest a whole scene. Russian director Sergei Eisenstein adjusting a knight's robe during the filming of the 1938 classic *Alexander Nevsky.*

direction first. While in Japan and China, the idea of relatively flat figures in a two-dimensional frame, and an emphasis on details within that frame until they have a huge power, is natural to the way their art has developed. In certain Chinese paintings, the canvas is left bare where there is supposed to be sky. . . .

TWO RUMOURS

O: I heard a rumour that you set up some carillon bell sounds in Times Square, coming out of the covered sewer grates. Is this true?

M: Fascinating! I wish it were. But no.

O: Perhaps you should do it. . . .

M: I *did* think of an experiment which *would* be fascinating to do. To record the bell tone—the carillon, in fact—of San Francisco Bay. Every body of water—it

doesn't matter whether it's a puddle or Lake Superior—has what they call a seiche tone. Even if you can't see it, the water is vibrating, undulating at a resonant frequency that is keyed to the size of the body of water. San Francisco Bay I think has a seiche tone of one hour and forty-three minutes. A wave will cross the bay and then come back in that time period. These are very large waves, undetectable by our normal senses.

On top of that are the waves—the chop—that we can see, and then little micro-waves that are just part of the texture of the water. If you set up a pole at some point in the bay, and had a laser beam that reflected off the surface of the water and continuously measured the distance between the tip of the beam and the surface of the water, you would be plotting a series of curves. You could print that out as a long series of wave forms, like the record of an earthquake seismograph. One of the wave forms would be this big seiche tone, which would vary over a long period of time, hours. Others would be quicker and more obvious.

Now you can take that wave form and speed it up and render it audible as a series of tones. I don't know what it would sound like, but the bay would have a (*hums*) tone. Then superimposed on that would be all these other tones of the smaller and smaller waves. It would be some kind of music.

O: That's something you could do for the Museum of Jurassic Technology.

M: Actually, the Exploratorium in San Francisco would be a good place. . . .

O: The other odd story I remember about you was that you once imitated a dog in a film's soundtrack.

M: (*Laughs*) It happened in *Return to Oz.* I was shooting the scene where Dorothy is rescued, at the very end of the film. She was caught in a flood earlier in the film, and at the end is still alive in the willows by the side of the river. Of course, she has really just come back from Oz. And you hear in the distance a dog bark. When I was shooting that, I was directing Fairuza Balk, who was playing Dorothy, and to cue her to wake up, I barked like her dog, Toto.

O: And that's in the film now?

M: (*Barks!*) Later, when we were assembling the film, that was one of the sounds the editors used in the track simply because it was there and it sounded okay. But it was still there when we were doing the mix for the previews. I asked, Aren't we going to change this dog-bark? The editors said, What do you mean? I said, Well, that's me! And they said, What? We thought it was the dog! So then they began a search for dog-barks. We tried many different versions, but in the end nothing sounded better, in some mysterious way, than that impromptu dog-bark.

O: I remember that while I was writing *The English Patient,* I needed to have a drawing of a dovecote in a letter that Hana writes. I'd once seen a dovecote in France, so I did a quick, five-second drawing, assuming I'd get somebody else to do a proper drawing later. The manuscript went off to Knopf, and they insisted on using my drawing, saying, Actually, that's just the kind of thing you'd find in a letter! I was shocked, because it was quite childish. And it's a bit embarrassing to see it still there in foreign editions.

DEVIL'S WORK

O: One of the things you claim is that it was cartoons, as well as stop-motion films such as *King Kong,* that caused a sudden leap in the creative use of sound in the 1930s. How did that happen, and why?

M: Well, it was a practical problem. Since animation is shot frame by frame, whether drawings like Mickey Mouse or sculpted animals like King Kong, it's impossible to have any sound that comes with them. You have to create the soundtrack, which both completes and creates them as three-dimensional beings, since they are not dimensional beings in themselves. One of the things that helps the audience in the suspension of disbelief is that the animated characters do make sound—therefore they must be real, in some way.

O: And this leads to a fictionalizing of sound. . . .

M: Exactly. Because there is no sound to begin with, you, the creator, are free to imagine anything. If we're filming a staged play, people speak, they move about, they pick up glasses, they put them down, they close doors, so they automatically have a physical presence and also generate their own sounds. With live-action films it was not immediately obvious that you had to do anything other than simply capture those very sounds. With animated films you have to create something that gives a sound where none was present. With fantasy films like *The Wizard of Oz* you have to do the opposite, remove what feels like the wrong sound and put something else in its place. I think those early cartoons, which were seen as not very serious things, planted a seed that sound could be used in metaphorical ways.

O: Who were the early filmmakers who picked up on this?

M: Jean Renoir and René Clair in France. Cecil B. deMille in the United States. Fritz Lang in Germany. Renoir in particular was *extremely* interested in *realistic* sound. He went so far in one direction that he almost came around the other side. There's a wonderful quote by him where he says that dubbing—replacing the original sound with something else—is an invention of the devil and that if such a thing had been possible in the thirteenth century, the practitioners would have been burned at the stake for preaching the duality of the soul!

Renoir felt that a person's voice was an expression of that person's soul, and that to fool around with it in any way was to do the devil's work. The devil is frequently represented as having a voice at odds with what you see. In *The Exorcist,* the voice that the young girl speaks with is not her own voice. This idea of devilry and duality and dubbing, there's something to be explored there. . . .

King Kong was a stage in the great creative leap in sound in the 1930s.

Renoir was also the first person, by his own account, to record the sound of a toilet flushing and put it in a film by taking a microphone and cable from the sound department, going down the hall to the toilet, and recording the flush. This was something no one had thought of before. It was for a film called *On purge bébé*—that's "Let's give baby an enema"—which was originally a stage farce, and Renoir's first commercial hit.

O: There's some organization in North America that gives an award for the best nature recording every year. One year there was a wonderful winner—a man won the award for recording flies buzzing *within* a piece of cowshit.

M: Hmmm . . .

O: You said Hitchcock also was someone who used sound in a new, imaginative way—something I'm not very conscious of when I see one of his films. I'm much more aware of his visual inventiveness.

M: There is a tremendous use of sound in Hitchcock. There's the famous moment—I think it's in *The 39 Steps*—when a woman is about to scream and the film cuts to a tunnel, matching the woman's open mouth, and a train emerges with a screaming whistle. At the moment when you would expect one thing, something else is put in its place.

There's also the great use of dialogue distortion in his early film *Blackmail,* where the heroine, who the night before has killed someone with a knife, comes down to breakfast with her parents and all the

words are muffled except for "knife"—as when her father says something like, "Please pass the butter *knife.*" It's one of the first uses of sound to get at an inner state of mind.

O: And then there was Orson Welles. . . .

M: He came from a highly developed theatre and radio background, where he had pushed sound as far as it could go at that time. Think of the famous use of silence in his dramatization of *The War of the Worlds.* So when he came to film, in the early forties, he brought with him his whole bag of tricks to simulate space with sound. Generally, in Hollywood, such things had not seemed necessary, because you already have the visual representation: simply by turning the camera on a scene, you are representing a spatial reality. In radio, you have to evoke everything through sound. Welles found that his radio techniques transposed quite well to film, and that he could combine the aesthetics of the radio play and the cinema. That's one of the signal contributions of his first film, *Citizen Kane.*

O: So, coming from radio—where he had had to *invent* terror, invent that imaginary visual landscape of a rainy street or an empty echoing stadium to create an essential atmosphere for the listener—he was using sound differently. He knew he could manipulate and exaggerate it to have an

Orson Welles during one of his famous *War of the Worlds* broadcasts.

effect. The soundtrack didn't have to be just a "recording." When the dying Kane whispers, "Rosebud," you feel and witness the *emotion* of that word going through the whole house. . . .

M: Yes. Exactly.

O: I haven't seen the film for a while, but is that a very conscious thing all the way through the film, that selective extravagance of sound?

M: Yes.

O: The focussing on sound as a kind of light.

M: It's very much like light. One of the fascinating things for me in mixing is that what we do with the palette of sound—what sounds we choose to emphasize, how we put a spatial ambience around those sounds, what we choose to eliminate—is very much equivalent to what the director of photography does with light. By highlighting the planes of a face, then making the background go darker and slightly out of focus, and then putting a light over there to pick out the ring that's on the table, which otherwise you wouldn't see, the director of photography is directing the eye, *in a painterly way,* emphasizing certain things, de-emphasizing certain others. But that is fixed at the time of shooting, there's not much you can do later to change it.

Who knows, now that we're entering this new age of digital manipulation, these kinds of things may become more and more possible—to change the lighting of a scene later on, depending on how the scene functions in the film.

We already have that ability in sound—by the placement of sound or by regulating how loud it is, we can change the "lighting" of a scene. Well, through sound, we can make the scene "darker," for instance, so that the atmosphere behind the scene will have the same emotional effect on an audience as if it had been shot in a darker light.

What is most present in my mind when I'm mixing is that concept of lighting, both physically—picking things out in the frame that are important or that give you a greater sense of actually being there with the characters—and emotionally, to emphasize certain story elements.

The more you get into the emotional end of things, the more you draw upon the metaphoric use of sound. Reality can only go so far and then you have to go beyond reality, beyond the frame. I've always found that I've underestimated how far I can push. It's rare that I put a sound to a film and it says, "Oops, no, that goes too far!" Usually it says, "No, do more!"

O: Have you done that to specific scenes in a film? Given them that darkness?

M: Yes . . . I'm trying to think of a good example. It's actually easier to darken things than it is to lighten them.

O: I suppose something like *The Talented Mr. Ripley*—which begins as a sun-dappled film. . . .

M: The sound designer Randy Thom has written some interesting things about exactly this subject, how sound can easily disorient, can depress, can darken, can render more edgy. Alan Splet's ominous and crushing industrial atmospheres in *Eraserhead* are probably the most outstanding example. On the other hand, it's not immediately obvious how sound can lighten things. Birdsong sometimes does. But that's a cliché.

It may have something to do with the fact that the dreams we have are not evenly divided between happy and sad. Most dreams are neutral, or mysterious and enigmatic, or frightening. Only rarely do you wake up thinking, What a happy dream that was! It says something about the function of a dreaming mind that it's there not to render you happy but to unsettle, reexamining or foreshadowing events in a strange, talismanic way. I don't know whether the two things are related at all, but there is enough similarity between films and dreams that there might be something to it. . . .

■

O: I recall you talking about how you created the sound of the desert in *The English Patient*. You said the real desert does not give good soundtrack.

M: The desert is a vast space. When you're there, the feeling it evokes is psychic as well as physical. The problem is that if you record the actual sound that goes with that space, it has nothing to do with the *emotion* of being there. In fact it's a very empty, sterile sound. You hear people's voices, clearly, but there's nothing else, unless there is a wind of some kind. So the trick in *The English Patient* was to evoke, with sound, a space that is silent. We did it by adding insectlike sounds that, realistically, would probably not be there. There was a whole palette of little clicks and *presences* that came from insects.

Also tiny sounds—as tiny as we could get—of grains of sand rubbing against each other, little things that would not record even if you had a microphone there—like those flies buzzing in the manure. We took those tiny things and made a fabric out of them.

O: Did you do anything to try and evoke distance or space, as well? A distant camel-bell? Or a voice?

M: Mainly through voice, through the placement of voice. That depended on how Anthony shot the scene. But if somebody was fifty feet away, we paid very close attention to how that voice would sound fifty feet away. If that didn't happen to be captured on the original soundtrack, we created an acoustic envelope around the voice to make it feel like it was fifty feet away.

O: Was that done during the mix?

M: Yes.

O: So there wasn't an earlier stage, before the mix, when that quality was put in?

M: No. All those additional fine-tunings of acoustic space happened at the mix, because not only is everything together then, but you're physically in the space of a theatre and can now tune it all exactly as you want it to be in the theatre when it is being shown to audiences.

O: In an early film like *American Graffiti,* when you were doing the sound, that kind of effect—the use of source music—was created by you and George Lucas at the time of the filming, wasn't it?

M: No. That was all created afterwards. After the filming but before the mix. We produced the radio show just as if you'd happened to tune in radio station XERB in the summer of 1962: it had Wolfman Jack talking, it had commercials, it had songs, it had people phoning in to request music. And then we took a tape of that radio show into different sonic environments, out in the real world, and played it back and captured what we heard on a second tape recorder. It was a process I nicknamed, for obvious reasons, "worldizing."

In the mix I had separate control of both the original radio show and the "worldized" version. By fading up the first track, I could emphasize the power and clarity of the radio show and the music, if that's what we wanted. If we wanted to push the sound into the background, we could shift the balance and emphasize the second track and, in fact, the third track. We did all the worldizing twice, which further randomized the sound so that if we wanted to we could make the sound into almost a mist, like a rainy mist, in the background. Almost not there at all, and yet filling the space around the characters. It's the sonic equivalent of photographic depth of field. If I'm taking your portrait, I don't want the background to be in focus, because I want to concentrate on your face. So I adjust the lens's depth of field to throw the background out of focus.

This had not been done so fully before in sound. It was the breakthrough on *American Graffiti*.

WATCH *HOW* THEY SAY IT

O: I'm intrigued by what you call "metaphorical sound" . . . the idea of emphasizing the visual by artificially focussing on a possibly disjointed or unrealistic layer of sound. Especially because there's also, simultaneously, such "authenticity" in the sounds you use in your films. You've described this as "the reassociation of image and sound in different contexts." How did you first become conscious of the possibilities of this?

M: I remember Roman Polanski coming to my film school, USC, in '66. He talked quite passionately about sound, but he talked about it in terms of celebrating the authenticity of the sound itself. An example he used was the drip of a faucet and what that tells you about a person, about the apartment they live in, about their relationship to many other things. The fact that that drip is there says many different things. I agreed with that.

It's always a balance for me, between something being authentic, and celebrating that authenticity, and yet at the same time trying to push the sound into other metaphorical areas. Think of the screech of the elevated subway train in *The Godfather* when Michael Corleone murders Sollozzo and the policeman, Captain McCluskey, in the Italian restaurant. It's an authentic sound because it's a real subway train and because it seems authentic to that neighbourhood of the Bronx, where the restaurant is located. We don't wonder what the sound is, because we've seen so many films set in the Bronx where that sound is pervasive.

But it's metaphorical, in that we've never established the train tracks and the sound is played so abnormally loud that it doesn't match what we're looking at, objectively. For a sound that loud, the camera should be lying on the train tracks.

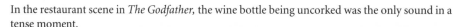

In the restaurant scene in *The Godfather,* the wine bottle being uncorked was the only sound in a tense moment.

O: I was watching that scene again recently, and what's wonderful about it also is that it begins with the intimate noise of a cork being twisted out of a wine bottle. It's such a perverse celebration of a minor detail at a tense point, that bottle being uncorked at the start of the fatal meal . . . and about four minutes later, there's the manic, screaming train sound and a double shooting.

M: That was very deliberately done, to make you pay attention to a tiny realistic sound and then have an overwhelming sound that you have to interpret in a different way—all on a subconscious level.

O: And after the gunshots you get opera! It's like the sequence has three or four musical acts. The whole composition of the scene is remarkable.

M: Another element in that scene is Francis's use of Italian without subtitles. It's very bold, even today, to have an extended scene between two main characters in an English-language film speaking another language with no translation. As a result you're paying much more attention to *how* things are said and the body language being used, and you're perceiving things in a very different way. You're listening to the *sound* of the language, not the meaning.

O: What was the word you used last night? Not aphasic but . . .

M: Yes, that's it: aphasic. You don't know what they're saying, so the only way to understand what the scene is about is to watch *how* they say it, through the tone

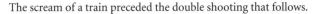

The scream of a train preceded the double shooting that follows.

of the voice and their body language. The sound exercises the mind in much more complex ways than appear on the surface of the scene, which is otherwise just a dialogue scene between three people. The use of unsubtitled Italian is making you pay attention to sound, setting you up for what is about to happen.

O: We are a limited viewer. We're not being told everything.

M: And also all this is predicated on Francis's decision not to have music during the scene. In the hands of another filmmaker, there would be tension music percolating under the surface. But Francis wanted to save everything for those big chords *after* Michael's dropped the gun. Even after he shoots, there's silence, and in your mind you hear Clemenza saying, "Remember, drop the gun. Everyone will be looking at the gun, so they won't look at your face." So Michael shoots them and then there's this moment of silence and then he drops the gun.

O: He doesn't even drop it, he tosses it! It's a much more extraordinary gesture than a subtle drop.

M: Yeah, it's as if to say: *Look at this gun!* The gun hits the ground, and then the music finally comes in. It's a classic example for me of the correct use of music, which is as a collector and channeler of previously created emotion, rather than the device that creates the emotion. Music in *The Godfather* is almost always used in this way. I think in the long run this approach generates emotions that are truer because they come out of your direct contact with the scene itself, and your own feelings about the scene—not feelings dictated by a certain kind of music. *The Godfather* is a good film to study for its use of music.

Most movies use music the way athletes use steroids. There's no question that you can induce a certain emotion with music—just like steroids build up muscle. It gives you an edge, it gives you a speed, but it's unhealthy for the organism in the long run.

So after being plunged into that astonished silence before the gun is dropped, the audience is confused emotionally. Is Michael a bad guy? A good guy? Here's somebody who has done the very thing he said he wouldn't do, which is to work for the family. Now he's *killed* somebody for the family. Are we going to watch this Kennedyish character now trample over the ideals he espoused at the beginning—

O: So the music comes in to guide us out of the scene. . . .

M: The music at that point says, This is an operatic moment. Michael is a character in an opera. Young, idealistic, now of his own volition going deep into the centre of the darkness and doing the thing that none of the other members of the family can do—he's sacrificing his own innocence. Because everyone knows him to be an innocent—the police, the other mob families. This kid is the last person that Sollozzo or McCluskey would expect to pull out a gun and kill them. So Michael trades in his innocence and commits these murders in order—he believes—to save the family. In the previous scene, where Tom Hagen and Sonny and Clemenza and Tessio are sitting around talking about what to do, nobody suggests, Let's kill them both. In fact, when Michael says it, they laugh: This is crazy! You can't kill a police captain in the middle of New York! But Michael, uncoiling the power of his will—which has lain dormant—explains in that wonderful scene where the camera moves in on him, slowly, how he's going to do it, and you see a kind of snake unfurling out of this Ivy League character, a snake that will remain draped around his neck for the rest of the film. And in the subsequent *Godfather* films as well.

O: Wasn't there a story about a Mafia henchman who thought the sound in the restaurant murder scene was very realistic?

M: Yes—there was an interview a couple of years ago in *The New York Times* with Salvatore Gravano, who had killed a number of people for the Mafia and then turned state's evidence. The interviewer was asking him whether Mario Puzo had ever had Mafia connections. And Gravano felt that *definitely* Puzo either had connections or had been in the Mafia himself. As proof he cites the scene where Michael kills Sollozzo and McCluskey: "Remember how Michael couldn't hear anything as he's walking up on them? Remember how his eyes went glassy, and there was just the noise of the train in the background, and how he couldn't hear them talk? That's just like I felt when I killed Joe

Colucci. . . . Somebody who wrote that scene had to have a feeling for that. I mean, I felt like I was pulling the trigger myself."

Gravano thought that only somebody who had actually killed would know that subtle piece of emotional information, therefore Mario Puzo had to have killed somebody, or had intimate contact with people who had killed. But, as it turns out—aside from the fact that Gravano was confusing the book with the film—it was just my attempt to fill in a sound space that would normally be occupied by music—something that came from a kid from the Upper West Side of Manhattan and had absolutely no Mafia connections anywhere!

I remembered the interviewer went on to ask Gravano if *The Godfather* had influenced the way he behaved.

"Well," he answers, "I killed nineteen people."

What did that have to do with *The Godfather*, the interviewer asked.

"I only did, like, one murder before I saw the movie."

"KA-LUNK"

O: I find it fascinating that you feel that with such "metaphorical sound" you can reach a deeper truth about the atmosphere of the scene. Can you think of other examples?

M: What immediately comes to mind is the use of sound in transitions in *The English Patient*. The transition from the Patient, after Hana has finished reading Herodotus to him . . . She leaves Almásy alone and subsequently she's playing hopscotch downstairs. You hear her throw the metal spile she's using to mark the square, and you hear the sound of her feet as she jumps. That sound continues, but it seems now to be much too much. And with the audience in that slightly confused state of mind, the film dissolves through to the scene where the explorers, in an earlier time, are sitting around the campfire and the Berber guides are playing their music and you realize that elements of this drumming have infiltrated their way into the hopscotch, and that that's probably what triggered this memory within Almásy. That he too heard the sounds of hopscotch, and there was something about its rhythm that took him back to the past.

O: Speaking of specific everyday sounds that can be made metaphorical, there is the famous use of the sound of the door closing at the end of *The Godfather.* I believe you spent a good deal of time testing doors. . . .

M: That's a small but interesting example of the kind of stuff that happens routinely. Something as innocent as a door-close. If you approach it coherently and seriously, you understand that there are many door-closes that would have been wrong for that scene. First of all because this is the last sound in the film—other than the music—and second because it is the decisive moment in which Michael is closing the door on his wife, and on a whole part of his emotional life, which ultimately leads to the tragedy of *Godfather II,* where you see the results of that decision on a very large scale.

The door-close, in the sense of what Polanski was talking about, has to be true to what we perceive objectively: the physicality of the door and the space around it. But it also has to be true to the metaphorical impact of that door-close, which is, "I'm not going to talk about my business, Kay." That *ka-lunk,* that articulated sound of solidity, has to express something of the finality of the decision.

O: What governs your decision to make that moment of sound symbolic or metaphorical as well as realistic?

M: The cork you mentioned in the restaurant scene in *The Godfather* is a good example. That just happened, but the way it was cut and the fact that nobody was talking at the moment the cork is being drawn from the bottle made us decide to emphasize it. One could have chosen not to emphasize that small sound, and to concentrate instead on the expressions of the diners. But something about the insistence of that little sound—the screw winding itself into the flesh of the cork—seemed to help structure the larger context of things and set us up for the shock and noise of the train and the shooting only minutes later. So I remember recording that squeak and pop with great attention to detail. . . .

NOVELS AND FILMS — THE REDUNDANT ABUNDANCE

O: The writer and filmmaker Henry Bean told me a story of a writer who had been approached by someone who said, "Can you believe what that film producer did to your book!" And the writer replied, "He did *nothing* to my book." Still, books and films often make bad marriages. What are the problems in adapting novels into films?

M: The most frequent problem is abundance. The amount of story in a novel is so much more than a film can present. In general, short stories are easier to translate into films than novels are.

As a rule, when you're adapting a novel to film, you have to ask, What's the short story of this novel? And then make certain fateful decisions. The obvious truth about film is that it's highly redundant visually. In *Madame Bovary*, Flaubert describes Emma Bovary's eyes and refers to their colour perhaps three other times. On film, every single frame of Isabelle Huppert's eyes says, This is the colour of her eyes, or, This is how her hair is, this is her costume.

There's a tremendous power in that, but if you have that kind of redundancy on top of the story abundance of the novel, you get . . . whatever the combination of abundance and redundancy is. We'll have to coin a new word. It's overwhelming, anyway. If the filmmakers are overly respectful of the way the novel tells itself and of every novelistic detail, it's a recipe for filmic trouble.

The kind of novel that makes a good film has a certain motion—whether that's physical motion across the screen or emotional motion, moving from one state to another. Or, one hopes, both.

O: I know you usually read the original novels that the films you work on are based on. *The Unbearable Lightness of Being, The English Patient,* the Oz books, and, in the case of *The Conversation, Steppenwolf.* And you also do research around some of them. So you begin your work long before the filming happens.

M: Yes. I try to expose myself as early as possible, not only to the novel but, if possible, to the author's source material. I try to get as far back as I can into the roots of the material.

O: Anthony Minghella did that when writing the script of *The English Patient.* He read up on desert exploration, finding some of the realities on which I had based my fiction. The different kinds of shelters the expeditions would construct in the desert, et cetera.

M: I also try to choose projects that dovetail with my own interests. That's a significant part of the process—where you are really casting yourself, in much the same way actors cast themselves in a role. In an ideal situation, such as Vanessa Redgrave in *Julia,* an actor chooses a part that represents some emotional truth to her as an individual, which pushes her somewhere she has not gone before.

O: This is very precisely what writers do, or should do.

M: You want the correct balance of those two things—if you place an actor in a situation in which there is no emotional resonance with anything in her life, you get a false performance. On the other hand, if somebody merely does what she's already done ten times, you get a formal, stylized performance that's very easy for an actor to fall into. The same would apply to film editors.

O: There's a line of Saul Bellow's—"I write to discover the next room of my fate." In this way, I think, many novels are self-portraits—or future self-portraits, self-explorations, even if the story is set in an alien situation. You can try on this costume, that costume.

M: Somebody once asked W. H. Auden, "Is it true that you can write only what you know?" And he said, "Yes it is. But you don't know what you know until you write it." Writing is a process of discovery of what you really do know. You can't limit yourself in advance to what you know, because you *don't* know everything you know.

■

O: When you worked on *The Unbearable Lightness of Being* as a supervising editor, making the final selection of the material, was it a difficult editing process? I ask this partly because it's a film that in a way remains a novel. It doesn't really have that short story line you said is so important to find.

M: The struggle on that film—it's a wonderful film, I saw it again a year or so ago, and it holds up very well, I think—was that the novel has the structure of somebody cross-country skiing across a landscape. Milan Kundera takes the story a certain distance, from one character's point of view, and then he switches to the other ski and goes backwards in time—not all the way, but maybe a third of the way—and then goes forwards again with the story, from somebody else's point of view, taking it farther than the first character. Back and forth and back and forth, but always ultimately moving forwards, using different people's points of view like a pair of skis.

O: And that's the structure of the novel.

M: Yes. I was fascinated to find out how we were going to deal with that in the film! Jean-Claude Carrière and Phil Kaufman, who wrote the screenplay together, created a very fine first draft that ironed out the time structure and told it continuously, from an omniscient point of view. I read this draft and thought it was great. Then I anxiously awaited the next draft, which was going to be where they rediscovered the episodic, different-point-of-view structure, in filmic terms. But that never happened. It became clear that there was so much to deal with that the narrative line had to be continuous.

That was what I think made it hard to discover the short story inside the film. Everything that was nonlinear in the book was now linear, and therefore the fracture points were very different, or even nonexistent.

The English Patient also had many different time sequences, but by contrast, Anthony Minghella's screenplay intricately manoeuvred the backwards-and-forwards in time—telling a personal story, a love story, against the historical palette of World War II.

In some ways the two stories—*Unbearable Lightness* and *English Patient*—are similar. When you look at all the possibilities of literature, they're surprisingly similar. But what was inherent within your book that was brought out filmically was the fragmented structure. I think there are more than forty time transitions in *The English Patient*. A huge number. Many more than in *Julia*, which also goes backwards and forwards, and many more than in *Godfather II*, which does the same thing.

Daniel Day-Lewis and Lena Olin, *left,* in a scene from *The Unbearable Lightness of Being,* 1988; Philip Kaufman directing them in a scene from the same film.

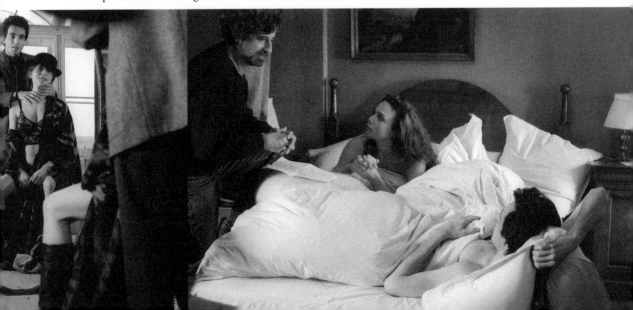

In *Unbearable Lightness,* those transitions were all eliminated, so it moved continuously forwards.

O: I love the book of *The Unbearable Lightness of Being*—it was stunning for me how it worked as a novel. And there were great things in the film. But whereas the sexual/personal story was alive and taut, and while some of the political scenes, like the arrival of the tank and the invasion, were powerful, I thought some of it didn't really have the sudden and wild anarchy of the book. Why was that?

M: I don't know. We never took that film down in length. It was a long first cut. And in the end I think the film is two hours and fifty minutes. It's about the length of *The Godfather*—just under three hours. At a certain point during the editing of *The Godfather,* Francis cut it down to two hours and twenty minutes. But it was clear it didn't work at that length. Then, when we restored the length, somehow, having gone down so deep, it didn't come back exactly to where it was before—we had learned things by going that far. We never did that on *Unbearable Lightness.* Phil—for his own reasons, probably correctly—didn't want to take it that far. Looking back on it now, I think we probably would have learned something if we had. There would have been scenes in collision with one another that were not written to be in collision. And even if they didn't work, that would have taught us something about how to reinvent the film in its longer length.

O: The film of *English Patient* is almost as long as *Unbearable.*

M: But with *Patient* there was a tremendous amount of experimentation in how the stories collide with one another. Of the forty transitions, I think only seven remained the way they were in the screenplay. Everything else was reinvented to take advantage of the film's strengths. Because *Unbearable* was a linear story, we didn't have the flexibility to shuffle scenes around the way we were able to do in *English Patient.*

THE TRAGEDY-OF-JOB MOMENTS

O: I know this is not a fair question. . . . Are there specific scenes you've edited that you're very fond of?

M: (*Laughs*) I particularly like the invasion scene in *Unbearable Lightness of Being*—what we were able to achieve integrating all kinds of documentary footage from 1968 with the new material shot with our actors, Daniel Day-Lewis and Juliette Binoche. Because the cold war was still on in 1986, Phil was unable to shoot in Prague. But there was easily forty hours of documentary material about the Soviet invasion of Prague, scattered all over the world. The challenge was to collect and distill that material, and it was a crazy quilt of textures; some of it was in colour, some of it was shot in 16 millimetre, some of it had been copied thirty times, some was original 35 millimetre black-and-white negative. We had to find a way to integrate our story into that footage—to have the two characters move through it—*and* tell the entire story of the invasion in twelve minutes; and we had to get into that footage from a film that had a very different "undocumentary" texture and very stylized look, and also to get out of it at the other end and back into our story in an interesting way, and not leave the audience with the sense that this was an aberration or an intrusion. Even though we were going into this very different technique and universe, it had to feel authentic and viscerally powerful—as if you, the audience, were caught up in these events as well.

O: Are there other scenes you remember editing a certain way which were then scrapped and eventually recut in another way?

M: The closest would be the final confession between Almásy and Caravaggio in *The English Patient.* Very late in the editing we altered it from a private dia-

Overleaf: Daniel Day-Lewis and Juliette Binoche in one of the street scenes in Prague from *The Unbearable Lightness of Being;* street scenes in Prague were shot to re-create the Soviet invasion and were mixed in with real documentary footage.

logue between two people to one where a third person, Hana, overhears the Patient's confession. She was not a part of that scene when it was shot. But inserting her presence into the conversation allowed her to have the important knowledge about who Almásy was—which Caravaggio alone had had in the screenplay and during the shooting—so that when she later administers the fatal dose of morphine to Almásy she does it with the weight of that knowledge. So we used footage of her from a scene we had dropped, where she was with Kip—and in one case we actually removed Kip from the frame, optically, to give Hana a whole frame to herself.

O: What was remarkable was how her emotion from that earlier scene with Kip was immediately altered, and now expressed something new in this different context. Also, that artificial link brought the various narrative threads in the film together. It's a wonderful example of lateral thinking during the editing process—this can be in a book or a film—that to me is as creative as the original composition. It's the art of shaking a scene up, turning it upside down, to discover other possibilities in the written or filmed work.

I also remember, in an early cut of *The English Patient,* a scene after Hana says good-bye to Kip, who is on his motorbike, where she walks back to the house. There was an amazing shot of her back—her whole body expressing great loss. A great shot. But in the next cut of the film it was gone. Her grief there, over Kip's leaving, was too close to the grief of the Patient's last scene. You couldn't leave it in, because you had to pace the film. You needed, I suppose, to save the grief for the next scene. You had to remove what was a remarkable shot for the value of the film as a whole.

M: Yes, that's what I call the "Tragedy-of-Job moments." They are like the good man Job, who does everything—and more—that God requests of him, but God perversely afflicts him and not the bad person who is Job's neighbour. Why me? Job asks. Well, it's because God can see the whole that Job cannot see, and in some mysterious way these afflictions are for the good of the whole, in a way that is invisible to the person.

From *The English Patient:* Hana overhearing Almásy's confession. Kip has been optically removed from the lower frame.

There was a moment in *The Conversation*—it had to do with Harry Caul's initial assembly of his tape recording of the lovers—that was in every cut of the film, and somehow any changes in nearby scenes had to be reflected in it. It was like a hinge scene. Over and over again I would be working on that scene, and it would accept the changes, it would accommodate itself to the whole. If you anthropomorphized, you could see the scene becoming prouder and prouder of itself, of how it did all this for the film! And yet there came a point when I said, You know, I think I'm going to remove this scene. Everything else is now so clear that this scene no longer needs to be in there. It's making the point that is made elsewhere in the film.

And as I was removing that scene, at two in the morning, it began to speak to me, as if it were Job, saying, Why are you removing me, me of all scenes who has been so faithful to you, who has tried so hard to accommodate your every wish? And I said, I know what you're talking about, and believe me, I've spent many hundreds of hours on you and yet I'm willing to throw all that work away for the benefit of the whole.

O: It's so similar to editing a book, in those final stages of trying to find the right balance for the emerging organic form. It's like pruning trees in a landscape. You've got fifteen trees and you take out numbers 3 and 7 and 9, and once they're gone you realize that—

M: You see a whole different thing.

O: You can see a different possible form and you discover that a whole new set of trees can go, or should at least be moved to a new place. . . . In literature, even in something as intimate as a poem, those early drafts can be just as wayward and haphazard as the early stages of a film. Look at the gulf between the untidy, seemingly almost useless, first draft of Elizabeth Bishop's "One Art" and the remarkably tight and suggestive final version of her fourteen-line villanelle. It becomes clear that all the subtleties of nuance and precision of form were achieved during the editing. So much so that it's almost difficult to recognize the link between the original lines and the final poem. I'm sure the gulf is just as great, even greater, in film.

M: Very much. Film travels at one mile an hour through its projector. So in *Apocalypse Now,* we shot over two hundred and thirty-five miles and reduced it all to two-and-a-half miles—a ratio of just under 100 to 1. That's high, but not unique: Michael Mann's recent film *The Informer* had a similar ratio. There will be long stretches in the evolution of a film where nothing seems to fundamentally change—plateaus.

And how you prune or chop will determine the very character of a film. There are two approaches to reducing the length of a film: There's what I call the spaghetti-sauce method, which is simply to put the film on the stove with some heat under it, and stir. You taste it occasionally and say, That's great! Now the carrots are working with the tomatoes in a good way, or, No, it's a little too thick, let's add some water! Gradually, organically, the volume of the film reduces to the appropriate level.

The opposite approach is more brutal. There was a brigand in Greek mythology, Procrustes, who lived on the road between Athens and Sparta. He had a cabin at a place where the road got very narrow, along the coast. Everyone who happened to pass his cabin was obliged to spend the night, and sleep on Procrustes' iron bed. While you were sleeping, he would either stretch you so that you were as long as the bed, or he would lop off things that stuck out, so that no matter how tall or short you were, by the time you left his cabin, you were the same length as everyone else who'd been there.

Well, Procrustes would say: Here we have a film that's three hours long, and we need it to be two hours long. Let's just—*chop*—and make it two hours. You do brutal, awful things to the film, but you quickly get down to two hours. The good thing about this process is that you now have the luxury of sitting down, watching the film, and two hours later getting up. Very occasionally it actually works. The editor Robert Parrish tells the story in his book, *Growing Up in Hollywood,* how *All the King's Men* was previewed seven times over six months with increasingly unsuccessful results until the head of Columbia, Harry Cohn, was about to take the film away. The writer-director, Robert Rossen, in desperation told Parrish to go through the whole picture and "select what you consider to be the center of each scene, put the film in the sync machine and wind down a hundred feet (one minute) before and a hundred feet after, and chop it off, regardless of what's going on. Cut through dialogue, music, anything. Then when you're finished, we'll run the picture and see what we've got." Parrish did it—cutting a two-hour-and-ten-minute picture down to a ninety-minute picture and it worked, made sense "in an exciting, slightly confusing, montagey sort of way." And *All the King's Men* went on to win the Oscar for best picture.

The bad part of it is that it's not an organic process, so there are big, bleeding stumps in the story. All of the subsequent work is to figure out what can be done to cauterize those wounds and yet keep the film at two hours. In the end,

HOW TO LOSE THINGS /? / THE GIFT OF LOSING THINGS?

One might begin by losing one's reading glasses
oh 2 or 3 times a day - or one's favorite pen.

THE ART OF LOSING THINGS

The thing to do is to begin by "mislaying".

Mostly, one begins by "mislaying":
keys, reading-glasses, fountain pens
- these are almost too easy to be mentioned,
and "mislaying" means that they usually turn up
in the most obvious place, although when one
is making progress, the places grow more unlikely
- This is by way of introduction. I really
want to introduce myself -   I am such a
fantastic lly good at losing things
I think everyone shd. profit from my experiences.

You may find it hard to believe, but I have actually lost
I mean lost, and forever two whole houses,
one a very big one.   A third house, also big, is
at present, I think, "mislaid" - but
maybe it's lost, too. I won't know for sure for some time.
I have lost one/long peninsula and one island.
I have lost - it can never be has never been found -
a small-sized town on that same island.
I've lost smaller bits of geography, like   and many smaller bits of geography or so
a splendid beach , and a good-sized bay.
Two whole citiees, two of the
world's biggest citiies (two of the most beautiful
although that's beside the point)
A piece of one continent -
and one entire continent.   All gone, gone forever and ever.

One might think this would have prepared me
for losing one average-sized not especially------- exceptionally
beautiful or dazzlingly intelligent person
(except for blue eyes)   (only the eyes were exceptionally beautiful and
But it doesn't seem to have, at all...   the hands looked intelligent)
                                  the fine hands

a good piece of one continent
and another continent - the whole damned thing!
He who loseth his life, etc. - but he who
loses his love - neever, no never never never again -

A
  x
B

One Art

The art of losing isn't hard to master;
so many things seem filled with the intent
to be lost that their loss is no disaster.

Lose something every day. Accept the fluster
of lost door keys, the hour badly spent.
The art of losing isn't hard to master.

Then practice losing farther, losing faster:
places, and names, and where it was you meant
to travel. None of these will bring disaster.

I lost my mother's watch. And look! my last, or
next-to-last, of three loved houses went.
The art of losing isn't hard to master.

I lost two cities, lovely ones. And, vaster,
some realms I owned, two rivers, a continent.
I miss them, but it wasn't a disaster.

—Even losing you (the joking voice, a gesture
I love) I shan't have lied. It's evident
the art of losing's not too hard to master
though it may look like (*Write* it!) like disaster.

The first and the final drafts of the poem "One Art" by Elizabeth Bishop, published in 1975.

we usually use some combination of both: the spaghetti-sauce method and the Procrustean.

O: In Canada, the spaghetti-sauce method is known as the maple-syrup system. We have to boil the collected material down to its essence.

M: Delicious. . . .

O: Miles Davis, talking about his music, said, "I listen to what I can leave out." That seems similar to what I've heard described as your "blue light" theory— how sometimes you artistically need to remove a key element of a scene.

M: I formulated this idea during *The Conversation*—probably because we wound up taking so much away. It went from almost five hours to less than two.

As I began to eliminate things, I would have the feeling that I couldn't remove a certain scene, because it so clearly expressed what we were after. But after hesitating, I'd cut it anyway . . . forced to because of the length of the film. Then I'd have this paradoxical feeling that by taking away something I now had even more of it. It was almost biblical in its idea of abundance. How can you take away something and wind up with more of it?

The analogy I came up with was the image of a room illuminated by a bare blue lightbulb. Let's say the intention is to have "blueness" in this room, so when you walk in you see a bulb casting a blue light. And you think, This is the source of the blue, the source of all blueness. On the other hand, the lightbulb is so intense, so unshaded, that you squint. It's a harsh light. It's blue, but it's so much *what it is* that you have to shield yourself from it.

There are frequently scenes that are the metaphorical equivalent of that bulb. The scene is making the point so directly that you have to mentally squint. And when you think, What would happen if we got rid of that blue lightbulb, you wonder, But then where will the blue come from? Let's take it out and see. That's always the key: Let's just take it out and find out what happens.

So you unscrew the lightbulb . . . there are other sources of light in the room. And once that glaring source of light is gone, your eyes open up. The wonderful thing about vision is that when something is too intense, your irises close down to protect against it—as when you look at the sun. But when there is less light, your eye opens up and makes more of the light that is there.

So now that the blue light is gone and the light is more even you begin to see things that are *authentically* blue on their own account. Whereas before, you attributed their blueness to the bulb. And the blue that remains interacts with other colours in more interesting ways rather than just being an intense blue tonality.

That's probably as far as you can go with the analogy, but it happens often in films. You wind up taking out the very thing that you thought was the sole source of an idea. And when you take it out, you see that not only is the idea still present, it's more organically related to everything else.

In Dostoevsky's *Crime and Punishment,* the one thing that is never talked about is the reason, the real reason, that Raskolnikov killed the landlady. If Dostoevsky actually explained why he killed her, everything else would be minimized and it would not be as interesting and complex. It reminds me of something my father said when people spoke about his paintings. He related it to a comment Wallace Stevens made: that the poem is not about anything at all, the poem is what it is. It's not there to illustrate a point.

"WIDEO"

0: You developed a wonderful theory about editing a few years ago, in your book *In the Blink of an Eye:* that often the best place to cut from one shot to another coincides with the actor's blinking, especially if the actor is good—since a blink naturally signals a closure to a thought.

M: From my early editing experiences I became convinced that there was a connection between the patterns of a person's eye blinks and the patterns of their thoughts. That blinks are the equivalent of mental punctuation marks—commas, periods, semicolons, et cetera—separating and thus providing greater articulation to our thoughts. I owe the equation Cut = Blink to the director

John Huston—he put forth the idea in an interview with Louise Sweeney in the early 1970s.

The upshot of all this is that I believe the pattern of cuts in a film, to be at its best, needs to reflect or acknowledge the pattern of thoughts of the characters in the film—which ultimately means the thought patterns of the audience. In arranging the sequence of shots, the editor is in effect "blinking" for the audience, and the resulting cuts will seem most natural and graceful when they fall where the blink would fall in an exchange between two people in conversation.

O: Since your book first came out, have your thoughts about the "blink" changed?

M: I discovered something, working on *Ripley,* that I was amazed I hadn't discovered before. Statistically, a blink will most often happen when the actor is speaking a nonvocalized consonant. I think they're called fricative consonants: an *s* or an *f, th,* but not *d*(uh)—*d* has a vocal component to it. If somebody is speaking, the blinks tend to happen on *s*'s and *th*'s—sounds like that.

O: Is it because those letters are more difficult to say?

M: I don't know. I've just discovered this. It may be that. It may be that the blink is waiting to happen and somehow, in the moment, there's a brief pause of some kind, because the vocal cords are not being used and you take that opportunity to blink. It's another aspect of the blink that would be worth a little study—watching to see what part of the alphabet coincides most often with blinking.

Practically what it means is that those fricatives are good places to cut because the same thing that makes a person blink, when he speaks those lines, is also making the audience "blink"—the audience is more receptive to a shift of attention at that moment. The cut just looks better. Feels better, rhythmically, within the cadence of speech.

O: We had a prime minister in Canada who had a tendency to lisp, so his speechwriters were told to avoid the *s*'s.

M: (*Laughs*)

O: When I came from Sri Lanka to England I was eleven years old, and I had a problem distinguishing the letters *v* and *w*. So I would say "wideo" or "wagabond." For the first three years in England, I'd always have to think twice before I said a *v* word or a *w* word. That's probably a more cultural kind of halt.

THE NON-FILM WAY OF LIVING

O: Tell me how you got interested in Curzio Malaparte's writing? Did you learn Italian in order to translate him?

M: I took a year of Italian in college and then studied in Perugia, so I had a pre-existing interest in Italian. And I speak French—I like the Romance languages.

In 1986, when we were in Lyons shooting the invasion of Prague for *The Unbearable Lightness of Being,* I ran out of things to read. I went to a bookstore and bought a book on cosmology. The author was explaining the very early stages of the universe after the Big Bang, and he confessed, "I could try to tell you about this moment, but it's better simply to recount Malaparte's story about the frozen horses of Lake Ladoga."

The story involved the siege of Leningrad, artillery bombardments, forest fires, hundreds of cavalry horses escaping in a frenzy from the flames only to end up flash-frozen as they reached the supercooled water of the lake. And to top it off, all this somehow related to the condition of the universe shortly after the Big Bang. I loved it! I had to find out who this Malaparte was.

Curzio Malaparte and friend.

Back in Berkeley, I went to the university library and found that of the three works of his that are translated into English, one of them was *Kaputt,* which contains the story of the frozen horses. Reading the rest of the book was like falling into a waking dream. I read everything of his I could get my hands on after that, including works that had not been translated into English.

After *The English Patient,* in the course of an interview with the magazine *Parnassus,* I compared the process of film adaptation to translation, in the sense that many of the decisions you make—when you go from a book to a script and then from a script to shooting and from shooting to editing—are like translating from one language to another, from the language of words to the language of images and sounds. But there is naturally within each language a different emphasis on certain things. You have to take that difference into account when you translate from one language to another.

After the interview, I thought, Hmm, it sounds good, but maybe I'd better do some translation to make sure that what I'm saying is true. So I went back to some of the Malaparte material that was only in Italian. I was happy to discover that I enjoyed translation, particularly right after having finished a film. You're so keyed up in making the film that when it's over, suddenly, after a year of work, you feel like you've fallen off the edge of a cliff. To continue that work, in a different form, was a very pleasing way to make the transition back to the non-film way of living.

O: The politics of Malaparte's life seem very complicated and ambivalent. We are never too sure where he stands. He's constantly changing sides.

M: "Complicated" is putting it mildly! His real name was Kurt Suckert—his father was a German who had married a girl from Milan. So he was Protestant German in an Italian Catholic world. He ran away from home at age sixteen and fought all four years of World War I on the side of the French against the Germans. He was so disturbed by what happened during the war that he joined

Brigitte Bardot and Michel Piccoli on the rooftop stairs of Villa Malaparte in Jean-Luc Godard's *Contempt,* 1963, filmed at the extraordinary villa on Capri designed by Malaparte.

the Italian Fascist Party in its early, idealistic phase. Later he was expelled for writing an exposé of Mussolini's rise to power after he felt that the original ideals had been corrupted. After World War II he became a communist, and then on his deathbed he converted to Catholicism apparently.

His adopted name—Malaparte—could be read as the "bad part" that does not fit in with the rest of society. There's still a great deal of controversy about him in Italy. Some see him as an egotistical opportunist. I think there's something else going on, a bruised idealism that could never find a home in this world. . . .

O: He was essentially a prose writer, and you're translating his prose into poetry. What's your reason for that?

M: It seemed to happen all by itself. It surprised me because I'm not somebody who naturally gravitates to poetry. I prefer to read prose, if given the choice. So I was surprised, but because it seemed to happen automatically, I let it.

With hindsight, I'd say it was probably due to the rich, almost overwhelming density of Malaparte's original text, the fabulous nature of his imagery, his frequent use of repetitions, and the cross-sensory nature of his metaphors: "the air filled with water and stone," "a bitter blue light."

I think one of the reasons his writing has found it hard to breathe in English is that extreme density of image. If you get into it—as I did—it's fine, but it's almost too much, too thick a potion. It's less thick in Italian because there's a musicality that relieves the thickness. But in English it doesn't have that. In a way, the fragmentation on the page into lines of poetry is a way of aerating it, reinfusing that musicality. It was also fascinating to me because I suddenly saw a parallel between the decision of where to bring a line to an end and the decision of where to end a shot.

O: I know. When I phoned you and told you how good and natural the line breaks seemed, and then to hear that you'd not done this before . . . I was amazed at that!

M: We confront this all the time in film editing: The point at which you decide to end the shot usually has very little to do with the grammar of the scene around it. You do not end a shot at the comma, so to speak. You end a shot sometimes right in the middle of a word, and go on to another shot with the dialogue hanging over. But the architecture of those shots, and where you choose to end the line, has to do with the rhythmic balance of the material up to that moment.

O: You can see another aspect of this in Robert Creeley—who is a master of line breaks in poetry. Where he breaks the line is utterly bound up with his voice and persona—so the craft represents him, draws a portrait of him, as much as the text does. The form in this way can mirror the speaker's state and nature. There's a wonderful statement about Creeley by the poet Sharon Thesen that describes this. "When you see/hear Creeley read it's almost like managing pain. . . . It's that probing consciousness, the turnings toward and away from what can literally be borne in or by the line . . . and it's all *in* the line. . . . His vocabulary is not large and florid. There's that intelligence that just will not exceed its form. . . . It pulls back with that lovely eloquent 'humilitas.'"

In your translating and editing of Malaparte's poems such as "Sleepwalking" or "The Wind," how faithful were you to the text?

M: Well, as faithful as a translator can be. There's an Italian adage: "*Traduttore, traditore*"—translator, traitor.

O: So you did at times betray his original text?

M: Yes, but I hope I betrayed the surface only in the interest of getting at a deeper truth. In one language an idea can be expressed in a single word and in another language you need five words for it. If you translated each of those words literally, there would be something wrong. So it might be better to find out what happens if you condense these five into a single word. And then what does that do to the architecture of the rest of the material? You probably have to make other adjustments as a result, and so on.

O: What surprises me about Malaparte is his surreptitious humor.

M: He's full of that. But you have to be alive to it. It's subtle—particularly for an American audience—so far from overt that it's easy to miss it. I find Malaparte's work is infused with this quality. . . . There's a fascinating description of a dinner scene in *The Skin,* which takes place just before the Allies move into Rome. Malaparte is serving as an aide-de-camp with the French army, and they're billeted on the hills overlooking Rome. Some French generals and Moroccan soldiers are having couscous for dinner. During the preparations for dinner there's an explosion—a grenade goes off and one of the Moroccans loses a hand. During the dinner the subject of Malaparte's experiences in his book *Kaputt* comes up, and one of the French generals protests, Why do these incredible things happen to you, Malaparte? I'm a general and I've gone through the whole war and nothing incredible has ever happened to me. You must be inventing these things. And Malaparte says, No, I don't invent them. I may be a magnet for them. But they happen.

There's a debate back and forth, and then Malaparte says, Well, in fact, as I've been talking to you, the most incredible thing has happened.

What is it?

He says, Well, as I was eating I discovered some human fingers mixed in with my couscous. Naturally, being a good guest, I didn't mention this and have been eating as if it were really prepared for me.

Everyone else at the table goes into a state of shock, and Malaparte says, No, no, look. You can see these little bones on the plate. What must have happened was that the Moroccan's hand landed in the pot in which the lamb stew was being prepared, and it was cooked along with the stew and served to me.

They're all revolted, but one of the guests, Jack, an American friend of Malaparte's, examines the plate and realizes that he's played a joke—that it's just lamb bones carefully arranged to look like a hand. After the dinner, Jack is slapping Malaparte on the back and saying, What a jokester! What a trickster! Yet with this mixture of the true and the concocted, Malaparte ends the story on a note of ambiguity. It's finally unclear whether they were human fingers or not. And perhaps the joke was on Jack, after all. But it's funny. And horrible. In his introduction to *Kaputt* Malaparte writes: "This is a gay and gruesome book."

Generally, the only accounts of the war experience from the fascist side came either from nonliterary people or from the Nazis themselves, and you had to discount what they said because they were Nazis. Whereas here was Malaparte, this much more neutral, ironic observer, telling you things you hadn't heard before, and in that particular way of his. That's what I responded to, I guess.

O: I remember a story about William Carlos Williams visiting Ford Madox Ford in France. They're walking in a field and Ford is expounding on his theories of impressionism and the modern novel and so forth. In his journals, Williams wrote: "For forty minutes Ford was going on and he didn't even notice that nearby there was a sparrow, terrified because we were approaching its nest." A magazine ran Williams's account on the left-hand page, and on the opposite page Ford's diary account of the same afternoon. And Ford's entry was almost entirely about that sparrow he'd seen on the walk. It wasn't anything to do with aesthetics. It was wonderful, full of details, his mind was totally on the three little birds in their nest.

THIRD

CONVERSATION

NEW YORK CITY

In the fall of 2000, I was a writer-in-residence at the Columbia University medical school in New York. Every morning I would take the A train to Columbia Presbyterian on 168th Street, the hospital where, in fact, Duke Ellington was admitted in the last days of his life. During those three months I invited some writers to come and speak to the class I was teaching. As there was a chance Walter would be travelling through New York in December, I asked him if he would address the students and medical faculty about his work in film. He agreed partly because he had been born in the hospital, as he said (always precise), "fifty-seven years and one hundred and fifty-two days ago." So I was able to introduce him one afternoon as an older and wiser Walter Murch.

The talk held his medical audience spellbound. He projected clips from various films, talking about how they were structured, and he projected slides to show how picture, light, sound, and electricity combine in the process of amplification in a theatre. His constant fascination with and knowledge of the sciences has always made him very much at ease with this kind of audience. A year later he would be giving a lecture in San Diego on the future of digital cinema to a gathering of three thousand neurosurgeons.

Elizabeth MacRae and Gene Hackman looking at dailies from *The Conversation* with Coppola.

The next morning after his talk at the hospital, we sat down for our third conversation. The sound of the steam pipes in the walls of the SoHo loft where we met constantly startled us with their loudness, a sort of haphazard and unseen gamelan orchestra. This time our talk focussed mostly on two films: *The Conversation* and *Touch of Evil* which Walter had spent the early part of 1998 recutting according to Orson Welles's recently discovered memo. *The Conversation* was the first feature on which Walter edited picture, and in many ways I think it's his most interesting (and probably his most independent) work in his ongoing collaboration with Coppola as writer-director and himself as editor.

Our conversation ended with a late Vietnamese lunch on Greene Street.

EDITING *THE CONVERSATION*

O: When you and Francis Coppola worked on *The Conversation,* the content must have seemed like the absolutely logical subject you would want to make a film about, a celebration and inquiry of "humble sounds." Really, the same obsession you had when you were eleven years old. Was it a film Coppola wrote on his own and you then got involved in, or were you involved at an earlier stage?

M: He wrote it in the late sixties. The idea for the film was a *Life* magazine article that Irvin Kershner, the director, had brought to Francis's attention. It was a portrait of Hal Lipset, a surveillance technician who worked out of San Francisco. Francis had seen Antonioni's *Blowup* a year or two before, and he had the idea to fuse the concept of *Blowup* with the world of audio surveillance. The central character, Harry Caul—loosely inspired by Harry Haller in Hermann Hesse's *Steppenwolf*—is an ordinary bourgeois person who is suddenly plunged into a world over which he has no control.

"A sense of doubling": hands and machines—Murch echoes Hackman's moves in the mixing room.

O: It's an amazing film. On one level it's a thriller, but it also has that ambiguity we were talking about earlier. And it's got such a chiselled and obsessed point of view.

M: Yes, since the story is relentlessly told from the single point of view of this ordinary surveillance technician. You know he's been hired by the Director of a faceless Corporation to secretly tape the conversations of a young couple who may or may not be having an affair. But since you only know only what *he* knows, you never really discover the whole story of what happened. You just make assumptions. And because he's a sound man, over the course of the film you, the audience, naturally begin to hear the world the way *he* hears it. That was a wonderful opportunity.

O: This is one of the great unreliable narratives in film. And it seems an obsession so close to yours. . . .

M: There were many times while making the film that I had a sense of doubling. I'd be working on the film late at night, looking at an image of Harry Caul working on his tape, and there would be four hands, his and mine. Several times I was so tired and disoriented that Harry Caul would push the button to stop the tape and I would be amazed that the film didn't also stop! Why was it still moving?

It's curious that recently I've been working on the Edison-Dickson film, doing exactly the same kind of thing that Harry Caul did on that tape.

O: The craft of Harry Caul and what you do as a sound person do seem very close.

M: I think Francis was probably studying me occasionally, as if I were a member of a strange tribe and he were an anthropologist! I was the sound person most accessible to him—I supervised all the postproduction sound work on *Rain People, Godfather, THX,* and *American Graffiti.*

O: Watching *The Conversation,* I feel Coppola has given us, in an odd way, a celebration of artists, of professionals. There's such a pleasure in the craft—in the scene following the conference on electronic surveillance technology, where Harry's four fellow professionals stand around chatting about their craft, and in the way they talk about Harry as one of the "notables." It's a portrait of a clan of artists.

M: Yes, that was very much on Francis's mind. I remember him saying at the time how fascinating it is, particularly in film, to watch a craft being exercised. A woodcarver. Or a stonemason. To simply sit and watch. How often does he sharpen the blade? Oh, that's interesting—he sharpens it every tenth stroke. There's a very tactile, visual quality to it all. And it's of considerable human interest at the same time.

O: It's the way that in a samurai movie we become much more interested in the warrior's detailed training in solitude than in the final battle.

M: Yes. And for Francis, Harry Caul's craft is, of course, very much like film-making: Here's the raw material, and how do you get the best out of that material? It's an insight into the way such a mind works. Also, there's a lot of Francis in Harry Caul, although when you meet Francis you don't think of him as Harry. Francis comes across as the expansive, voluble paterfamilias. He'll welcome you to his table. He loves to have lots of people around and he loves discussion, to be the host, to cook dinner for you—all those social things that run absolutely opposite to the lonely Harry Caul in his motel-like apartment, playing a saxophone alone. But in fact there's another side to Francis that's very much like Harry Caul.

Also Francis himself has a highly developed technical side. Had his life gone another way, I can easily see him getting even more deeply involved in technology: "Harry Coppola." The story that Harry's rival, Bernie Moran, tells at the party in Harry's loft—how Harry bugged the neighbours' phones when he was twelve? That's actually a story about Francis when he was twelve.

Also, every filmmaker is a kind of voyeur. It just happens that Harry's voyeurism is very narrow—only the sound spectrum. But as soon as you become a filmmaker you are naturally always looking for subject matter and looking at new ways of seeing things and snooping on aspects of people's lives: not only subject matter but *approaches* to subject matter. I think it was easy for Francis to understand Harry Caul and his craft, out of his own experience.

That's been one of Francis's great strengths—finding ways to get his films to tap into his own personal experiences. I think sometimes that when films Francis has made have gone wrong, or not been as fully developed as they might have been, it's because he hasn't found a way to use his own life and experience as a reservoir from which to nourish those particular films. Then it tends to become a more technical exercise. But certainly in the *Godfather* films and *The Conversation* and *Apocalypse Now,* he was able to convert the making of those films into a kind of personal battleground and enrich the subject matter of the film itself.

0: Even though they are surrounded by "big" plots, most of Coppola's characters—Willard, Michael and the others—are solitaries, compulsively private. They are one-way mirrors, looking out, seldom revealing themselves, in some way at war with the outside world. That's where the drama lies.

M: My personal image of a Coppola film is a close-up of a very human face against an incredible backdrop of historical action. And having the two things work together without unbalancing each other.

0: I remember when you were accepting the Scripter Award for Anthony's adaptation of *The English Patient,* you read out the scene numbers in the screenplay and then you read out the order of the scenes as they finally played in the film. The eventual order was something like 1, 42, 2, 98—everything seemed to have changed, in the course of editing. Is that something that has happened in most of the films you've done, or was that an unusual occurrence?

M: In editing, the order of scenes often changes from what it was in the script. *The Conversation* was changed a lot. But in terms of its entanglements, I think *The English Patient* was the most changed. In *The English Patient,* there's a double variability—you're going backwards and forwards into several different time frames, and the point of view is not fixed: you can jump to a scene between Caravaggio and Hana as easily as you can to one between Kip and the Patient. Yet they're all in the same environment. Whereas *The Conversation* was limited by its somewhat linear time frame and by the nature of Harry Caul's singular point of view. You *only* have scenes in which Harry Caul is present. You are looking either at Harry or at something he is looking at. I should say listening as well as looking.

O: When you were editing *The Conversation,* was there a sense that you could have shaped it ten different ways, constructed new involvements? Because I get the sense watching it that the plot could swerve backwards or sideways into all kinds of unexplored material. Was it a very difficult edit?

M: A peculiarity of the project was that a good ten days of material was never filmed—Francis and the production team just ran out of time and money to shoot the entire script, and he had to go off to do preproduction on *Godfather II.* His advice to me at that point was, Well, let's just cut what we have together and see if we can find a way to compensate for that missing footage. So from the beginning we couldn't structure it the way the screenplay called for. I'd say there were about fifteen pages of script material that were not shot.

O: Was it a small complexity of plot that was missing from the shot film, or was it something major? How did you work around the missing scenes?

M: We had to be pretty inventive. For instance, in one scene Harry pursues Ann—the young woman who was his surveillance "target"—to a park, where he reveals to her who he is and what his concerns for her are. Francis shot the park material, but the material leading up to it, including a chase on electric buses, was never shot.

O: In the film, that conversation in the park is part of a dream sequence.

M: Because since we had no fabric with which to knit it into the reality of the film, it floated for a while, like a wild card, until we got the idea of making it a

dream of Harry's, which seemed to be the way to preserve it within the film. . . . When you have restricted material you're going to have to restructure things from the original intent, with sometimes felicitous juxtapositions.

O: Were there other scenes like the park sequence where you needed to adjust or even reshoot material?

M: In the end, the only additional shot we had to film, to make it all work, was a close-up of Harry's hand pulling a reel of tape off the tape recorder, so we could reveal that Meredith, the woman who seduces him at the party, has stolen the crucial tape. In fact, the idea of Meredith as an agent of the Corporation was created in postproduction, and it clarifies and shapes the whole story.

O: It's almost as if you're inventing the script, discovering it, as you work on it.

M: Inventing elements of it. That was necessary, given that there was unshot material.

O: When films are worked on in this way, they seem to give off a novelistic air. I felt the same way watching Wong Kar-wai's *In the Mood for Love,* where I believe he created a "story" during the editing from a much larger canvas of possibilities that he had filmed. And in *The Conversation,* we get the sense that there's a complete story behind the selection of material—it's back there in the distance. That's similar to the kind of thickness that a novel gives off. We are not held hostage by just one certain story, or if we are, we know it is just one opinion: there are clear hints of other versions. Not many films do that. I think *you* achieve that effect by always suggesting through sound that something is going on off screen—in *The English Patient,* the sounds that come from outside the torture room when we are inside suggest other worlds and other plots: we don't see them, but we hear them through the layering of sounds. In *The Conversation,* something like that is achieved by altering and colliding the order of events.

M: One thing that made it possible to do that in *The Conversation* was Francis's belief that people should wear the same clothes most of the time. Harry is almost always wearing that transparent raincoat and his funny little crepe-

Overleaf: Surveillance by Gene Hackman and John Cazale in *The Conversation*. *Above:* Maggie Cheung and Tony Leung as the "husband" and "wife" from Wong Kar-Wai's *In the Mood for Love*. The voyeurs: Grace Kelly and James Stewart in Hitchcock's *Rear Window*, 1954.

soled shoes. This method of using costumes is something Francis had developed on other films, quite an accurate observation. He recognized that, first of all, people don't change clothes in real life as often as they do in film. In film there's a costume department interested in showing what it can do—which is only natural—so, on the smallest pretext, characters will change clothes. The problem is, that locks filmmakers into a more rigid scene structure. But if a character keeps the same clothes, you can put a scene in a different place and it doesn't stand out.

Second, there's a delicate balance between the time line of a film's story—which might take place over a series of days or weeks or months—and the fact that the film is only two hours long. You can stretch the amount of time somebody is in the same costume because the audience is subconsciously thinking, Well, I've only been here for two hours, so it's not strange that he hasn't changed his clothes.

As soon as this issue becomes overt, of course, you have to address it—if somebody in the story gets soaking wet, then of course he'll have to change his clothes, or if he's at a different kind of social function a week later, of course he'll be wearing a different set of clothes. Short of that, it's amazing how consistent you can make somebody's costume and have it not stand out.

Elizabeth Hartman and a skeleton in Coppola's 1966 comedy, *You're a Big Boy Now.*

O: Film—even more than theatre, I think—insists on a unity, in some odd way. Not just in costume or location but even in sound.

M: Mm-hm.

O: I mean, if a different, distinct sound or room tone is suddenly introduced, unless it's explained or established it can appear inexplicably foreign. There's a forced consistency in film.

M: Right, which is necessitated by the fact that films are shot out of sequence.

Actually, one of the main structural changes in *The Conversation* was necessitated when we realized that the audience found what Harry Caul *does*—his regular work—so mysterious that it was not only hard for them to understand it but hard to understand the twists of *this particular* situation in which he finds himself. There were many screenings we had along the way where the audiences were completely flummoxed!

In the original filmed version, when Harry decodes the tape he's made of Ann and the young man, Mark, he *immediately* uncovers the line, "He'd kill us if he got the chance," then goes to return the tape to the Director. As an experiment we divided the scene in two. In the first part we had Harry working on the tape in a routine way, without uncovering the key line. The next day he goes to deliver the tape to the Director. But the fact that the Director's assistant—a very young Harrison Ford—seems a little too anxious to get his hands on the tape gives Harry—and us—pause. Harry takes it back to his studio to listen to it more closely. Now we have the second half of the scene where he uncovers the fateful line—which now has greater meaning in this new context.

This structure allows the audience to follow the train of events more clearly. But it took us some time to realize that there was a problem and then figure out what to do about it.

O: For me, *The Conversation* felt like the first American film of our generation that was really *European.* It was a new perspective, a new focus. In *You're a Big Boy Now* and *The Rain People,* I saw that something strange was happening, but this was the one that was so gutsy, in terms of, Okay, we're going to talk about this from this obsessive angle and we're *not* going to deal with, or think about, the John Ford vista.

M: Exactly. The inspiration for Billy Wilder's *The Apartment* was a tangential character in David Lean's *Brief Encounter*: the man who agrees to lend the lovers his apartment for the night. Wilder wanted to take a peripheral character from one film and make him a central character in another. What is it like to be that character? Harry Caul is very much in line with that. In a "normal" film, Harry would be the anonymous person recording the tape: you would see him only briefly as he comes into the office and hands the tape in, is paid, and leaves.

Francis was interested in following an anonymous person and really investigating the fabric of his life. It was a courageous act on his part never to flesh out the story of the murder that finally happens. We know there are two suspects, but what and who they are, and what their real jobs are, and what their relationship is, *we* don't know, because Harry doesn't know. And even *Francis* didn't know: he felt that if he knew, he'd somehow be infected with that knowledge, and he'd be obliged to shoot it, to have it just in case. And if it existed, the impulse to put it in the film would then be almost irresistible. So he willingly said exactly what you said: I'm not going to think about that at all. It was courageous and risky.

It made the film more awkward to edit, because we didn't have lots of conventional plot material. In the end, the film was a delicate balance between a character study of this rather colourless man—Hermann Hesse's Harry Haller—and a dramatic mystery of corporate takeover and murder—a Hitchcock kind of idea. It was very much in Francis's mind, from the beginning, to try to make an alloy of Hermann Hesse and Hitchcock, to forge an unlikely alliance between those two sensibilities. The struggle of the film, at every level, was how to achieve that balance.

What we found was that if the balance shifted ever so slightly towards the murder-mystery aspect, our test audiences became impatient with the character-study parts: they seemed unnecessary—Get rid of that! But we had nothing to replace them with. . . . On the other hand, if we stayed more with the characters, the murder mystery was so partial that it seemed unnecessary. It seemed like something chosen by the filmmakers to beef up—

O: An intellectual plot.

M: Right.

O: But it's what I love about the film! It's that wonderful balance of those two things: a mystery genre and an intellectual character study. I thought what was interesting about it, watching it again, was that it was like *Rear Window*—the central character is a voyeur, an eavesdropper who later on is the one invaded by the person he's watching. And it's like *Vertigo,* which has that strange, subliminal obsessive subplot that you don't know if Hitchcock was even really aware of, which rises up and exists there, equal with the mystery.

M: My memory of getting the structure of that film as right as we ever got it is of a knife-edge alchemy between two elements that don't naturally flow together: copper and tin easily go together to make bronze, but this was something else. The metal of character study and the metal of murder mystery don't easily melt together.

O: I know. I began *The English Patient* by reading a nonfiction book about a spy who goes across the desert during World War II. A friend of mine had told me about a spy her father was tracking in Cairo. Read this book called *The Cat and the Mice,* she said. There was Ken Follett's novel too—*The Key to Rebecca*—based on the spy's adventures. But in the nonfiction work it was the man who guided the spy across the desert who seemed to me much more interesting than the spy, though there were only a few lines describing him. And I knew, like Billy Wilder did, that *this* was the guy I wanted to write about . . . and this was Almásy. I was not really interested in a spy story, I was interested in Almásy's character, but I also wanted the drama of the spy story to hover on the horizon as I wrote.

■

O: How long did it take you to edit *The Conversation*?

M: A little longer than *The English Patient*. They finished shooting *The Conversation* in March of '73, and the mix and everything was done about eleven months later. More than usual, but less than some. It also had a very long first assembly, like *The English Patient*: four and a half hours. To complicate matters, I was doing two things at once—mixing *American Graffiti* and editing *The Conversation*. I was new to the job, it seemed crazy, but doable. Now, looking back on it, I can't imagine tackling something like that! I was also newly a father for the second time, and Aggie and I had just moved house.

O: You did the sound on *Graffiti* while you were editing *The Conversation*?

M: Editing *The Conversation* during the day and mixing *Graffiti* at night—some combination of that. Richard Chew was my associate editor on *Conversation*. He was able to take up the slack, thank God. If I had to be gone for a period of time on *Graffiti*, he was able to keep the editorial pots boiling. Richard went on to edit *One Flew over the Cuckoo's Nest* and win an Oscar for editing *Star Wars*.

O: When you put together the DVD version of *The Conversation* twenty-five years later, did you see it as an opportunity to finesse any of the editing?

M: No. We didn't touch the picture at all. We remastered the soundtrack though. It was originally mixed in 1974 as a monophonic optical track, the kind of sound that had remained virtually unchanged since the late 1930s. By 1976, with the introduction of Dolby stereo, we were able to mix higher-quality sound, and in stereo. Since then, of course, there's been tremendous progress technically: we've seen the introduction of digital sound and all the different kinds of sophisticated computer-controlled multitrack systems. *The Conversation* was, technically speaking, plain vanilla. Artistically, it was another matter. We were trying to push the envelope. A very small envelope.

If you release an older film on DVD, you're almost obliged to remaster the soundtrack so that it can withstand scrutiny by the magnifying glass of today's sophisticated equipment. Luckily, we found the original masters of the music—now twenty-eight years old. They had been recorded on three-track magnetic tape. The idea at the time was that the three tracks would allow us to shift the balance between the bass and the treble parts of the piano, to give different colourations of the mono sound.

But today, if you play the three tracks through a theatre system, it reproduces a very nice stereo field. So we were able to present the music in stereo for the DVD. That then obliged us to re-create some of the atmospheres, and an occasional sound effect, in stereo.

O: It's strange to realize that *The Conversation* came between the first two *Godfather* films, as opposed to being pre-*Godfather*.

Roman Coppola, flanked by his parents, carries the Palme d'Or won in 1974 at Cannes for *The Conversation*; Murch and his wife, Aggie, walk behind.

M: In a sense, it *was* pre-*Godfather*. *The Conversation* was a script that Francis had written and developed long before *The Godfather*. In fact, he had intended to make *Conversation* right after *Rain People*. But the financing fell apart, and *Godfather* luckily came along to fill the gap. If that hadn't happened, American Zoetrope would probably have had a short life.

Nonetheless, as soon as *Godfather* was over, Francis put *The Conversation* into production, almost as a wedge to keep himself from being crushed between the *Godfather* films. There was tremendous pressure on him financially, and then creatively, to do a sequel to *Godfather*. And he took it upon himself to do it right: to show that sequels can be films that stand on their own.

Anyway, the *Godfather*s had such power, both within the industry and the culture at large, that Francis was desperate to stake out his own personal turf, in between, so as not to be known just as "the *Godfather* guy." The decision to make *Conversation* right after *Godfather* turned out to be creatively the right thing to do. And strategically it was wonderful, since both *The Conversation* and *Godfather II*—very, very different films—were nominated for Best Picture at the Academy Awards in 1975. People thought, This guy can do everything!

THE INVISIBLE PARTNER

O: There's a distinctive use of music in all your films. In *The Conversation*, there's that scene where Harry works on the tape, and slowly turns the tape machine dials off one by one, *click, click, click, click,* after he clearly hears the line "He'd kill us if he got the chance"—and then you allow the piano to come in at that point. It's such a grace note, underlining a clarifying moment: Harry now understands something. And the music signals the end of Act One. Curtain. For me, it has the same effect as the appearance of music after the silence that follows Michael's first killing in *The Godfather*.

M: You're right, it's a very similar situation, though the films are very dissimilar. In that scene in *The Conversation,* you go through a good five or six minutes with no music accompanying what's happening, other than the music that's actually on the tape. It's only at the moment when Harry realizes, to his chagrin, Oh no, this apple is poisoned, that the music comes in. As I said, music seems to function best when it channels an emotion that has already been created out of the fabric of the story and the film.

O: Obviously you're very careful not to overuse music. But you must have been tempted to use much more of Jim Morrison's music in *Apocalypse Now*. But even that's restrained. Most filmmakers would have drowned themselves in his music.

M: It's funny, we did an experiment. . . . At a certain point in the film's evolution we thought we would use Jim Morrison's music much more, but as it turned out no matter where we put it, it always seemed too much on the nose, even though the music was written long before and had nothing to do with *Apocalypse Now* in any direct sense. Yet you felt as if Jim Morrison was right there behind the screen, telling you exactly what was happening. No matter how hard we tried, there was something about that music that seemed to be commenting on the action. So we pulled back and only used it at the very beginning and at the end.

O: Where did the great drumming music come from, in *Apocalypse Now*?

M: Mickey Hart, who was the percussionist for the Grateful Dead, organized a group called the Rhythm Devils. Francis asked them to do a percussion track for the entire film. They were to look at the film and improvise as they watched it.

O: That's what Louis Malle got Miles Davis to do when he "played" the sound-track to *Ascenseur pour l'échafaud* [*Elevator to the Gallows*] . . . in the late fifties.

M: And that's just what the Rhythm Devils did. Twenty percent of the music in *Apocalypse Now* is Mickey Hart and the group, sometimes in isolation, other times integrated into the electronic score.

O: Does music always tend to be written and brought in at the last stage of a film?

M: In *The Conversation* the music was done in a very intelligent way—I was surprised later on to find out this was not the usual method. Francis gave the script to the composer, David Shire, long before the film was shot—highly unusual, although I recommend it if the director and the composer have a good relationship. Francis asked David to pretend that this was a strange kind of musical: The screenplay is the book, so now come up with tunes for it. David wrote two or three of the themes that are in the film, based just on his reading of the screenplay. Francis was able to play those themes for Gene Hackman and the other actors at the time of shooting, so they could hear the music that might be played with the scene. They could hear the scene's colouration—so they didn't have to *act* that colour. It gave them a great deal of freedom to have that advance knowledge, to pitch themselves against or with the music, to know how the music would fill in their performances, the yin to their yang.

O: Balanchine, talking about Stravinsky's score for the ballet *Apollo,* said "the score was a revelation. It seemed to tell me that I could dare not use everything. That I too could eliminate."

M: It's incredible to me that it's done in any other way, when you think how critical music is in film. But music is almost always written after the fact, with the composer reacting to events already filmed and edited together. How much better if the music is present at the birth of the film, born along with the screenplay, the two of them interweaving through the process of shooting and post-production. . . .

Later, when I was editing *Conversation,* I could place the music where it felt right, and David might say, Oh yeah, I agree with that, or, No, I don't like that, or he'd go away and compose something else and give me that to work with, so there was constant feedback between the script, the music, and the film, as it was evolving. Each was able to nourish and influence the other, in ways that don't happen in most conventional films. Usually the music not only comes in very late but is almost spray-gunned on to the film: Now stand back! The music guy comes in all suited up with a big spray gun and blasts it red! Your alternatives at that point are either: I don't like it, or I like it. Maybe shift its location. But at that stage you really can't change the fundamental nature of the music. Nor has the music had an opportunity to shape the film.

That's why the music sometimes ends up being thrown out—because it wasn't given a chance to grow with the film. Then you have panic, and some other poor composer is called in and told: We have two weeks before the film has to hit the theatres! It's like putting out an oil fire with dynamite.

My experiences working with Anthony Minghella and the composer Gabriel Yared on both *English Patient* and *Ripley* are the closest to that *Conversation*-type collaboration of music and film.

O: I remember when Anthony shot the deathbed scene between Hana and the Patient, he played the aria from the Goldberg Variations on set, even though that was replaced with other music later on.

M: That's a technique that was used a lot during the silent era, when there was no recording at the time of shooting. When sound recording came in, that was used less and less, for obvious reasons: it would leak onto the dialogue track. Kubrick used it during the filming of *Spartacus,* I believe. And maybe *2001*. Certain directors still make great use of it. But you have to then re-record the dialogue.

O: One of the things that struck me about what you and Anthony did musically in *The English Patient* was that if there's music on the soundtrack, the audience later realizes it's part of the reality of the scene. For instance, we hear Benny Goodman's jazz as part of the soundtrack, and it's only later that we realize it's a record being played by Caravaggio for the Patient. The music becomes more than an outside force—it grounds the music in the actual scene. I think there were a couple of moments in *Ripley* that worked that way too.

M: Yes. That's the great power of source music—music that comes from within the scene, either because an orchestra is playing and you see the orchestra or because somebody has a radio or record player on. It has a musical effect on the audience, but they are insulated from feeling overtly manipulated musically because the sounds are explained by the scene. It seems almost accidental: Oh! This music just happened to be playing while they were filming the scene; it isn't read as having anything to do with the subtext of the film. Of course, it does. But your conscious impression is that it doesn't. Sound effects work very much the same way.

O: So it feels like a lucky accident.

M: All source music and sound effects aim for that ideal of the lucky accident. We filmmakers didn't have anything to do with it! It just happened! And the audience appreciates it this way. It sneaks past their immune system, so to speak. Whereas a musical score doesn't. It has to pass through some sort of blood/brain barrier. When you hear it, you recognize that you are now being manipulated musically—and you reposition yourself slightly. A new voice has entered. Whereas source music can enter a scene without being perceived as a new voice. It just seems, as you said, a lucky accident.

What we were doing in *The English Patient* was playing with the twilight zone between those two realms. We wanted you to hear the Benny Goodman as score, but then it collapsed, it condensed, the water vapour of that music became liquid when you saw that it was coming from a record player within the scene. That has a curious effect on an audience—almost the opposite of what I was saying. But I enjoy playing with those things. Like all those techniques, there is a fine line: If you overuse it, then it becomes predictable and it's not so welcome anymore.

O: I also remember that in the early drafts of the film you used a very good version of the Goldberg Variations when Hana is playing the piano, and later you had to change the recording to a not-as-good one—to make it more realistic. Or she would have been playing as well as Glenn Gould!

M: Yes, and we detuned the piano, to imply that it had been exposed to the weather for months.

THE MINOR KEY

O: If you think about the characters in the films you've worked on—you've got Willard, Michael Corleone, Tomas from *Unbearable*, Ripley, and Harry Caul— it's a ne'er-do-well bunch! There's an almost insistent need in you to make us love such people.

M: And the English Patient too.

O: And the Patient, yeah.

M: It's interesting, isn't it? I don't know whether *love* is the right word. Understand, sympathize, perhaps. I don't know how much of that pattern you've identified is my choice and how much is chance. Clearly everyone involved is fully aware of the problematic aspects of the characters. . . . But that's what makes it interesting—there's a wonderful challenge in showing the deeper or less obvious aspects of people who, on the surface, are unlikeable or even boring. Everybody has a story, and people who are usually labelled "uninteresting" or problematic usually have the more interesting stories. There is a mystery about them.

O: Even with a strong script about such deeply flawed characters, you as an editor also have to present them emotionally and intellectually in some fair way, so they are complicated and dangerous but cannot be dismissed easily or quickly. . . . It seems you'd need to have a real empathy for that point of view.

M: I agree. To the extent that these are characters played in a minor key, I'm interested in the minor key. They come at you sideways, whereas major-key characters come at you directly—

O: As in *Spartacus.*

M: Yes. I guess I am drawn to stories where you have to get under the skin of rather unlikely and sometimes unlikeable characters.

Source music in *The English Patient:* the piano was detuned to suggest that it had been exposed to the elements.

How you do that, as an editor, ultimately comes down to selecting the shots, and moments within shots, where the character looks appealing yet problematic at the same time—conflicted, in other words. If you have a choice of seven different shots, which one shows that conflict best? There are many tiny but telling details the editor includes or eliminates in order to make the audience aware of the deeper aspects of character.

For instance, if you are wearing a hat, as soon as you tip the hat slightly back on your head, it gets noticed—you're sending a message via the angle of the hat: I'm a happy-go-lucky guy. Or if you ram the hat down on your head, you're saying, I don't want to talk to anybody. Or if you tip it forward, you say, I'm aggressive. . . . But if you're trying to be earnest, the tipped-back hat doesn't quite send the right message.

In film there are endless versions of this, where a look, an aspect, an attitude, a gesture is fortuitously correct or incorrect, and either amplifies or contradicts the message the filmmakers want to convey.

I'm using "hat" as a metaphor: one moment is always going to be the most revealing, in the best sense, of the inner character, at that point in the film.

0: I would forgive Harry Caul a lot of things for that moment when he looks at the paper mobile hanging on the string in front of him and just blows it, with a small breath. It's such a tender, intimate scene. So much is happening in that little moment, which is nothing really.

M: That's a very good example. He comes into the scene, in a wide shot, and that little mobile is hanging at an angle, so it's almost invisible—you don't notice it. Then he bumps into it, his head nods forwards, and he hits it. It's right around that point that I cut to a slightly closer shot of that same action, where that little dangling thing pirouetted in the most interesting way. If I'd just held the long shot it wouldn't have been as interesting.

0: I saw *The Conversation* when it first came out, and watching it again recently I was waiting for the last camera movement, when Harry Caul is pulling his apartment to pieces—

M: The oscillating camera—

O: Which I assume is where the bug he's looking for possibly is.

M: It is and it isn't. I think if there were literally a camera in his room, he would have discovered it. But that camera movement does give you that effect of another alien presence in the room with him. The camera is definitely not a neutral "hat." Most of the time the camera asks us not to think about the particular angle from which it's photographing, but to think about the action—it just happens that the chosen angle is the most revealing for this particular action. Whereas in that shot in Harry's apartment, the camera is aggressively a presence.

O: We were talking last night at dinner about how in the last half of the film there's practically no dialogue, though it's something we're not really conscious of.

M: Yes. From the moment the guests leave the party in Harry's loft, and we're left with Harry and Meredith, the woman who seduces him and steals the tape, the normal give-and-take of a dialogue film—where meaning is conveyed in words—begins to bleed into something else quite different. It becomes very spare in its use of dialogue. I think that encourages the audience to listen to sounds as if they are speech. In other words, you begin to search the soundtrack for meaning because there are no words "in the foreground" distracting you. You pay closer attention to the sounds that are there. There isn't a noticeable difference between the sound effects in the first half and those in the last half of the film. But what is different is the gradual evaporation of dialogue, leaving in the end just "the conversation" itself, and the sound effects. You pay attention to the stars on nights when there is no moon. When the moon is shining, all you can see is the moon. Dialogue is the moon, and stars are the sound effects.

Curiously, I wasn't consciously aware of this when I was working on the film. But when it came out, and people started saying that it had an interesting soundtrack, I wondered, What are they talking about . . . ? Okay, it's about a sound man, and that encourages you to take his point of view. Still, I didn't fully understand until I realized that the absence of dialogue in the second half of the film makes you listen to the sounds and give them a significance they would not otherwise have. It seems obvious in retrospect.

O: It's interesting how that awareness of an absence sometimes occurs subconsciously even while reading a book. In the middle of William Faulkner's *Light in August* there's a brief—just a page long—conversation between Joe Christmas and the woman, Joanna Burden. It's a very quiet conversation, and nothing much goes on, but I was in tears in that scene. And I didn't know why. It was only later that I realized that's the only time in the book when Joe Christmas has a real conversation with someone else. He is so utterly alone. He doesn't really talk to anyone in the book. So their talk feels shockingly intimate, and it emphasizes the absence around the scene. It would be like Harry Caul suddenly communicating openly with someone in the middle of the film.

WHAT'S UNDER THE HANDS?

O: Gene Hackman as Harry Caul gives a remarkable performance of a guy who won't reveal anything about himself, yet somehow we are magnetized by him. How does that work? I know when you were cutting *The English Patient,* you had a central character who was essentially in bed all the time—yet somehow you had to make him dramatic. I noticed that whenever you cut to him in the bed he'd be moving, in some small way, he wouldn't just be lying still, he'd be shifting within the sheet or leaning forwards to get something, so he was very active while supposedly bedridden and static. When you edited *The Conversation,* did you do anything similar to make Hackman's character so magnetic? It was a great performance!

M: Yes, it was. The very smart thing that Francis exploited is the human hunger for mystery: if somebody says, I'm not going to show you what's under my hands, you become fixated on what's under his hands. Even if your hunch is that there's nothing, you won't be satisfied until you've seen what is—or isn't—under his hands.

And that's what happens when you present somebody, like Harry Caul, who won't tell you anything about himself. He has nothing in his apartment that will give any clue as to what's going on inside him. His girlfriend, Amy, tries to get him to talk about himself and he says he's a kind of a freelance musician. Then she says the worst thing she could have said, which is: "I want to know about you." That's when he gets up off the bed and leaves.

Revealing just enough of that secret dynamic was the real challenge for Hackman. He usually likes to play characters who have at least one opportunity to bust loose. But in *The Conversation* everything was constrained, hidden. The job of the editors, conversely, was to make things as clear as possible, because what Harry does—his work as an electronic eavesdropper—*is* hard to understand, by its very nature.

Francis was very articulate about this at the time of shooting. He knew people were fascinated by *process*. So he dwelled deliberately on all the minutiae of Harry's work—and that's one of the things that suck you into Harry's life and get you to identify with him.

O: I agree. It's like Bresson's *Pickpocket,* where he shows you the poetry in the details of the craft. There's nothing more interesting than that.

M: Exactly.

O: Everything that happens in *The Conversation* is to do with communication, or noncommunication. Harry's obsessed with translating what people say inti-

A detail and a scene from Robert Bresson's 1959 film, *Pickpocket.*

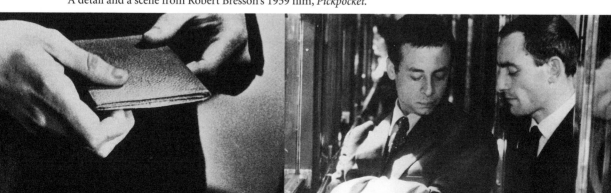

mately, in secret, but he himself says nothing, reveals nothing. The English Patient doesn't move, Harry Caul doesn't communicate.

M: Yeah. . . .

O: All aspects of Harry's life, even his rooms—his apartment, the loft—have locks and distinct boundaries—

M: Harry's life is segregated into neutral rooms—the motel-like appearance of his home is identical to the hotel room where the murder is committed. Also, he has his costume—

O: The caul of a raincoat you were talking about before. But even his work space—which is his "heart"—ends up as a little cage, with this amazing DMZ of an empty loft around it. Was all this conceived beforehand?

M: It was developed as Francis wrote the screenplay and interacted with the various department heads—the costumer, Aggie Rogers, and production designer, Dean Tavoularis.

O: What was that interesting but rather bewildering element about Harry's relationship with the other people in the apartment building? His landlady puts a bottle of wine inside his door . . . ?

M: That was part of a subplot that *was* interesting but in the end superfluous. The bottle of wine is the only fragment of it left. In the shooting script, people in the apartment building discover it's Harry's birthday and invade his apartment with a birthday cake, then start complaining about the plumbing in the building and elect him to be their representative to go talk to the owner of the building about fixing it. We discover a further level of secrecy in Harry's character when we find out Harry himself is the owner of the building. He goes to see his lawyer and asks, What am I going to do? The tenants want me to complain to myself.

Coppola's notes for the script of *The Conversation.*

CONVERSATION NOTES

there is always the idea that the sins a man performs are not the same as the ones he thinks he has PERFORMED.

Harry confesses that he has performed a sex act on himself; and doesn't begin to see the greater sin — the one he performed on the two young people.

the opening might be built out of fragments of various conversations. So that when we first meet the two young people they seem like just another conversation until we see that the microphone is trained on them: THEY ARE important ONLY BECAUSE SOMEONE IS LISTENING.

the whole Assignment would have had to be APPROACHED GEOMETRICALLY, like the film itself.

Firstly it would take two high-Directional microphones, one one either END of the RECTANGLE to be able to cover them.

BLIND SPOT

A

B

A

B

blind SPOT

DC. #2 —

48" off floor

6 pA

1725 in duct

O: So this subplot was shot?

M: All that was shot. But it was cut for reasons of length. And to try to maintain that balance we talked about between the character study and the murder mystery.

O: I thought the love scene where he's seduced by Meredith after the party in his loft was remarkable. The only intimate touch we really see between them is when she kisses his *ear*! And all the love talk during their foreplay is really coming from the tape. . . . There's no conversation. And the minute the tape ends, the love scene ends.

M: That was all in the screenplay. Francis was interested in having things exactly as you describe them—a fragment of dialogue on the tape seems to comment on something we are seeing in the loft. The relationship between the tape and the visuals is musical. We hear the girl on the tape taking pity on a homeless man sleeping on a park bench—while Harry is lying on his cot, in agony about her fate. "I love you," the girl says to the boy on the tape, as Meredith is whispering into Harry's ear.

These things are complicated to work out. They eventually depend on the exact orchestration of all the elements. How precisely things happen at any moment is determined largely in the editing, but Francis was very clear about what he wanted to achieve, and he shot the material in such a way to allow it to happen.

O: For me a similar and even more stunning moment occurs in *The English Patient*—which wasn't even in the screenplay—when Almásy and Katherine are caught in a truck during the sandstorm. It's part of a flashback and reveals the first awareness of their attraction for one another. He has touched her hair and she has not moved. She turns instead and puts her fingers on the glass of the truck window, the shot dissolves, slowly—*into the present*—and we briefly see Almásy's disfigured face under her hand. So it becomes her hand caressing his face across time in a tender gesture. It is emotionally haunting, because "in the present" Katherine is no longer alive.

"NIGHT WAS NIGHT": RE-EDITING
TOUCH OF EVIL

O: I often saw the original version of Orson Welles's *Touch of Evil* on late-night television, and I always drifted away from it. I recognized something strange was going on, but it never felt a consistently focussed film. There was "interference" taking place. . . . Then in the late nineties I heard you were re-editing the film. And—very exciting—that you were basing your work on Welles's famous memo written after he was fired by Universal, before he'd finished it. When I saw your new, reworked version of *Touch of Evil,* I found it a much darker, more radical film than the original. How did this project come into being?

M: It came out of the blue—a phone call from Rick Schmidlin, whom I didn't know. In fact, very few people at that time knew who he was. He'd done promotional films for Harley-Davidson, just enough story to get to see guys driving around, buying and riding Harley-Davidsons—"A Trip to the Rockies" et cetera.

But he loved film, and film history, and he particularly loved Orson Welles's work. In the early 1990s he read a fragment of Welles's memo in *Film Quarterly,* written in carefully modulated tones of suppressed outrage after Welles saw what the studio had done to *Touch of Evil.* The complete memo had been lost for some years, but the fragment had such a powerful effect on Rick that he made it his mission to find the complete, fifty-eight-page memo—which he did—and then convince Universal to recut *Touch of Evil* accordingly.

Rick had some contacts at Universal—he'd done some laser disc restorations for them—and he just walked in and kept banging on doors until he finally found someone high up enough in the executive food chain to know what he was talking about, to get excited about it, and to put it into production.

He called me and asked if I was interested. Well, I'd just finished a film, and I had no idea what I was going to do next, so I asked him: Was the original negative in reasonably good shape? (It was.) Was there a good magnetic master of the soundtrack, with separation of dialogue, music, and sound effects? (There was.) And, Let me see the memo! I was hooked as soon as I started reading it.

"As if Orson was sending us notes"
by Rick Schmidlin

About three years ago, I was at the Los Angeles County Museum and heard Walter Murch lecture on sound. After the lecture, they presented *The Conversation.* That was probably the single most important lecture I had ever heard, and *The Conversation* inspired me to do what I would later do.

When I was given the green light to re-edit Orson Welles's *Touch of Evil,* based on his memo, it didn't take a rocket scientist to know who I wanted to re-edit this film. I got Walter's phone number through a friend and called him at home. I said, Walter, this is Rick Schmidlin. You don't know me, but I'm going to be producing a re-edit of Orson Welles's *Touch of Evil,* and I can't think of any intellect that could match Orson Welles's better than yours. Would you be interested? Walter said, Mmm. Send me the memo and I'll take a look.

So I sent him the fifty-eight-page memo. About a week later I got a phone call, and he said, Can you come up to northern California and meet with me to discuss the project? I immediately drove up there. As I drove past San Francisco and headed up Highway 1, I remembered one of his instructions was, When you come to a crossroads and there's an X—that's where you make a left. Walter lives in a town that doesn't even have a marker to tell you how to get into the town! You fend for yourself.

I followed Walter's instructions and came to this beautiful 1880s farmhouse, with a lagoon that has the largest variety of birds in the world. I got there at lunchtime. I sat at the kitchen table with Walter and Aggie and their daughter Beatrice. And he talked about—of all things—a single reversed camera angle that he said existed in *Raging Bull*! And could I find out anything about a print with this version that he saw in Europe—it puzzled him what this reversal shot might mean to the context of the scene. I still haven't been able to find out about it.

At the end of lunch, Walter pulled out the memo and started reading it, from page 1, right down to the last of the fifty-eight pages. At the end, he put down the memo and said, I'll do it.

A month and a half later I was in Walter's converted barn next to the farmhouse. Over the weeks, it was fascinating to watch him work. Some mornings I would arrive and he would be standing at the Avid in his bathrobe—sometimes just pajamas—hair mussed up, and I knew that he had gotten an idea at four or five in the morning and had been editing continuously since then.

One of the most interesting things that happened was when we found that a twelve-page sound memo existed—and we were able to locate it. The studio would fax the pages up to us. It was strange . . . as if Orson was sending us these notes!

To say the least, working with Walter was the most rewarding experience in my life. I learned about mathematics. I learned about patience, structure, discipline, creativity, passion, humanity, humility, family, poetry, prose. And also what it was like to be in a house that does not have a television set.

O: How did the famous memo get written?

M: Welles had been permitted only one screening of the film, after the studio had worked for months making many changes, straightening out his original crosscutting structure and writing and shooting four new scenes, directed by Harry Keller. They were supposed to explain the situation more clearly and make the film more accessible to the audience for a Universal B picture in the late 1950s. Welles wrote his notes during that screening. I can only imagine how he felt, sitting there, writing away furiously in the dark. . . .

By the morning he had typed up fifty-eight pages of comments—astute, insightful, restrained, boiling with passion under the surface. But he was aware he was addressing his thoughts to the heads of the studio—notably Ed Muhl—who were his declared enemies. So you can see him trying not to express outright blame for what had happened, no matter what he thought privately. It's heartbreaking to read! Both for the obvious waste of talent and insight of one of our great filmmakers. And because, with hindsight, we know *Touch of Evil* was to be Welles's last film within the Hollywood system he'd so dramatically entered nearly twenty years earlier.

The memo is inspiring also for its raison d'être—which was to lay out the things Welles felt were wrong with the studio version of the film, and what he felt could be done to correct it, within its own terms. And it worked out to contain approximately fifty practical suggestions, beginning right away with the removal of Henry Mancini's opening music—"I assume the opening music is temporary"—and concluding with suggestions for how to treat Marlene Dietrich's famous eulogy for Quinlan, played by Welles, as his body floats in the garbage-strewn stagnant water of the canal: "What does it matter what you say about people? He was some kind of a man."

In the end, we were able to accommodate all fifty changes, even though all we had was the original negative and the magnetic soundtrack. None of the

One page of the fifty-eight-page memo Welles wrote during the screening of *Touch of Evil,* then typed up after being allowed to see the film only once.

I assume that the music now backing the opening
sequence of the picture is temporary. . .

As the camera moves through the streets of the
Mexican border town, the plan was to feature a
succession of different and contrasting Latin
American musical numbers - the effect, that is, of
our passing one cabaret orchestra after another.
In honky-tonk districts on the border, loudspeakers
are over the entrance of every joint, large or small,
each blasting out its own tune by way of a "come-on"
or "pitch" for the tourists. The fact that the
streets are invariably loud with this music was
planned as a basic device throughout the entire
picture. The special use of contrasting "mambo-
type" rhythm numbers with rock 'n' roll will be
developed in some detail at the end of this memo,
when I'll take up details of the "beat" and also
specifics of musical color and instrumentation on
a scene-by-scene, and transition-by-transition basis.

In the version I was shown yesterday, it's not clear
where you have decided to place the credits. A
brief report on this will show whether or not my
old ideas for sound and music patterns in this
opening reel are still of some potential value.
Since a clear description of this original plan will
occupy some space and take some little time to put
together, I'll postpone this pending your reply.

outtakes had been saved, of course, though they were available when Welles wrote his memo. What helped immeasurably were some of the new digital techniques—unimaginable when the film was originally shot.

Shortly after I began, a friend asked, What are you up to these days? Oh, I said, I'm doing Orson Welles's cut of *Touch of Evil.* And he said, You're not doing anything, I hope, to the beginning of the film. I replied, That's the first thing I'm changing.

A choking sound could be heard . . . I explained I was following Welles's directions. There was a long silence. He said, That's like hearing that God just called and said he wants to change the Bible.

O: Did you alter the content of the shot?

M: Just the opposite. Welles wanted to remove the main titles that had been superimposed over it, and he wanted a different soundtrack, something composed of snatches of source music—from brothels, cantinas, car radios, tourist traps—that shift and blend into each other as the camera drifts through the streets of this border town. The aural equivalent of the camerawork, in other words.

We were able to remove the titles, since we luckily discovered a "textless background" in one of the cans of negative. This was then digitally rewoven into the fabric of the film, so you can't tell where the transition takes place.

The original Henry Mancini title music was perfectly good in itself, but the problem was that it set up a stylistic expectation that the film never followed. The music, full of bongos and brass, makes you imagine a Peter Gunn or James Bond–type detective, suave, handsome, effective—but nobody in the film is like that.

Instead, we were able to construct something that I hope is close to what Welles wanted: overlapping fragments of source music, a device the film uses throughout: Afro-Cuban interwoven and alternating with rock and roll. The music throughout the film goes back and forth as the action repeatedly crosses the American-Mexican border.

Touch of Evil is, in a way, an investigation of the idea of "borderness." What is a border? What are our expectations of the people who live there? Welles plays tricks and upsets those expectations. In an earlier, non-Welles draft of the screenplay, the American detective was a Texas Ranger. He was upright and his Mexican counterpart was the corrupt, slothful, lecherous cliché. Instead, it's the

Welles directing Charlton Heston and Janet Leigh in *Touch of Evil*.

American detective, Quinlan—Welles—who is corrupt, overfed, shabbily dressed, reactionary, and racist. By contrast, Vargas, the Mexican narcotics investigator played by Charlton Heston, is square, liberal, uptight, moralistic, and a workaholic unable to consummate his honeymoon—with Susie, the luscious Janet Leigh—because of his commitment to solving the crime.

In many and various ways Welles was playing with oppositions, turning them upside down when it suited him. And what's nice about the new version of the film is that the opening shot now acts as a prelude to the events that follow. It settles you into your chair and presents you, in miniature, with all the themes and ideas that the following piece of cinema is about to investigate. So even if we'd made no other changes past that first shot, I think the film would be perceived as a different film, because you enter it in a different way.

O: That sense of erased borders is there throughout the film. Even the border between indoors and outdoors doesn't exist. When Charlton Heston is indoors making a phone call, you see what's going on out on the street: the two men he needs to talk with are actually outside, walking past. Or he's in the car when his wife, Susie—Janet Leigh—comes out above him onto a fire escape of a building he's driving by. So many times we move fluidly from indoors to outdoors and back again. It's the first film I've seen where that is so evident, and done in such a casual way. It isn't a case of cutting from A to B.

M: It was one of the technical breakthroughs of the film. In many cases they were using a handheld camera—a French *Camérette*—and shooting on real locations at night. Night was night, it wasn't fake night. This allowed a great freedom. Welles actually wanted to shoot in a real border town, but that presented too many logistical and economic problems for the studio. So he filmed it in Venice, California, reinventing it as a border town. Still, it was a real location and it really was as shabby and derelict as it looks. Of course, he emphasized that where he chose to: garbage blowing in the wind and floating in the canals.

O: There are also amazing similarities to *Psycho,* which followed two years later.

M: Yes. In fact, Welles was apparently bitter about *Psycho*'s success. It was made by the same studio—Universal—and many of the same craftsmen who worked on *Touch of Evil* worked on *Psycho.* Janet Leigh plays the same kind of victim. She gets raped in *Touch of Evil,* and murdered in *Psycho,* in similar motels. The psychotic motelkeeper—Dennis Weaver—is harmless in *Touch of Evil,* but he's deadly in *Psycho,* as played by Anthony Perkins.

O: And *Psycho* was much more popular.

M: Which explains some of Welles's bitterness. *Touch of Evil* contributed all of these elements . . . yet *Psycho* created a sensation. They are very different films,

Welles was bitter about *Psycho*'s success: Janet Leigh, *left,* played the same kind of victim in *Psycho* as in *Touch of Evil,* in a similar motel, in a film made by the same studio. *Right:* Orson Welles as Hank Quinlan and Marlene Dietrich as Tanya

on a certain level, but on many other levels they're similar. I'm sure that Hitchcock learned a lot, looking at *Touch of Evil.*

O: I loved that elevator scene in *Touch of Evil.* The elevator is too crowded and Heston decides to walk up the stairs, and leaves the group (and the camera) in the elevator. We ride up and meet Heston again—two floors up.

M: It was a real elevator, and there was no way then to get a camera inside it and have people talk. Impossible. But he did it. The French *Camérette* was a portable 35 millimetre camera, and he got it into the elevator, handheld. The sound was unusable, because the *camérette* is not a silent camera, but they re-recorded the dialogue later.

I'm sure Godard and Truffaut, who were big fans of *Touch of Evil,* learned from that scene how they could achieve exactly what they wanted—at once both a fresh sense of reality and ingenuity.

O: Welles is also very careful in his use of specific time . . . beginning with the clock bomb being set at exactly three minutes and—

M: Twenty seconds—

O: And you know that at three-twenty something is going to happen.

M: I was giving a presentation of the recut version in Denmark, and somebody perceptively mentioned that a hidden advantage of this new approach to the beginning is that as long as there were titles running, and as long as there was title music, you knew, subconsciously, that the bomb wasn't going to explode. Whereas without titles and with a fragmentary soundtrack there's no knowing exactly when three minutes and twenty seconds is up. The bomb could explode at any time.

So the moments when the car with the bomb approaches the camera are much tenser now than they were in the earlier version. The bomb car also has a musical signature, a certain song on its radio, that helps to identify it and tell you it's getting closer even when you haven't seen it yet.

O: No last chords of music now, *tick-tick-tick-tick,* and then the explosion.

M: Right.

O: Was there anything in Welles's memo that you tried that did not work? A scene that might have worked theoretically, on the page, but in fact did not work in practice?

M: Nothing. Nothing. That was the remarkable thing. The studio had allowed him to see it only once, without stopping. His fifty-eight-page memo is the result of that one screening of the film, when he saw new scenes he'd never written and never shot that had been added to the film.

Put yourself in his place—being forced to look at even one new scene written by somebody else and directed by somebody else, inserted into your film—it would be so devastating. But there were four new long scenes, so it was amazing that he was able to suppress that disorientation and keep writing, and that night generate a fifty-eight-page memo.

When I started working on the project, I never expected that we could do everything he wanted. In my experience even if you have all the necessary resources, you're lucky if seventy-five percent of the ideas pan out—a good rate of success for *anybody's* notes about a film. But in this case every single one made the film better. Although there were some notes that mystified me, initially. It was only after I'd completed the work, and seen them within the context of the whole film, that I realized what Welles was after.

O: Like what?

M: The best example of this is the seemingly trivial removal of a close-up of Quinlan's sidekick, Menzies, played by Joseph Calleia. In the memo, Welles says that he wanted it removed "because of a mistaken use of the wide angle lens which distorts Menzies's face grotesquely. There is no use upsetting the audience this way. The scene played all right without this weird close-up." As I read that, I thought, What is he up to here? Welles used that same lens quite often in the film! But at that point my job was just to try to do what he said.

The close-up in question occurs in a scene between Vargas and Menzies, at the crucial moment where Vargas has confronted Menzies with evidence of Quinlan's duplicity. Menzies, who has been standing, collapses, and his agony is revealed in this close-up. Almost instantly, he jumps back to his feet and defends Quinlan, but the damage has been done: Vargas has seen him acknowledge the truth, and—just as important—Menzies has seen Vargas see this. As a result, everything that Menzies does in the last half-hour of the film is done under duress: not authentically, because he believes it to be best, but because he *must,* having revealed his weakness to Vargas. Menzies has a metaphorical leash around his neck.

Another section of Welles's memo discussing the studio's editing.

the Grandi-Susan scene be re-examined with
an open mind. No great effort will be needed   *intercut*
to find the proper footage for inter-outting
from the wealth of material available from the
various scenes which play by the flaming car.
It's my opinion that the entrance of Quinlan
should be saved for this. I think that moving
the conflict between Quinlan and Vargas closer
to the street scene in front of the hotel will
aid clarity and much improve the narrative line.
But this is only one of several solutions.
Quinlan's arrival through his line "whoever did
it, ye jackass" and the out of the blazing car
would also make a most effective transition.
You would then return to Grandi (by a quick
dissolve, if you prefer) for his line "We used
to have a nice, quiet town around here..."
This would play beautifully. The subject of
Grandi's anxiety would have been dramatically
illustrated, we would not have left the scene
of the explosion until after all our principals
had been established, and the device of cutting
away from Quinlan (olearly the most significant

2ND intercut

By cutting out this close-up, we also cut the leash. He never collapses in the scene with Vargas, continuing to defend his boss to the end. But we—not Vargas—see the doubt and anguish on his face. Vargas does not see it because of the staging of the scene.

Everything that Menzies does from that moment on—and he plays a crucial role in the undoing of his boss—is done authentically: he *chooses* to do it, rather than being coerced. This increases the standing of Menzies's character in the film, raising it to a level of equality with Vargas and Quinlan. Welles has elsewhere described *Touch of Evil* as a story of love and betrayal between two men, Menzies and his boss Quinlan. The removal of Menzies's close-up plays a significant part in realizing this vision for the film.

It's interesting that in the memo Welles doesn't get into any of the underlying reasons for making this change. Remember, he was writing to his enemy, the head of the studio. If he were to admit that he made a mistake in the conception of the scene, it would have given the studio more power over him. So he hides his real reason in a technical fog, blaming it on the use of the wrong lens.

There are frequently moments like these in the making of films, where huge issues of character and story are decided by the inclusion—or not—of a single shot that reverberates throughout the film.

Well, at the time the memo didn't achieve its ends. Welles didn't get what he wanted. But forty years later we were able to do everything that he asked. It's not a completely different film, it's a more fully realized version of itself, which is what a good film should be.

O: One likes to think he would be very pleased right now.

M: I hope so. He once said in an interview in *Cahiers du Cinéma:* "For my style, for my vision of the cinema, editing is not simply one aspect: it's *the* aspect. The notion of 'directing' a film is the invention of critics like you [*Cahiers du Cinéma*]. It isn't an art, or at best it's an art only one minute a day. That minute is terribly crucial, but it occurs very rarely. The only time one is able to exercise control over the film is in the editing. The images themselves are not sufficient.

They're very important, but they're only images. What's essential is the duration of each image and that which follows each image: the whole eloquence of cinema is that it's achieved in the editing room."

THE WRONG ECHO

O: The climax of *Touch of Evil*, using a microphone instead of a rifle to hunt down the guilty, is also ingenious. . . .

M: Kind of like the opening of *The Conversation* . . .

O: The microphone as a potent weapon.

M: In that denouement of *Touch of Evil*, Welles worked out something that's very close to my heart because it's so similar to the beginning of *The Conversation*—namely, to make the resolution of the story depend on different shadings and perspectives of sound.

Quinlan and Menzies are walking through this maze of oil derricks, at night, and—unknown to Quinlan—Menzies is wired for sound with a radio mike hidden under his jacket. Some distance away, Vargas is following them with a radio receiver, picking up their conversation, hoping that Quinlan will incriminate himself.

When you're close to Quinlan and Menzies, they sound normal. When you're with Vargas and his tape recorder, they sound distorted, like voices over

In *Touch of Evil,* Orson Welles as Hank Quinlan and Joseph Calleia as Sgt. Pete Menzies walk on the bridge. Charlton Heston, as Mike Vargas, *center,* stalks them underneath; *right,* Vargas with his tape recorder, using "a microphone instead of a gun to hunt down the guilty . . ."; *far right,* Vargas finds his wife, Susie, drugged and in a seedy motel.

a telephone. And when you are far away from both the hunter and the hunted, you hear the voices in a sort of echoey field of sound. It's all very dynamic, with no musical accompaniment.

This attention to detail pays off fantastically well when Quinlan and Menzies walk over a bridge and Vargas is forced to go under one of the archways of the bridge to stay close to them. And now Quinlan's recorded voice, heard over the tape recorder, echoes within the archway. Quinlan suddenly stops, suspicious—he hears his own voice with the wrong echo on it. And he begins to work out what's happening—that his buddy Menzies is carrying a hidden microphone and his enemy Vargas must be under the bridge with a recorder.

So that echo—that particular quality of sound—causes the plot to unravel: Quinlan accuses Menzies, there is a struggle, Menzies is shot, then Quinlan goes after Vargas, and then is shot himself by the dying Menzies. Welles hung the whole ending of the film on the ability of the people in it, *and* the audience, to understand a subtle nuance with the sound. That it's the wrong echo. It's fantastic!

O: Did you talk to people like Janet Leigh and Charlton Heston, or anyone else who worked with Welles?

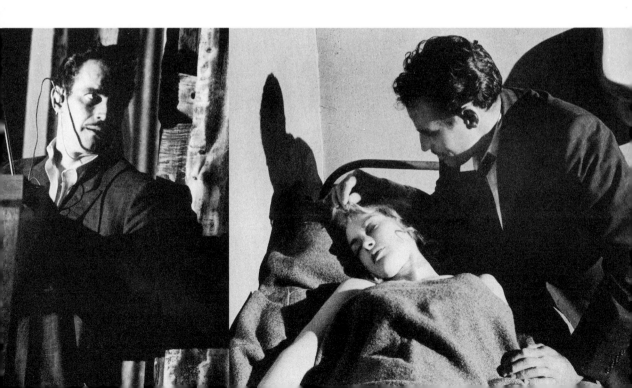

M: We talked to them afterwards, when the work was done, and we screened the film for them. Janet Leigh was very emotional—it brought everything back to her, what they had all set out to do so idealistically at the beginning.

During the editing we did talk to Ernie Nims, who was the head of post-production at Universal in 1958. He had been an editor for Welles on a film called *The Stranger,* made in 1946, and had a good relationship with him.

The studio had told us that everyone associated with the film was dead, but Rick Schmidlin, very much the detective, had a hunch and called up Information in Los Angeles, asking for Ernie Nims. Nothing in the 213 area code, or 818, but he struck gold in 310. "Is this Ernie Nims?" "Yes." "Are you the Ernie Nims who was head of postproduction at Universal?" "That's me!" "Did you work with Orson Welles?" "Orson Welles! The only genius I ever worked for. He was twenty years ahead of his time!"

For Ernie, all the trouble that Welles got into came from that: His thinking was too advanced for the times.

Ernie was eighty-nine years old when we talked to him, and it turned out he had stashed away in his attic a number of documents relating to the film that were a great help to us: Welles's notes on the use of sound, which weren't part of the fifty-eight-page memo. Also memos that Welles had written to Ernie about their strategy for the film, how to outwit the studio. I have a suspicion that it was thanks to Ernie's intervention that the original version of *Touch of Evil* was as good as it was. Given the animosity with Ed Muhl, the old studio head, things could have been much worse.

On another hunch, Rick looked up Ed Muhl and found him alive and kicking in the 818 area code. He was over ninety and completely unrepentant. He felt that Welles was a poseur who never made a film that earned any money.

0: In a way Welles is a touchstone not just for great originality but an example of how and where a young director can go wrong.

M: Absolutely. His life says, Even if you're only twenty-five you can do this, because I made *Citizen Kane* when I was twenty-five. It is possible. That's a great encouragement to young people. On the other hand, his life was so star-crossed, the struggle so played out in public view for so long, that you can read it as a cautionary tale: Here's how to succeed, but here are the traps to avoid.

In the end, I'd say his presence as an iconic figure is due not only to his successes but also to his failures—and to the particular kinds of successes and failures they were.

THE MOST CHARACTERISTIC ANGLE

O: You tell the story about Orson Welles pretending the wrong lens had been used in *Touch of Evil.* As an editor, when you receive footage, how much of an issue is the choice of lens used during filming? Does the director discuss such technical matters with you? Or are these the kinds of considerations you become aware of only when you cut the film?

M: The choice of lens is crucial. There's a chemistry between each actor and a certain lens. That's a reason for shooting makeup and costume tests with the principal actors before you start the actual production. One of the things we're doing is studying the chemistry between the angle of the lens and the planarity of the actor's face.

Certain actors will look most *themselves* if they're photographed with a certain lens at a certain distance. It has something to do with the translation of a three-dimensional object—the human face—into a two-dimensional photograph. We've all known people who look better in person than they do in photographs, and vice versa: people who look ordinary in real life and intriguing in photographs. This is the same kind of thing.

A telephoto lens tends to flatten out its subject, and a wide-angle lens does the opposite: it will curve out a flat subject.

I remember George Lucas being fascinated by the depth of Robert Duvall's features, his deep-set eyes and rounded forehead. It was one of the reasons he

Robert Duvall in *THX 1138:* "There's a chemistry between each actor and a certain lens."

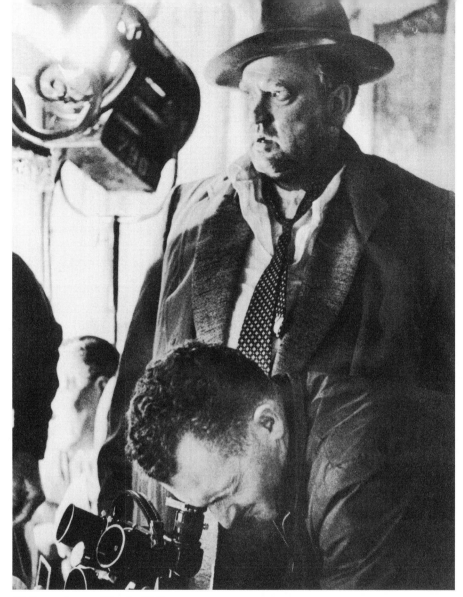

Welles on the set of *Touch of Evil.*

cast Duvall in *THX 1138*—apart from the fact that Duvall is a wonderful actor.

The nine-year-old Fairuza Balk, who played Dorothy in *Return to Oz*, had a beautiful face that just leapt off the screen if you photographed her with a 45-millimetre lens at four and a half feet. I remember that because of the poetry of "forty-five at four and a half"—which is what I would call out frequently when we were doing a close-up of her.

Q: Do you ever make suggestions about lenses to the director?

M: That's usually a discussion between the director and the camera department. It's the editor's job then simply to receive the material and make it work in the best way possible. When I assemble the scene and discover, for example, that there's one place where I'm using the B camera and the actor does not look so good with that lens, I may write a note to the director and suggest, If you ever have a half-day where you're doing some pick-up shots, it might be good to reshoot this line with this actor as just a prime close-up.

We look at ancient Egyptian painting today and may find it slightly comic, but what the Egyptians were trying to do with the figure was reveal the various aspects of the person's body in the most characteristic aspect. The face is in profile because that reveals the most about the person's face, but the shoulders are not in profile, they're facing the viewer, because that's the most revealing angle for the shoulders. The hips are not in profile, but the feet are. It gives a strange, twisted effect, but it was natural to the Egyptians. They were painting *essences,* and in order to paint an essence you have to paint it from its most characteristic angle. So they would simply combine the various characteristic essences of the human body. This was a piece of spiritual art. It wasn't trying to reproduce photographic reality, it was trying to reproduce and combine all the essential features of a person within one figure.

That's exactly what we do in film, except that instead of the body of the person, it's the work itself. The director chooses the most characteristic, revealing, interesting angle for every situation and every line of dialogue and every scene. He then overshoots that material and gives the editor an additional range of choices. We're doing the same kind of shifting between angles. It may be, five hundred years from now, when people see films from our era, they'll seem "Egyptian" in a strange way. Here we are, cutting between different angles to achieve the most interesting, characteristic, revealing lens and camera angle for every situation. That seems perfectly normal to us, but people five hundred years from now may find it strange or comic.

FOURTH

CONVERSATION

S A N   F R A N C I S C O

Our fourth conversation took place over a few days in California in January 2001—our first meeting in downtown San Francisco, the second in the small town on the coast where Walter lives with his family.

We began by comparing influences and how we are influenced. Walter discussed two essentially different kinds of filmmakers, symbolized by Coppola and Hitchcock, before slipping into a memory of one of the key moments of his career—as a young editor on *Julia* for the master director Fred Zinnemann—a time he spoke of with great affection. (After Zinnemann died, he was to create a short film about him, called *As I See It.*) Walter spoke too about his father—the painter Walter Murch—and how his father's work and career left a firm impression on his own life and work. As we talked about this and that, we realized it was Inauguration Day for Americans. In a nearby lobby a sparse, disgruntled crowd watched a television that showed the rainy proceedings taking place three thousand miles away.

On the second day, in Walter's house, we returned to explore more intricate instances of sound and film editing. The complexity and carefulness of his mind, and his immense passion for the work, were clear as he spoke about

Murch in a grave on the set of *Julia,* 1976.

divergent and convergent plots in films, and the constantly shifting relationship between directors and editors. When we broke for lunch, he sat down at the piano in his living room and played what he said was "the music of the spheres," based on his theory that the distances between planets can be patterned on or related to the spacing between the keys on a piano. This was strange and wonderful music.

Leaving that evening, I commented on the beautiful post-dusk grey light. Walter responded, "And this is the exact level of light that is broad daylight on Saturn."

INFLUENCES

O: There's a general question I was going to ask you. I'd like to get back to what influences you in other people's work. You haven't referred much to other filmmakers or editors save for the European New Wave, early in your life. And I suppose I too would be hard-pressed to say who influences me among my contemporaries. I can say a book like Derek Walcott's *Another Life* opened a door for me, or a book of poems by Robert Creeley or Adrienne Rich, but usually if I read my contemporaries I read them to enjoy them and get lost in the work, to be moved or not, but I never feel consciously influenced by them. What tends to influence me more is the specific project at hand—all the existing problems and issues that surround the book I'm trying to write—*these* influence me. Is this something that you feel?

M: Yes. It's very difficult for me to see films when I'm working. I get too easily depressed. If they're bad, I begin to despair for filmmaking in general. It seems proof that it's impossible to make a film. You're always plagued by the question: Can *we* do this? So to watch a film that doesn't work is dispiriting, in a large sense.

O: For the editing of it or the whole film?

M: The whole film. Also, when I watch a bad film, I often see it doing things that the film I'm working on is doing. It's like being a hypochondriac listening to medical discussions on the radio: Yes! I've got a rash right there too! That cough I had two days ago, it's proof! But this is a kind of madness, and it leads me to make wrong equations: Since such-and-such a technique is in a film that doesn't work, it means that if we're using a similar technique, our film won't work either. Of course that's not true. Something that's used in a good way in one film can be used to poor effect in another, and vice versa.

On the other hand, if I see a film that I love, I think: I can use those techniques—and I become like a magpie. It's like that crazy period in Victorian architecture when they ransacked the world—These pineapples from southern India are marvellous, let's put them here! So when I'm working on a film, I like to see documentaries, and I like to see theatre. I'm excited by the fact that in theatre things can go wrong at any moment.

O: It's unedited.

M: Yeah, it's unedited! People can forget their lines, they can fall offstage, or something miraculously wonderful can happen that was not prepared in advance. And may not happen again. Whereas film—it's always the same. You don't have to worry that on the third showing of the film the actors are going to forget their lines.

For me, film is more omnivorous. Hermann Hesse talked about this—about how a writer is influenced. He said there are various stages of influence. Kind of like chakras. The lowest, least noble method of influence is, say, reading Hemingway and then deciding to write like Hemingway. This is natural, it's something we all go through, but you have to go beyond this to higher and higher levels until you reach the point where you're influenced by reading something like the equivalent of the back of cereal boxes. Somehow just purely mundane or accidental things have such magic to them that they influence you and make you see things.

I tend to think of film in that way. When I'm working on a film I try to open a certain part of my brain and ask myself, What's going on in the world?

O: Those humble sounds you spoke about earlier . . .

M: And sometimes not so humble. I remember very clearly the moment I got one idea for a sound in *Apocalypse Now.* It was after the filming, at a party up at Francis's house—I think it was Marty Sheen's birthday. He was a baseball fan, and Francis had made Marty think he was going to miss a baseball game by delaying the party. Then at just the right moment he revealed that there was a helicopter waiting to fly Marty to Candlestick Park to catch the game.

We were all walking down to say good-bye as the waiting helicopter started its engine up. It went *whooh whooh whooh,* a kind of turbine sound, as it began to whirl up. I immediately saw the existing cut in the film, from the line "Charlie don't surf" to all the helicopters on the beach, with their rotors. It had been, up to that point, "Charlie don't surf"—then *bang!*—suddenly the film cut to whirling helicopters and there was a lot of noise. But I thought, It would be interesting to introduce this turbine sound about five seconds earlier, so while you're watching the scene on the beach at night, you start to hear an inexplicable sound that gets louder and louder and louder, until, when it's quite loud, Robert Duvall says, "Charlie don't surf," and then it cuts to the mass of helicopters. You're not quite aware of what the sound is or where it's coming from until the cut happens, and then you realize, if you think about it at all, Oh, that's what it was.

O: When I was working on *The English Patient* one thing I did *not* want to read during research was great desert writers. I intentionally didn't read Thessiger or Doughty or Lawrence. I was mostly reading essays full of data about the surface of the earth at the Royal Geographical Society. Articles discussing sand dune formations, the depth of certain wells that could be relied upon during a trek. As in your situation, this felt more like unedited material, unfictionalized data.

M: Some filmmakers, when they're at home, love to have many television monitors going, showing films all the time, so their home is peopled by classic films, part of the atmosphere, to foment the creative activity. To me, that's an impossible way of living—by my own lights, it's ultimately destructive of the creative process. Things become too self-referential—look at what's happened to modern painting or modern music in the twentieth century. All new compositions refer to previous compositions in arcane ways. You build an incredible sand castle, a house of cards with references within references within references. You can see it happening now with films, and I don't know if it's such a good thing. It's fun, occasionally, but not as a steady diet.

Eliot's *The Waste Land* is like that. James Joyce is like that. To really get them you have to know all this *stuff.* Well, those in particular are wonderful works of literature, but ultimately, for the health of the creative process, I wonder if it's been a good path to follow. . . .

If you go very deep, however, it's another matter. That's why the great composers of the nineteenth century kept going back to folk music, to roots and fragments of things that had deep meaning for them and for the society in which they lived. Even if that meaning wasn't overt, it gave the music a life form. I would much rather find in film the equivalent of that than make superficial reference to films that are only a few years old.

Shadows on the sand: on location in the dunes of Tunisia during the filming of *The English Patient.*

O: As a writer, it's easier for me to watch film without that element of critical judgement in my head—I still see it as magic. Whereas if I'm working intensely on a book I probably would not be reading a really good novelist. I could read a good writer from another century, but not a contemporary. I'd probably read a terrific genre novel like Walter Tevis's *The Queen's Gambit,* or nonfiction. (I was told recently that Yeats when writing poetry would read the prose of John Milton in order to prime himself!) I can learn from film especially because it is *not* part of my world. Though I'm more likely to be influenced by the craft in a film's editing than in a film's content. I wonder if you, similarly, are influenced by the other arts? Are you influenced by novels or music—or by science?

M: Yes. They're there as spark points. They're part of the phenomena of life. I try to imbue all aspects of reality with that magic. Sometimes I read intention into purely accidental things. That's been part of my approach to life for as long as I can remember.

When I'm editing a film I'm always browsing radio stations as I drive to work, and suddenly I'll hear something in the music that connects with an image in the film. I might literally then find that piece of music, and put it in the film and see what happens.

■

O: If you had to choose, say, ten films that have altered editing and sound in some way, what would they be? This is one of those terrible lists! I suppose *M* and *King Kong* would be on your list. But what films do you think have influenced and altered the direction, or shown further possibilities?

M: I'll try to think. My mind doesn't really work that way. With some effort I can talk about the history of influences, in an impersonal way. But on a personal level, it's the back of the cereal box again. . . .

O: Stuff outside the genre.

M: Yes. Or just things that to an outsider would look like nothing. I remember the beginning of *Seconds*—a film by John Frankenheimer. I saw it at school,

Peter Lorre in Fritz Lang's *M*, 1931, a film that influenced sound and editing.

when I was a film student. There was a shot at the beginning—a handheld shot going down into the main floor of Grand Central Terminal, a very wide shot, a hidden-camera kind of thing.

This was an ordinary monophonic film of the time, nothing technically spectacular about it, but the sound of the air—just the sound of a vast space filled with people—accompanying that shot made me suddenly realize how much can be achieved with the right *atmosphere* of sound. It told me all I needed to know about the power of atmospheric sound. There was also a great drill sound at the very end—the slightly liquid sound of a drill going into a skull—after the image had cut to black.

Seconds was not an influential film, historically. And I don't know that anyone looking at it today would be struck by what I'm talking about. But I was primed to receive the information it was sending me.

I also must have seen *Touch of Evil* around that time. I don't remember a thunderbolt moment, like I remember with *Seconds,* but clearly Welles's use of source music and sonic perspectives *must* have registered, must have deposited a layer of rich silt somewhere in my mental geology.

O: By the way, the other day I was watching John Ford's *Stagecoach*—

M: I haven't seen it since the mid-sixties.

O: You should look at it again in relation to the idea of source music. Late in the film, when John Wayne is led by the woman, Dallas, into the bordello area of the town, they're walking along a path and different music comes from each of the bordellos as they pass them. It's rather similar to the use of street music in *Touch of Evil.* I remember being told that Welles watched *Stagecoach* three times before shooting *Citizen Kane,* but the influence seems more evident in *Touch of Evil.*

I think we tend not to be influenced by the major works, the Big Waves. No writer is really influenced by *Moby-Dick.* I remember reading a review of a biography of Scott and Zelda Fitzgerald. There was a description of how, when they were living in Paris, they didn't like sharing the elevator with other tenants—it meant they would have to wait for it—so Zelda tied a scarf to the elevator door, so that it would remain on the fourth floor all the time. No one else could get it. There was something about the panache of that and the spoiled behaviour of it that I kept thinking about when I was writing my memoir *Running in the Family.* My book took place at the other end of the world. But this minor fragment of a biography fed the tone of my book.

M: There's an inverted version of that: the idea of the staircase that you wrote about in your literary magazine, *Brick.*

O: Yes. As a child in Sri Lanka, I knew only one house that had a staircase—

most of the houses were bungalows. So whenever I came across a staircase in a book of fiction, that childhood recollection of a staircase would get superimposed onto the scene from *The Count of Monte Cristo,* or whatever book I was reading.

M: Yes! You imagine that very staircase, even though it's completely wrong on one level—but that's the staircase you imagine. I expect that a lot of creativity comes out of those kinds of juxtapositions. The improbable juxtaposition of *The Count of Monte Cristo* and that Sri Lankan staircase is especially rich. And if Dumas could peer into your head and see the staircase that you were imagining, he would be horrified! That's not what he meant at all! But in fact it really is very rich.

There's a wonderful quotation from Goethe—he must have been frustrated at some point about the difficulty of communication. He said, "Utterly futile to try to change, by writing, someone's fixed inclination. You will only succeed in confirming him in his opinion, or, if he has none, drenching him in yours."

O: There's a poet in Vancouver who said, "I'll see it when I believe it!"

M: Exactly. I'm sure Goethe didn't think that way most of the time, otherwise he wouldn't have kept on writing. He was talking in black-and-white terms: Agree with me or not! The richest zone of communication is in the grey area, around things like your staircase, where the reader is somewhat receptive to what the author writes but also brings along his own images, and ideas, which in a creative way do violence to the author's vision and ideas. A synergy results from what the writer presents and what the reader brings. That communication, initially present in neither the sender or the receiver, is greater than the message of the writer alone or the thoughts of the reader alone.

It's similar to what happens with human sight. Your left eye sees one thing and your right sees something else, a slightly different perspective. They're so close and yet different enough that when the mind tries to see both simultaneously, to resolve their contradictions, the only way it can do so is to create a third concept, an arena in which both perspectives can exist: three-dimensional space. This "space" doesn't exist in either of the images—each eye alone sees a flat, two-dimensional view of the world—but space, as we perceive it, is created in the mind's attempt to resolve the different images it is receiving from the left and the right eye.

NEGATIVE TWENTY QUESTIONS

M: There's a great game—I forget whether we've talked about it—Negative Twenty Questions?

O: No, we haven't talked about it.

M: It was invented by John Wheeler, a quantum physicist who was a young graduate student of Niels Bohr's in the 1930s. Wheeler is the man who invented the term "black hole." He's an extremely articulate proponent of the best of twentieth-century physics. Still alive, and I believe still teaching, writing.

Anyway, he thought up a parlour game that reflects the way the world is constructed at the quantum level. It involves, say, four people: Michael, Anthony, Walter, and Aggie. From the point of view of one of those people, Michael, the game that's being played is the normal Twenty Questions— Ordinary Twenty Questions, I guess you'd call it. So Michael leaves the room, under the illusion that the other three players are going to look around and collectively decide on the chosen object to be guessed by him—say, the alarm clock. Michael expects that when they've made their decision they will ask him to come back in and try to guess the object in fewer than twenty questions.

Under normal circumstances, the game is a mixture of perspicacity and luck: No, it's not bigger than a breadbox. No, you can't eat it. . . . Those kinds of things.

But in Wheeler's version of the game, when Michael leaves the room, the three remaining players *don't* communicate with one another at all. Instead, each of them silently decides on an object. Then they call Michael back in.

So there's a disparity between what Michael believes and what the underlying truth is: Nobody knows what anyone else is thinking. The game proceeds regardless, which is where the fun comes in.

Michael asks Walter: Is the object bigger than a breadbox? Walter—who has picked the alarm clock—says, No. Now, Anthony has chosen the sofa, which is bigger than a breadbox. And since Michael is going to ask him the next question, Anthony must quickly look around the room and come up with something else—a coffee cup!—which is smaller than a breadbox. So when Michael asks Anthony, If I emptied out my pockets could I put their contents in this object? Anthony says, Yes.

Now Aggie's choice may have been the small pumpkin carved for Halloween, which could also contain Michael's keys and coins, so when Michael says, Is it edible? Aggie says, Yes. That's a problem for Walter and Anthony, who have chosen inedible objects: they now have to change their selection to something edible, hollow, and smaller than a breadbox.

So a complex vortex of decision making is set up, a logical but unpredictable chain of *if*s and *then*s. To end successfully, the game must produce, in fewer than twenty questions, an object that satisfies all of the logical requirements: smaller than a breadbox, edible, hollow, et cetera. Two things can happen: Success—this vortex can give birth to an answer that will seem to be inevitable in retrospect: Of course! It's the ——! And the game ends with Michael still believing he has just played Ordinary Twenty Questions. In fact, no one chose the —— to start with, and Anthony, Walter, and Aggie have been sweating it out, doing these hidden mental gymnastics, always one step ahead of failure.

Which is the other possible result: Failure—the game can break down catastrophically. By question 15, let's say, the questions asked have generated logical requirements so complex that nothing in the room can satisfy them. And when Michael asks Anthony the sixteenth question, Anthony breaks down and has to confess that he doesn't know, and Michael is finally let in on the secret: The game was Negative Twenty Questions all along. Wheeler suggests that the nature of perception and reality, at the quantum level, and perhaps above, is somehow similar to this game.

When I read about this, it reminded me acutely of filmmaking. There is an agreed-upon game, which is the screenplay, but in the process of making the film, there are so many variables that everyone has a slightly different interpretation of the screenplay. The cameraman develops an opinion, then is told that Clark Gable has been cast in that part. He thinks, Gable? Huh, I didn't think it would be Gable. If it's Gable, I'm going to have to replan. Then the art director does something to the set, and the actor says, This is my apartment? All right, if this is my apartment, then I'm a slightly different person from who I thought I was: I will change my performance. The camera operator following him thinks, Why is he doing that? Oh, it's because . . . All right, I'll have to widen out because he's doing these unpredictable things. And then the editor does something unexpected with those images and this gives the director an idea about the script, so he changes a line. And so the costumer sees that and decides the actor can't wear dungarees. And so it goes, with everyone continuously modifying their preconceptions. A film can succeed in the end, spiralling in on itself to a final result that looks as if it had been predicted long in advance in every detail. But in fact it grew out of a mad scramble as everyone involved took advantage of all the various decisions everyone else had been making.

On the other hand, the film can break down, too. Some inconsistency—emotional or logical—can pose a question that nothing in the "room"—that is to say, the film—can answer. The most obvious of these failures is the miscasting of a lead character: his presence in the film poses a question that's inconsistent with everything else. But films can ultimately fail for much more subtle reasons—death by a thousand cuts: the interference of the studio, bad weather, what the grip had for breakfast that crucial morning, the fact that the producer is going through a divorce, et cetera. All these things are in complex ways encoded into the body of the film. Sometimes for good, and the film is enriched by the process. Sometimes not: then it's aborted, abandoned during production; or stillborn, finished but never released; or released, fatally handicapped, to dismal reviews and no business.

This comparison of filmmaking and Wheeler's game goes some distance, I think, to answering the perennial question: What were they thinking when they made that film? How did anyone ever think that could work?

Nobody sets out to make an unreleasable film. But the game of the film can pose questions that its creators finally can't answer, and the film falls apart as a result.

O: I saw it late in the editing stage of *The English Patient.* The sequence—which had already been filmed—in which the characters respond to the news of Hiroshima was not going to work. And you and Anthony had to scramble and look for what could be an alarm clock instead of the breadbox.

M: Right. That's a classic example. The key, the little spark that turned into the solution, was something my assistant, Edie Bleiman, said: Well, a bomb is a bomb. She realized the crisis of Hiroshima, which is so important at the end of your novel, could be replaced by the crisis of the bomb that kills Hardy, which sends Kip, at the death of his friend, into a state of depression that even his love for Hana cannot rouse him from—this similar, more personal crisis could serve as the template.

The film was so much about those five individual people: the Patient, Hana, Kip, Katharine, Caravaggio—that to suddenly open it up near the end and ask the audience to imagine the death of hundreds of thousands of unknown people . . . It was too abstract. So the bomb of Hiroshima became the bomb that killed Hardy, someone you knew. Everything else reorganized itself from that new starting point.

O: It's taking a real and technical problem and solving it with a metaphor.

M: Right. And it happened that Edie was the one who saw the metaphor: that we had two bombs in the original story, and that if we didn't have the big bomb, we could just as well—better, even—use the smaller bomb as a metaphor for the big bomb.

O: It is strange, however—and this is perhaps one of the lacks in film—that we can't jump to the world outside the main story, to the larger canvas. It's almost as if irony would kill the intimate drama that has been created. Kurt Vonnegut talks somewhere about how as long as "the lovers" are together at the climax of the film it will be seen as a happy ending, even though a thousand enemy jets from Mars could be approaching the country.

M: Yes, perhaps film has much more inertia than prose. A book can nimbly switch tracks in a way that would wreck a film.

ENFORCED IDLENESS

O: You have said that having assistants grounds the artist, as opposed to the artist's being in isolation. We have, for instance, the great masters of medieval art being surrounded by their assistants, in contrast to the solitude of the contemporary artist. . . .

M: The situation's changing so rapidly in filmmaking. Digital technology allows, more than ever, a single vision to work itself out, and that carries a particular danger because you need fewer collaborators. Right now we're in a transition period when it seems we need even more collaborators because we have to work in both film and digital, but I can see that down the road it's possible that a film crew will be a very, very small bunch of people. The director Mike Figgis talks about his ideal: a "two-suitcase film," where all the equipment can be put into two suitcases. In the early days of Zoetrope, in the late sixties, there was a similar goal: All the equipment had to fit in one van. Trends come and go.

O: You hire a new group of assistants on every project, don't you? It's always new people, I believe, so you don't fall into a rut. Do you feel a necessity to bring something new to the pot, every time you work on a film?

M: I don't work with new assistants on every single picture. But compared to some editors, who work always with exactly the same team, I've worked with many different people over the years. I enjoy the variety—I thrive on it, actually—not only because new people bring new ideas but also because *I* have to redefine, reexamine *myself* and my sometimes hidden assumptions. How do I work? Why am I making certain choices? Is that really the best way to do it? I also like to introduce new technology, to experiment with new procedures, for the same reason.

It's part of my general predilection for things that somehow randomize the process and make it more interesting, keep me on my toes, and in the end more humanly productive.

O: Louis Malle talked about how, between any fictional films he did, he always made a documentary on his own. He took a camera, and he shot it himself. I think perhaps it's the same kind of thing—entering a different reality, an alternative set of rules, or pacing so you are continually in the process of learning, of even changing essential principles.

M: Do you do anything similar yourself, between books? I guess this conversation is something like that.

O: I find I need to get away from written language. After working on my first long book, *The Collected Works of Billy the Kid*, I needed to turn away from words, from my own brain's vocabulary. So I made a documentary film. I've done that a couple of times—worked in film or theatre or dance—so I would eventually come back to literature with a refreshed sense of language. A new voice.

M: One of the side benefits of moving Zoetrope up to San Francisco in 1969 was to take the filmmaking out of a self-contained film universe. In Los Angeles it's very easy, if you get to a certain level in your profession, to live, breathe, eat, think, sleep film. And to have so many offers that you're working all the time—without that ability, given by time and space, to reinvent.

In San Francisco there's not that much work. There aren't that many producers up here. There's a kind of enforced idleness between projects that allows you to develop other interests and then, in the best sense, to plow the results of those interests back into the next film.

TWO KINDS OF FILMMAKING

Q: Somewhere you draw a distinction between two kinds of filmmaking: the Hitchcock idea that a film is already complete in the creator's head—"I invented it in my solitude, and I now just have to go out and make it"—and the Coppola concept that thrives on process, where one choreographs and invents and gathers during the process of filmmaking. Do you see one kind of film-making taking over from the other as technologies improve? You've worked with both kinds of filmmakers. . . . Someone like George Lucas, for instance, seems closer to the Hitchcock style.

M: Yes, the very first people I worked with professionally were the epitome of those two different approaches. Francis is a practitioner of and is fascinated by

Hitchcock trying to get results from a very young Gregory Peck and Ingrid Bergman during the filming of *Spellbound*, 1945.

the human and technical *process* of making the film. George, in comparison, is somebody who has a complete vision of the film in his head. For him, the problem becomes how to get that vision, practically, onto the screen, in as unadulterated a form as possible.

Both approaches involve a process. But the most important distinction is whether you allow the process to become an active collaborator in the making of the film, or use it as a machine and try to restrict its contributions. The most extreme practitioner of the latter approach is Hitchcock. The equivalent in another discipline would be an architect like Frank Lloyd Wright who has all of the building on the drawing boards, down to the colour of the bedspreads in the room, and his only concern is to make the contractors who'll do the work "get" what he already has. Any variation from it is seen as a defect. The perfection already exists.

The other approach—Francis's, for example—is to harvest the random elements that the process throws up, things that were not in the filmmaker's mind when he began.

I'm overstating in order to clarify the distinction. In fact, nobody is completely hot or cold in this regard, and I don't believe everything that Hitchcock writes. I've seen the breakdown of the *Psycho* bathroom scene, which supposedly was storyboarded down to the *n*th degree, and followed exactly. Just from knowing what I know about filmmaking, I know that what is in the film was not storyboarded exactly like that. . . .

It has to be said—both systems have their risks. The risk of the Hitchcockian system is that you may stifle the creative force of the people who are collaborating with you. The film that results—even if it's a perfect vision of what somebody had in his head—can be lifeless: it seems to exist on its own, without the necessary collaboration either of the people who made the film or even, ultimately, the audience. It says: I am what I am whether you like it or not.

On the other hand, the risk with the process-driven film is that it can collapse into chaos. Somehow the central organizing vision can be so eaten away and compromised by all the various contributors that it collapses under its own weight.

Hitchcock directing Janet Leigh during the shower scene in *Pyscho*, 1960.

O: It seems now that with the digital systems you have the ability to edit more personally. You can improvise privately and try a variety of possibilities—the way you can with a manuscript—tinker, move back and forth. . . . Whereas you did not have the same freedom when you were actually cutting film—which was a more arduous task.

M: That's true, to a degree. But I've always tried to listen closely to that little voice in my head which says: Why not go down this other path? It's just a question of the time you have to take those different paths. With digital, you can do more exploration in less time. But the real question is: Are you the kind of person who likes to explore?

It's not unlike the distinction between fresco and oil painting. With fresco, once the pigment hit the plaster of walls and ceilings, that was it, you couldn't paint over it, you couldn't change directions. The fresco was painted in its final location. Everything had to be very carefully planned, in advance. You also had to have the imaginative experience to know that a particular copper pigment would turn green with time even if it looked brown to begin with.

Oil painting on canvas, when it came into use sometime in the 1400s, gave the painter the ability to edit: to paint over, to change an apple into a melon. Also, a canvas was portable and reusable, and the pigments were applied in the colour that they remained when dry.

I think this oil-versus-fresco distinction is true of all creative processes: some writers plan extensively and their first drafts are their final drafts, whereas it seems that you, Michael, are almost the polar opposite of that.

O: If I had a blueprint of what I was going to be working on for the next five years I would die of boredom by day three. I would hate to be locked within a given scenario. As a writer you have the licence to surprise yourself, veer off the path. You can always go back and remove mistakes, erase subplots that don't work. Nothing is written in stone, so why limit yourself to a pre-planned story?

M: But the distinction is more vivid in film, because filmmaking happens at such an intense rate and involves many people collaborating, and is produced in a nonlinear, out-of-sequence way—so that to the casual observer it's not obvious what's going on.

Even sculpting in marble, where it would seem the artist has to have a pretty good idea what he's going to do from the start, has the possibility of improvisation. Michelangelo talked about discovering the sculpture inside the block of marble as he worked on it, so if he saw a certain vein of marble that became a different colour deeper in the block, he'd change what he was doing in order to take advantage of that.

O: In the images in the temple paintings of Sri Lanka, you are made to follow the horizontal line of the narrative in the panels. And as you follow it you realize there's an archway of a door there, and the painter has gone up and then over it. Or if he comes across a different kind of stone, he will work around it, or work it into the piece. So the real world is incorporated into the structure of the work of art.

M: I particularly love that part of the process when an element of chance enters. Even in the editing stage, when everything's already been shot. I'm always trying to open myself up to what seem to be chance juxtapositions of images that may not have been indicated by the script but are revealed in the process of working with the material as it's actually shot.

O: How might chance influence a scene during the shooting of a film?

M: When Francis was shooting *You're a Big Boy Now,* his script called for the boy to finally confront his father, with whom he's had a longstanding difficulty. The father is an avid golfer. The way Francis wrote it, the boy comes home, says to his mother, Where's Dad? Oh, he's out in the back practicing golf. The boy goes out, but the father barely looks up from practicing his putting to confront what seems to the boy life-or-death matters.

"The element of chance": Coppola chose not to reschedule the golf scene in *You're a Big Boy Now,* and shot it in the rain.

They were shooting at a suburban house somewhere on Long Island. Francis's vision was of a man on a sunny day practicing golf in the backyard. But on the day of shooting it poured with rain. What do you do? Reschedule because it doesn't look the way you had it in your mind? Not Francis—he decided to have the father practicing golf in the rain.

The scene played almost exactly as it was written, except for that chance ingredient of a huge rainstorm. It showed that the father loved golf so much that he would play it in the rain, and so little wanted to talk to his son that he would persist even in such weather conditions.

O: Didn't weather play a similar chance role during the filming of *Apocalypse Now*?

M: The typhoon that actually destroyed many of the sets can be seen gathering force in the *Redux* version, where the boat stops at the medevac camp. That scene was shot entirely in the rain, though that was not the original intention. It gives a dismal, dank hopelessness to the men and women trapped there, and the sex that follows. That was before the typhoon got so bad that they temporarily abandoned shooting.

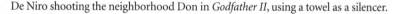

De Niro shooting the neighborhood Don in *Godfather II*, using a towel as a silencer.

O: There's a scene in *Godfather II*—one that I always wait for. It's where De Niro shoots the neighbourhood tyrant. He unscrews the lightbulb to darken the hall, he wraps a towel around the muzzle of the pistol, and as he begins firing the towel catches fire. It feels utterly accidental. And you think, Was that planned? Was it prepared? Did they pour gasoline on the towel to achieve that? Or is the effect created by quick cutting? De Niro is still shaking the pistol back and forth to put out the flame when the cut happens. But there's the sense that the murder is going out of control in a small way, and it feels *real,* a genuine accident caught on film. That's the only moment of something chancelike in his whole determined plotting of that murder.

M: It's an inspired moment, and it certainly does seem like chance. In fact, Francis wrote it into the screenplay, so it was planned from the beginning. He got the idea of the flames when he read that towels were sometimes used as silencers in those days.

O: What makes it powerful is its air of a caught accident, even if it's carefully prepared. It's the power of a quick unfinished detail—like that cigarette package being tossed into the air in slow motion during the robbery in *Something Wild.* The quickness of it buries the moment into your skin, makes it unforgettable.

M: Or the tobacco blown out of Charles Vanel's hand a second before the nitro explosion in *Wages of Fear.*

O: The other scene like that, because we are unprepared for it, is Grace Kelly's entrance in *Rear Window*—her walking out of the dark like a murderer—a suggestion of murder music on the soundtrack—to kiss a sleeping man before he's hardly awake. It's her first appearance in the film and we have no idea who she is—so the boundary between affection and danger has never been thinner.

And there's that remarkable moment in Ingmar Bergman's last movie, *After the Rehearsal.* When the final words have been said, there's this shockingly quick and blunt cut to black. We are allowed no beat of meditation. It's harsh and, in an odd way, bracing, strangely moving, because we've been pushed unexpectedly away from the usual time alloted for an emotion. I've always wanted to try to end a book that way. . . . I think Donald Westlake did that startlingly in *Comeback,* one of his Parker books.

WHY DID HE LIKE IT BETTER?

M: Fred Zinnemann had an interesting approach to directing—a unique combination of the previsualized and the improvisational. He had been both a documentary filmmaker and an assistant director, and these two attitudes coexisted—sometimes uneasily—in his work as a director of feature films.

O: How did you meet Zinnemann?

M: Matthew Robbins phoned me and told me Fred was asking who had edited *The Conversation.* I was out of work at the time, so I wrote a letter to him saying I'd heard he was making *Julia*—coincidentally I had just read *Pentimento,* Lillian Hellman's book— and I'd love to edit it if he would like to meet. So I flew to New York, in the spring of '76, and we hit it off. He was shooting *Julia* in England and France, so for the first time I would be working outside the country, on a studio project, with people I didn't know beforehand—although they became friends during the course of making the film.

O: How old was Zinnemann then?

Director Fred Zinnemann at seventy, in his waders, on location during *Julia,* 1977.

M: He was about to turn seventy. *Julia* was an American project—Lillian Hellman and her partner Dashiell Hammett were both American figures. But her story about her friend Julia, who was finally killed by the Nazis, took place in Europe. It was very much a European production. Fred, although he'd spent many decades of his life in America, was born in Vienna and had been living in London since the early sixties. So I think he was anxious to get an American editor, to bring an American sensibility to the film.

O: He was really the first person you worked with who was outside your generation, wasn't he?

M: Yes. While shooting the film, he got an invitation to the fiftieth anniversary of the film school in Paris that he'd attended in 1926, as a nineteen-year-old. He said, This is something that makes you feel old! He was a member of cinema's second generation. First were the Griffiths and the Chaplins, the people who started making film just after the turn of the century. They were the ones who got him intrigued by cinema when he was in his teens. He started making films with Billy Wilder in 1925, as a teenager, in Berlin. Then there was a third generation—Welles, Kubrick, Stanley Donen, Arthur Penn—and I guess my generation was the fourth. It was a great privilege for a young person, as I was then, to link up professionally with someone as talented and experienced as Zinnemann. It put me in touch with a sensibility and an approach very different from those of our "film school" generation.

Murch with Zinnemann on the set of *Julia.*

Q: How did Zinnemann combine the elements of chance and control?

M: He loved chance so much that he frequently shot the rehearsals of a scene. That meant everybody on the crew had to be fully prepared in advance. Usually what happens is that there's a rehearsal and the first one or two takes are shot just to see how everything is going to work. By the time you get into the third or fourth take things start to really click. Then maybe Take 7 is particularly good and Take 8 you shoot, and then you're done.

But Zinnemann liked to actually shoot the rehearsals—before Take 1. Which meant there was no time for all the people doing the lighting, the costumes, to get a sense of things. He wanted chance—but at the same time he wanted everyone to be fully prepared. As a result, people were frightened a lot of the time that something would go wrong and they would lose their jobs.

I remember one scene where we were shooting inside a train. A real train car, on a soundstage, so there wasn't a lot of room to move around because Fred wanted that sense of confinement. Since the camera operator could not use the large geared control that he normally used, he had a smaller tripod, with a little handle on it, to move the camera.

There was to be a close-up on Jane Fonda, who played Lillian Hellman, seated. She gets up to reach for a hatbox, and the camera was supposed to follow her as she moved to that second position, and then hold on her for a line of dialogue. In the middle of this move, the handle of the tripod came off in the operator's hands. With Zinnemann, the only person to say "Cut" was the director. So Chic, the operator, grabbed hold of the camera—put his hands on the camera itself—wrenched it up into the second position, and managed to get it into place for the line of dialogue. But the middle of the shot was all crazy, because the handle had come off.

Zinnemann seemed oblivious to this. He said, "Cut. Print that. Let's go on to the next one." Chic came up to him, with the handle in his hand, and said, Sir, I'm afraid there was a problem—the handle came off in my hand. Zinnemann's eyes narrowed and he repeated, "Cut. Print. We're going on to the next setup." I happened to be on the set at the time, and Chic looked at me and rolled his eyes as if to say, You're the editor! You're going to have to fix this one!

You had the feeling that Zinnemann was so intensely dedicated to people being prepared that if they weren't he was willing to use a faulty shot in the film to teach them a lesson: I will damage the film so that forever after you will remember the time the handle came off in your hand! Of course, in the end, he didn't do that. I found a way to cut around the problem, as Zinnemann knew I would. But I was amazed. If you'd worked with him before, you might know what was going on in his mind, you could find ways to anticipate it—but for the people who were not used to working with him, it was a little mysterious! But he made wonderful films so clearly it worked for him.

Later he confided to me. He said, My problem is that I began as an assistant director. It's an unusual path to being a director. And I'm like a fire horse: when it hears the alarm it responds with a snort. So when I'm directing, a large part of me is still an assistant director: How are we doing with time?

Every director has to think about this, but there's a trade-off between being on schedule and getting the right material and creating a collaborative, convivial atmosphere on the set.

Also, early in his career he had made a number of documentaries and documentary-type films, like *The Search* and *The Men.* In the early thirties, he had apprenticed with Robert Flaherty, the director of *Nanook of the North,* the first feature-length documentary. And he loved it when actors bumped into the furniture, when they were not yet familiar with the scene and didn't know where they were going. He loved that kind of randomness. He said, In life, events are always happening for the first time, they're not happening for the seventh time. What he particularly hated was a too-well-oiled performance, where everything was working too perfectly.

O: I remember in *The Nun's Story* a scene in the African hospital where one of the nuns gets killed. . . . It's a terrifying scene. It feels as if things are genuinely going out of control in front of your eyes. It's documentary-like in the middle of what is quite a classical film.

M: The two approaches are not contradictory, but they are creatively opposed—the way a thumb and a forefinger are opposed. Zinnemann's nickname among the English crew on *Julia* was "The Iron Butterfly"—he was courtly and polite, but he had a strong idea of who was in charge and from whom the ideas should come. This was a particular struggle between him and Jane Fonda, who was used to more give-and-take between the director and the star. On the other hand, he had that documentary side to him, that wild element, and he did set things up so that a rawness would occasionally happen.

We were shooting some of *Julia* in the Lake District of England—part of the idyll between Lillian and Julia when they are in their early twenties. The two of them are on a beautiful sailboat, on a sunlit lake. We were filming it from a barge that was typically full of coffee mugs and half-eaten sandwiches, coiled wires and all the paraphernalia of filming—totally out of keeping with what we were looking at.

At a certain point, in one of the most beautiful shots, the prow of the barge came up into the frame. Right when you were thinking 1920s, beautiful boat, two girls—suddenly, half-eaten sandwiches and creosoted wood rise into the scene. What to do? On my own, I asked for an optical to be made of the shot. Because the boat was always moving, it was very easy to optically compress the image, removing the offending barge, and then pull back out.

Shortly afterwards Fred came into the editing rooms and said, I heard you've ordered an optical. Why? I explained that the beautiful shot was spoiled when the barge came into the frame. I showed him the optical, then the original shot. He said, I like the original better! People will never be looking at the barge, they will be looking at the two beautiful girls on the boat.

I argued back that the optical was invisible, why take a chance on ruining the sequence, it's a period film, what if someone does notice it, et cetera. It became one of those little creative tugs-of-war.

He studied me with a kind of impatient amusement and then said, All right, because you're so invested in this, I'll tell you what we'll do. We'll finish the film my way—without the optical—and show it to Dougie Slocombe—the

Zinnemann in a sailboat with Jane Fonda, who played Lillian Hellman, and Vanessa Redgrave, who played Julia, in the Lake District of England.

director of photography—when it's all finished. If he mentions it, then we'll recut the negative and put your optical in.

At that stage we had three or four months to go before we were finished, and every time I saw that shot, I cringed. We previewed the film for audiences—no one commented on the barge, which was ominous—then we went to the lab to make the final answer print, which is the reference standard for all subsequent copies of the film. After screening the print for Dougie, Fred asked him, What did you think of the scene on the lake? Marvellous, marvellous! We were so lucky with the weather. Was there anything you'd like to change? Change? No, no! Absolutely marvellous, I just love it. Fred looked at me, I looked at him, and that was that. To this day, if you screen the film, the tip of that camera barge comes up into the frame.

That was very characteristic of Fred's approach, but for the life of me I couldn't see what advantage there was in having this thing come into the frame. Why did he like it better? He liked it better because . . . *something* . . . I'm still chewing over that one!

O: I think Coppola has that similar quality of bringing opposites together—the thumb and the forefinger. . . . The shape of his stories appears classical, yet within them there are things tipping over. He's described himself as the circus ringmaster. I love your story of Coppola getting Mickey Hart and his drummers to watch *Apocalypse Now* and drum their way live through the whole thing—it's a perfect example of how he gets everyone to participate.

M: Exactly! From the assistant director's point of view, it's a tremendously wasteful process. Why do you spend all that money and time—for what? You may get something that's a small percentage of that effort.

I remember talking to Zinnemann about Francis's approach. On *The Conversation,* he would shoot many takes—sometimes going into the twenties. I told Fred about Francis's reasoning: Yes, actors do get familiar with the scene by Take 7, then you go through a long number of takes where they become bored with it. Eventually, out of that boredom comes a frustration and the scene gets reinvented in an interesting way. You do go through a middle passage, but Take 25 may have something wonderful that's the result of this crucible.

O: Stanley Kubrick did a lot of that.

M: Yes, even more—sometimes eighty takes. And Fred said, We're after the same thing, I just like to achieve it earlier . . . by shooting rehearsals!

We remained friends after *Julia,* seeing each other when I was in London or he was in Los Angeles. He died a few years ago, at almost ninety. Although there were parts of him that were mysterious to me, I feel a special kinship with Fred. I do love control. And I do love randomness.

FAMILY LIFE

Q: It seems to me that many of the conflicts that exist in a great director like Zinnemann exist in many artists of our time. That strange mixture of the radical and the conservative, the documentary and the classical. It's funny, I was telling a friend of mine, David Bolduc, an artist in Canada, about interviewing you, and he said, Well, there's *another* Walter Murch, you know . . . there's a wonderful painter called Walter Murch. He knew your dad's work well. He noted that in several ways your father's work as an artist contains those opposites.

M: Yes, my father was driven similarly by contradictions in his painting. He was a representational painter, so he acknowledged the authority of the object, which definitely was a minority position in the New York art world of the forties and fifties. He was saying something by his choice of objects and how they interacted with one another, and he deliberately chose objects that contrapunted each other in sometimes humorous, sometimes ambiguous ways. Your first impression on looking at any of his paintings, particularly from a distance, is that they have a kind of photographic reality to them.

   The closer you get to the paintings, however, the more they completely fragment. If you get close enough and look at any square inch of them, they look like Jackson Pollocks, with all kinds of drippy paint techniques. He would even stub his cigarettes out in paintings. You can see the fragments of tobacco covered over with oil paint. Or he'd put a painting down and set cans of paint

Walter Tandy Murch, *far left*, painting: "...The air that exists between the object and my eye ... that's the only thing that I want to paint"—and standing on his canvas to distress it and create texture. Murch remembers his father's canvases being in the halls for weeks with cats, children and visitors walking on them. His father called the distress marks "hooks"—focal points around which he would plan an image.

on it, so you see the rings of the cans on the canvas. Or he would stand on a painting, and grind dirt into it.

Before he ever started on a painting, the canvas would have to go through a period of abuse. We lived in an old apartment on Riverside Drive in New York, and the long hallway of the apartment was frequently carpeted in unpainted canvases for weeks at a time. The life of the apartment, with cats and people and kids, would just continue. People would be tramping back and forth on the canvases, accidents would happen, things would get spilled on them. Then he would go through them and find the most interesting section of—

O: Distress.

M: Distress, right! Then he'd put that up on the easel and on top of that he'd paint these realistic still lifes. But somehow the ghosts of those random events would work their way into the objects. He called those distress marks "hooks." A canvas for him, without that distress, was a canvas that had no hooks on it and without them the image was in danger of simply sliding off the canvas. But if these unplanned events were already on the canvas, they provided focal points around which pictorial events could happen—even though it all looks very deliberately planned.

So the distressing was there right from the beginning and it continued all the way through the process of painting.

O: It seems to me that you as an editor are dealing with a similar blending of the rough, raw material you've assembled and the formal shape it needs to reach at some stage within the work. You have to order it in some way, in spite of the fact that you've got forty thousand fragments and miscues, and somehow also keep that dangerous element in the film.

M: You can't be *completely* open to outside influence, because then everything falls apart, it doesn't have any spine, it can't endure. But if you're not open to *any* outside influence, then your work is in danger of being too hermetically sealed, trapped within a preexisting vision that renders it ultimately not lifelike, in the deepest sense.

O: Your father clearly seems to have had an influence on you, in terms of the kind of artist you've become. Did you respond to the example of him as an artist?

M: He certainly showed me that it was possible to live a life of both order and excitement, as an artist, and be a good father and husband. He worked at home, so when I came back from school every day, there he was, painting away. I went through a period in my life where we were comparing dads at school. The other kids would say, My dad runs an office. Or, My dad drives a truck. My dad runs a big piece of machinery. My dad is the head of a corporation—the implication being that the kid could go into the office and use all the staplers or ride the truck: there were fringe benefits to having dads. I kept thinking, My dad works at home. There is no office. . . . Of course there were huge benefits—but I saw that only later.

   And it certainly had an influence on me—I guess what Rupert Sheldrake would call morphic resonance. If only because that's the world I grew up in, and you tend to perpetuate something of that in your own life.

   My father came from a musical family in Toronto. His mother, father, and three brothers were musicians, professional and amateur, and there was the assumption that everyone in the family would be musical. He played the violin until his teenage years, and he was good enough that he was on the radio in Toronto in the 1920s. But it wasn't him, and he went through a period in his

late teens when he didn't know what he was going to do. His mother observantly suggested art school. So he went to the Ontario College of Art. Took one step across the threshold, breathed in the atmosphere of turpentine and pigments, and thought, This is it! There was no question from then on. It's probably a unique example in the history of twentieth-century art of a painter who became a painter because his mother suggested it. But she was right.

O: Are your father's aesthetics something you feel close to? Or that you needed to react against?

M: No. Very close. He painted still lifes, and when you went into his studio, the little models, the objects themselves, were probably two feet away from him. But he tended to paint them as if they were monumental. Even though the paintings themselves are small, you get the sense of a monumentality to the objects in them. I think that was a result of his keen awareness of space. Even though in this case the space was only two feet.

He said to me once, I don't paint the object, I paint the space between my eye and the object: that space contains the object the way the mould of an object contains the object. I am painting space and I am also constructing

The two Murches at work: Walter Tandy Murch in New York at the easel and Walter Scott at his Avid in California. This is a customized setup using an architect's table so Walter Murch can stand. *The Radio,* 1947, oil on canvas, Walter Tandy Murch, and *The Lightbulb,* oil on canvas, 1961. *overleaf,* The bomb from Hitchcock's *Sabotage,* 1936, a film based on *The Secret Agent* by Joseph Conrad.

something on a two-dimensional piece of canvas that has its own dynamics, irrespective of the objects that are being painted.

And that's exactly the way I think about sound recording. If I go out to record a door-slam, I don't think I'm recording a door-slam. I think I am recording the space in which the door-slam happens.

O: It's the context for that noise.

M: Yes. I put it in a context. And try to have that context work within the implied space of the image, and also the larger implied space of the story.

THE UNANTICIPATED COLLISIONS
OF THINGS

O: As an editor you, like your father, appear to be very traditional, classical, and yet you're constantly celebrating the new technical possibilities of your craft—whether it's digital or something else. You're always interested in the new. Especially in this time when we are straddling film and digital techniques, what you call "the double-chandelier phase"—half gaslight, half electricity. And yet earlier, you said we're still in the Middle Ages as far as film is concerned, we're only halfway there.

M: Well, the Middle Ages was a time of great innovation. Technology is certainly in a period of transition, and you have to hold on to some of the old things because that's the only way you can do it right now. Yet you have to welcome in the new, whether you like it—which I do—or not.

Also, interesting things frequently result from hybridization, awkward though they may sometimes be at first. To many people in Europe—in France particularly—English is an awkward language. It's the bastard child of the Romance and the Germanic languages and has elements of both in almost equal proportion. Yet to those who love the English language, its particular strength is that very historical hybridization. You can choose to tilt your style towards the short, single-syllable, Germanic, Celtic end of things, as Hemingway did, or you can tilt it, the way Henry James did, towards the Romance-language roots. And you can vary it as you will.

Obviously there are frustrations in hybridization, but at the same time there's an incredible richness that comes from the unanticipated collisions of things. On a day-to-day working basis, for instance, my photo-board system gives me visual juxtapositions that I find very provocative.

O: When did you conceive of the idea of using photo boards?

M: On *The Conversation,* in the early seventies. Personal computers didn't exist then but I had index cards, which are a simple form of database. But writing out the details of each shot took more time than I wanted. I thought, Wouldn't it be nice if I could attach a little frame of the shot, in the upper corner of the card, to remind me. I never carried the idea further, but it occurred to me then. I didn't start the process of using photos until I worked on *The Right Stuff* in the early eighties.

O: Did you edit that?

M: No. But I did some of the preliminary culling of the documentary material used in it. And because there was so much material, I started taking representative pictures of each shot to help organize it all. That was how it began. I didn't develop the system in its fullest sense until *Unbearable Lightness* in 1986.

O: Can you explain the system?

M: One of the first things I do when I get a script is to break it down into sequences—the closest thing to these would be chapters in a book—which are my best guesses at what an audience seeing this film would understand as dramatic scenes.

O: Like Almásy's plane crash into the desert at the start of *The English Patient.* That would make up one chapter or sequence?

M: Exactly. Then you cut away from that scene to the train, with Hana, and you're off somewhere else. At that moment you're at the end of one sequence and the beginning of another. There are on average about thirty to forty of these sequences—or chapters—within a typical screenplay. And I number each of those sequences in the order in which they appear in the screenplay. But for practical reasons, since those train scenes may be scattered throughout the story, we shoot all the material to do with the train at the same time, because trains are so expensive.

Then, as the film is shot, I select a short series of representative stills—two to five, usually—from each camera position, called a *setup,* and print them, with the setup number in the lower left corner. The crew may shoot anywhere from seven to thirty setups each day. The pictures are then stuck onto a piece of stiff board about two feet wide by four feet high—each sequence having its series of boards. In the end, when the film is finished shooting, there will be thousands of these pictures—about forty to each board on perhaps a hundred boards which I keep stacked together in sequence order.

I can then hang the appropriate boards on the wall of my room when I'm editing a sequence, and have a visual display, organized numerically, of all the material that was shot for that sequence.

0: And the boards themselves are organized by script sequence?

M: Yes, but the photos on the boards are there in the order in which they were shot. So there is order and chaos mixed together.

A photo board for *Apocalypse Now.* On every film since *Unbearable Lightness,* Murch takes a series of representative stills—two to five—from each camera position (setup), prints them with the setup number in the lower left corner, then sticks them on a foamcore board. Each sequence has its own series of boards.

This means that the boards give me visual juxtapositions, vertically and horizontally—which is what I find so provocative. I see *this* image at the right edge of the first board, next to *that* image on the left edge of the next board. That juxtaposition may never have been intended by the script, but because there they are, next to each other, it tells me: This is possible. There's a little ticking bomb there that says: Photograph X could be, in the film, next to photograph Y—you never thought of that, but it's possible.

There may be several "iconic" frames within each shot. Essentially I'm trying to answer the question: Why did the director shoot this shot? In still photography it is what Cartier-Bresson calls "the decisive moment." One frame in particular, from the several thousand exposed for each shot, will catch my eye as being more representative of what the director was looking for. A glint in the actor's eye, a twist to the mouth, the way the camera was positioned with the light.

As I'm assembling the film, I'll be trying to find the exact moment each shot reaches its optimal maturity: I want to hold every shot on screen long enough for it to deliver the goods, but cut it off at a moment when it also has the potential to lead to something else.

Part of a photo board for *The English Patient*.

Let's say that I've provisionally chosen a particular point to end the shot. I'll then turn around and look at that whole wall of photographs and—without my being consciously aware of it—my eye will leap to an image that answers the question I was asking at the end of the previous shot: Oh! It would be good to see *that* image next!

O: So it's not a logical or rational jump.

M: Well, there is a certain logic to it, ultimately, but at the moment of making the choice it is more spontaneous, like performing a musical improvisation.

O: You're surprising yourself.

M: Exactly. There's just the *right* amount of turbulence in this system. There is a pattern, and there will be sections where the photographs are all about the same thing, but sometimes they jump around. I like that. I want to introduce— within the relative rigidity of all my databases and notes and structures and numbers and everything—I want to include this element of randomness.

O: This is William Burroughs as film editor.

M: Right! I'm sure, if you wrote down, under each of the photographs on those boards, the dialogue that was being spoken, and then put it in that order, it would read like some of William Burroughs's books!

A PEBBLE, A CRICKET, A WRENCH

O: Like Fred Zinnemann, you've worked on documentaries as well as features. I was recently involved in responding to a friend's long documentary and I witnessed that traumatic and difficult stage where you need to radically restructure it, cut it down, reshape it, without giving it a false sense of speed or plot.

M: You face that problem even with theatrical films. But the problems can be acute in documentary films—I'm thinking right now of the documentary section in *The Unbearable Lightness of Being*, where we had forty hours of documentary footage and had to fuse a tiny fraction of it with images of the film. How do you reduce the key moment in a nation's history, for which you have so many hours of material, into fifteen minutes? It was a question of time, simply spending time with the material and selecting striking images. Not just visually striking, but striking in all senses. Then finding ways to put those images together so they enhanced one another, both by resonance and by contradiction. If you find something very white, look for something very black, and put the two next to each other.

That's where you start. What you're constantly trying to find, as you distill it, is ways that these images can go together at deeper and deeper levels. What will immediately attract your attention—unless you're very lucky or very wise—is something on the surface. What makes you pick up a particular peb-

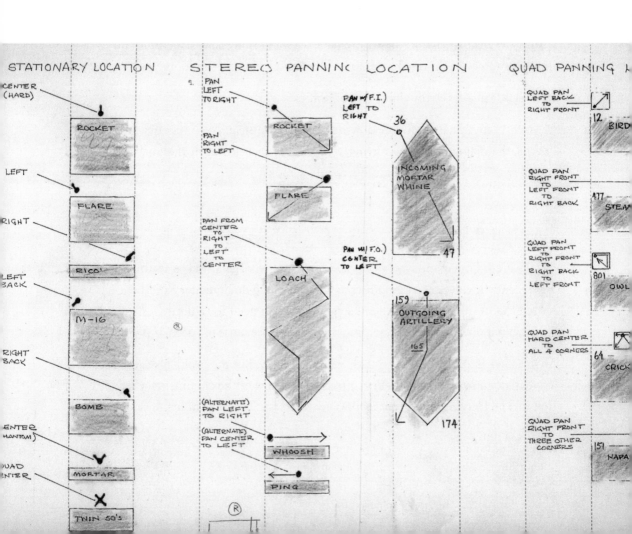

ble? You're walking on the beach and thinking about the political situation in the Congo and you pick up a pebble. Why did you pick up that pebble? Something made you do that.

It's similar. . . . Why do I select that shot? Something about it made me select it. Once having selected it, a process of organic crystallization begins. I can think of no higher tribute to a film than that—that you sense simultaneously that it's crystalline and organic at the same time. Too crystalline and it's lifeless, too organic and it's spineless. The human body is made of amorphic crystals—our DNA is an amorphic crystal which provides just enough structure to make it persist in a world that is trying to undo it. Yet it's random enough to be adaptable.

Sound cue sheets for the mix of *Apocalypse Now,* drawn by Murch.

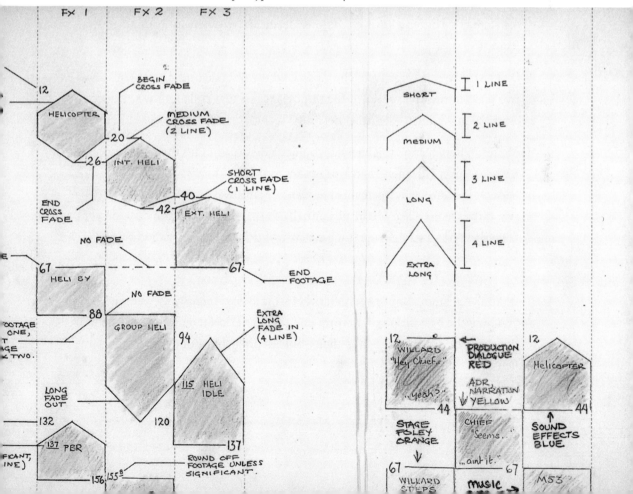

One of the reasons I lobby for the increased collaboration of everyone who can have a voice on a film is that through collaboration you add facets to the work. The work is going to be seen by millions of people, over many decades and under very many different circumstances, and even though the film is a fixed thing, you want it to be multifaceted so that different people will see different things in it, and come away rewarded.

The best, easiest way to get that multifacetedness is to allow the collaboration of lots of people, as well as Chance, which is sometimes Fate in costume. Each of those moments of collaboration, each contribution by someone other than the director, adds a slightly different perspective to the work, some chisel mark slightly at an angle to the central vision. And each of these moments, these facets, has the potential to make the work "sparkle" in a creative sense, and make it more accessible to a greater variety of people over a longer period of time.

If, instead, the film is a single, monolithic vision, the viewer has no option other than to submit to it on its own terms, bow down to it, or turn away from it.

O: The theatre director Paul Thompson, who works on and directs collaborative plays in theatre, speaks of the importance of that collaborative balance as essential in adding to the "thickness" of a scene.

M: Yes. Where he says thickness, I would say density, but it's the same idea. You try to get things to where there's substance to them. When you hit them, they hit back. At the same time, there must be clarity. I am always striving for a clear density. If the scene is clear but insubstantial, I think about what I can do to, in your friend's words, thicken it up. If it has density but opacity, I try to add clarity.

O: You've written about needing cricket sounds for *Apocalypse Now,* and how you built the overall sound up from one singular cricket, reproducing it so that the sense of crowdedness was there, but keeping the sounds all in the same key. . . .

M: We wanted a hallucinatory clarity, which you don't get when you go out in the field and record a thousand crickets. You get something, of course, with that kind of recording, and it's something that I use all the time in films: a shimmering curtain of sound. But at this particular point in *Apocalypse* we didn't want *that*. That was too real, too ordinarily real. We wanted something that was hyperreal. We got it by recording individual crickets very close, then electronically multiplying them till we had a thousand crickets. It's as if they each had their own little radio mike on. Then we had a thousand tracks of crickets.

O: And their pitch was the same.

M: Yes. One cricket is very much like every other cricket. That allows you to superimpose them all on top of one another and not get chaos. If you had thirty different

Murch with Babe, who is wearing a microphone designed by Alan Splet to capture snorting sounds for *The Black Stallion.*

kinds of insects, recorded them all separately, and then played them all together, multiplying that by a thousand, it would be something else. It would not have harmonic unity to it.

O: We're getting back to that issue of a "point of view"—even in sound. If I'm in the tropics and I hear a certain bird shrieking, my ear will remove all the other, minor noises, I will be able to focus on, to pick up that bird shrieking. You, as a sound editor, are making that selection for the viewer.

M: Yes. That's an ideal example! On the first feature film that I mixed—Francis Coppola's *The Rain People*—there was a scene with a woman—played by Shirley Knight—in a telephone booth alongside the New Jersey Turnpike. In advance, I thought, I'll record lots of traffic and it'll give the sense that you're beside the freeway. I did this, but very soon realized it was counterproductive. To make its point the recording had to be played at such a level that it ruined your ability to concentrate on the dialogue in the telephone booth. I didn't want to give up the idea of locating the woman in a place—beside the highway—but I wanted to hear what she said, because that's what the scene is about: she's talking to her husband and telling him the reasons she's run away from home.

I discovered that if I used what you might call a *precipitant* sound, something we associate with a specific environment but that is itself distinct, then the other sounds come along automatically. What I did was record somebody dropping a wrench fifty feet away—as if fifty feet away from the booth, in the garage of the service station where the woman in the movie is stopped. It was important that it was far away, and that it was a certain kind of wrench dropping on a certain kind of polished concrete. If you've ever been in such an environment, you know what that sounds like and you know that such sounds are commonplace in service stops near big highways.

That little sound was able to bring along with it, imaginatively, all the traffic. But the traffic sound exists in your mind. I spent a lot of time trying to discover those key sounds that bring universes along with them. I tend not to visualize but auralize, to think about sound in terms of space. Rather than listen to the sound itself, I listen to the space in which the sound is contained. . . .

O: As in the way we hear that bell in the distance, subliminally, while the English Patient eats a plum—so we become conscious of the landscape between his bedroom and the bell, which seems half a mile away.

M: And by implication, yes, all the birds and the insects that live in that world. And, by contrast, it is very different from the racket you've heard in the film up to that point, of the convoys going through the mountains and planes being shot down out of the sky and trains jiggling back and forth. You're now in an environment quiet enough to allow you to hear a distant bell. The bell brings a whole raft of associations along with it. There are religious connotations and geographical and cultural connotations, in addition to the purely spatial. The crickets we were talking about earlier: Where are they? They're nowhere. They're in Willard's head. They are spatial, but it's a mental space.

"THE BLUE LOOKED DEAD"

M: The chemistry of soundscapes is mysterious and not easy to predict in advance. You go into the final mix of a film knowing that certain things are possible, but not knowing exactly how they're going to work themselves out. I remember in *THX 1138* we were trying to achieve a great contrast between two environments: the silence of the white limbo prison and the chaos beyond it. In the silence of the prison you hear only distant cooing sounds—which I recorded at the Exploratorium, here in San Francisco—ambiguous machines very far off and so remote that you can't really tell what they are. And occasionally thunder, on a whim, just because the space is so big.

After many hours of walking, the characters THX and SRT—Robert Duvall and Don Pedro Colley—get to the edge of the prison, this white space. The light falls off, and magically there's a door. . . . They open it out of curiosity and are sucked into a corridor of people rushing like cascading water, hundreds of people, just rushing.

To create that sound I went out and recorded similar environments: people coming out of football matches, roller derbies, marathons, lots of people moving very fast. I recorded waterfalls, sewage pipes, rushing air—all those kinds of sounds. As I'd done in *The Rain People,* I piled them all on top of one another, thinking more and more and more equals more. I was going to conquer this once and for all! When we played everything together, however, a funny perceptual thing happened. The needle of the recorder went way off the meter. We couldn't see the needle anymore, the sounds were so powerful. But our impression was that it wasn't very loud. It was frustrating after all that work. How does $1 + 1 + 1 + 1 + 1 = 2$?

There was something about the chemistry of those sounds: they were all rushing sounds but none of them had *edges,* so that the ear couldn't seize them. Objectively measured, there was lots of energy, but subjectively, because there were so few edges to the sound, it wasn't particularly loud.

Then I remembered—these are the mysterious things: why did I think of this?—that a few months earlier I'd been at the Academy of Sciences at two in the morning, recording footsteps. For some reason I'd put the recorder at one end of the African Hall, and stood at the other end and just shouted incomprehensible, guttural speech. It echoed in a beautiful way: the recorder was 150 feet away, the sound bounced off the marble and glass surfaces, in the dark, at two in the morning.

I remembered that track and thought, I'll add that one to the mix. The effect was instant, overwhelming loudness. I had to pull the faders almost all the way down, and it was still too loud. Even though the meter was just sitting there quivering slightly, in the middle.

Again a paradox. We were experiencing great loudness, but electrically there was not very much energy. In retrospect I realized that what I'd done was provide one of those precipitant elements, like the wrench dropping, like the bell in the distance. This voice provided edges because—*ack ack ook ook ark*—it had starts and stops to it. Those edges collected all the energy of the sounds around them and delivered them in a startling way. So I was able to play the scene—electrically speaking—quite softly. But your impression is that it's very loud, because of the presence of this sound that precipitates the energy of the sounds around it.

The lives of people who orchestrate symphonic music must be full of such discoveries, handed down as observations . . . such as, Oh, if you combine the oboe with the violin you'll get this effect that far outstrips the amount of energy you're putting into it, because of the synergy between these two unlikely elements. Cooking is full of these discoveries too. Cooks are always trying to find unusual substances that, if you put them together, seem to excite the taste buds in new ways, because of the talent of that one contradictory taste to precipitate the elements of another: He added crushed olives to the cake icing! If you remove the precipitant, you're removing a very small element, but it makes what's left kind of bland.

It happens in the chemistry between sound and picture as well. A certain sound colour will make you see colours in the picture in much more vibrant ways.

There was a crisis with *Apocalypse Now,* back in '78, when it turned out that we didn't have the rights to Georg Solti's recording of "The Ride of the Valkyries," which is what we'd been using. Decca Europe refused to give it to us. We were very close to finishing the film and the fear was that we wouldn't get the rights, and then what would we do? We triaged the situation: continuing to petition Decca for permission, making arrangements with the San Francisco Symphony to record the music again, and trying to find an old recording that was close enough to Solti's that maybe we could get the rights to. That last task fell to me.

I went to Tower Records and bought all nineteen recordings of "The Ride of the Valkyries." I sat with a stopwatch and a metronome, figuring out which recordings followed roughly what Solti had decided to do metronomically with the music. In the end, I eliminated all but one—Erich Leinsdorf conducting the L.A. Philharmonic. I thought, It's not quite the same, but it's close enough and maybe, if we're lucky, I can make some adjustments to the picture. . . .

I transferred the Leinsdorf recording to film, put it up against the picture, ran them both together, and within ten seconds knew that it wasn't going to work. Not because of any metric problem—in fact it was quite close to Solti's rhythms—but because of the colouration Leinsdorf had chosen. At this point he had decided to highlight the strings . . . whereas Solti had chosen to highlight the brasses. . . . At that moment in the film you're looking down out of a helicopter, past a soldier, onto the waters of the Philippine gulf. There was a peculiarly wonderful acidity to the blue of the ocean that synergized with the metallic brass of Solti's recording. With Leinsdorf, the strings had none of that brassiness—they were soft and pillowy—and as a result the blue looked dead. It was no longer the same blue. So I abandoned the search. It was impossible.

Luckily Francis eventually got through to Solti himself. He explained the situation, and Solti said, Of course, dear boy, why didn't you ask me in the first place? Solti called the people at Decca and we got the rights to use the music—though it happened so late in the process that we were unable to get hold of the original tapes. What's in the film is simply a lift off a disc, off the 33⅓ LP.

Anyway, you can't predict what's going to work. We don't know enough about the physics of it yet, or the psycho-acoustic physics of it—how the mind works in its perceptions. It has something to do with mass and frequency and edges, the way a painting has to do with colour and light and line. The interaction of those three things.

A WRONG READING

O: In a film where there's one point of view, or even more than one point of view, is it possible to get a different perspective through the soundtrack—not just from what we're watching, but through sound as well? From how we might suddenly hear differently? Or does sound, because by its nature most of us hear it, have to be very democratic?

M: No! In fact, sound is so malleable. Films told from a single point of view, if they didn't have the malleability of sound to mollify that, would be almost unendurable.

O: Okay. That's what I was wondering. We talked earlier about how the style of "leaping poetry" is mirrored in the subliminal connections and surprising juxtapositions you can forge in film. We read an episode in *The English Patient* from Hana's point of view, but earlier we've been in Kip's head when he's going to defuse a bomb. This is not something we're very conscious of when we read—shifting over from one to the other—but it's happening all the time, activating and creating that thickness. I think sound is very close to that kind of leaping style in a book.

M: Yes. And in complex ways. As in *The Conversation,* where you don't know *what* the point of view is at the opening. It's clear only that you are high up, looking down on Union Square in San Francisco, hearing those soft, billowy sounds of the city at lunchtime. Then, like a jagged red line right across the view, comes this distorted—you don't know what it is—this digital racket, @#@*&%. . . . You will learn what it is soon enough, and you will learn that what you assumed was a neutral God's-eye point of view is in fact the point of view of a secret tape recorder that is recording all of this, picking up these distorted sounds that are the imperfectly recorded voices of the targets, the young couple's conversation sometimes muffled by the sounds of the square. But this

The long zoom down into Union Square in *The Conversation.*

is a shell game, a little mystery that progresses over the course of the film until you finally put the pieces together and realize what it is.

O: It's interesting because that abstract sound then gets cleaned up and interpreted and therefore becomes Harry's point of view, but in the end he totally misinterprets the one important sentence he's recorded.

M: Yes. He hears it in all kinds of different acoustic situations during the film—when he's working on the tape at the lab, when it's being replayed through the wall of the hotel, and just before the murder you hear a muffled version of it. When the tape is stolen from him by the Director—Robert Duvall—you hear it echoing down the corridors of the office building. You don't know what that sound is until finally it coalesces into the sound of the line itself, "He'd kill us if he got the chance."

Then, most unexpectedly, we discover that Harry has—all along—mentally altered the cadence of the line, which is hypersubjectivity, because of what happened in the past, where people were killed as a result of his actions. So he *chooses* which of the characters are likely to be innocent victims—the attractive young couple, particularly the girl. He doesn't want her to be hurt the way the previous people had been hurt, so once he finally decodes and clarifies the line—"He'd *kill* us if he got the chance"—it becomes a mantra that in every situation reinforces the message he needs to hear: These people are the victims.

At the end, when it's the Director who is murdered, we hear the line again. Now it's, "He'd kill *us* if he got the chance," implying: If he's going to kill us, we need to kill him. A line that has an innocent meaning at one time has a non-innocent meaning at the end. Harry has used all his technical filters to clarify the line. What sabotages him is the mental filter, the subjective filter that chooses to hear an inflection that isn't really there, because of his own past history.

DIVERGENT/CONVERGENT

O: How sound represents a point of view is fascinating in the way it can complicate the narrative stance. It's the way the tone of voice or a point of view in a novel represents the state of mind of a character, without authorial intrusion. It infuriates me when lines from a book are quoted to show the style of the writer, when they really represent the personality or voice of the character. In Anthony Minghella's film *Ripley* you have the scene where Freddie comes into Ripley's apartment and starts playing the piano, perversely, boorishly, and we witness it totally with Ripley's sensitive hearing. In a scene in a book, the moment quoted may not represent the author's style at all. It represents simply the state of mind of whoever holds the narrative ball at that moment.

M: Exactly.

O: I was wondering whether in film you can also have many points of view, or is there a limit? I'll give you an example. When Anthony first talked about doing *The English Patient,* he said you couldn't have more than one person having a flashback. If all four of the characters start having flashbacks, as they do in the book, it will get too confusing.

M: Yes, you have to be careful about it. I'm thinking of the film *Election,* which has four narrators. The teacher, Matthew Broderick, narrates it; the girl, Reese Witherspoon, narrates it; then someone else, the class jock; then a fourth person, the renegade lesbian sister. One would say in advance that something like that wouldn't work. But it does, brilliantly. The filmmakers managed to pull it off.

O: Can the point of view move around in film?

M: My rule of thumb is that there are two ways to deal with multiple points of view in a film: divergent or convergent.

O: Can you explain?

M: What I call the *divergent* method is when you start with all the characters in the same time and space—an Aristotelian structure. After that you can follow them individually wherever they go—as long as you've seen them all together at one point, right at the beginning. That allows you to pungently characterize these people in relationship to one another in time and space: physically, we get to see them standing next to each other and judge how they carry themselves, but also emotionally, how they relate to one another. Once the audience has that imprint, if it's well done, then the film is free to have different points of view.

The beginning of *The Godfather* is a good example of a divergent structure, where all the key players are assembled at the wedding that starts the film; also the beginning of *American Graffiti*, where all the key players are at Mel's Drive-in, so each of them is introduced as dramatically, efficiently, and interestingly as possible, *and* you see them relative to one another. It's like a convention where people come up to you wearing little name tags that say: Hello, my name is Kurt, I'm the artist, I don't know whether I want to accept the future that is laid out in front of me. Hello, I'm John, I'm the hot-rod racer who is afraid of the future. Hello, I'm Toad, I wanna get laid. So you get telegraphic, quick, not very complex, but true characterizations of those people.

The first time you see Fredo in *The Godfather,* he's drunk. Fredo is the weakling of the family. Michael, by contrast, never drinks alcohol. What does

Diane Keaton as Kay and Al Pacino as Michael in *The Godfather*.

that say about him, as a person and as an Italian, as a member of this family? Fredo, well, he's amusing, he's funny, but he's ineffectual. That's clear from the start, and it becomes clearer not only over the course of *Godfather I,* but in *Godfather II* as well.

But if somebody new is then introduced, a third of the way through the film—someone with his own point of view—you'll begin to wonder, Who is this? Why should I care about this person? If that person was not part of that Aristotelian beginning, the danger is that the late introduction will seem awkward or intrusive.

O: So if Kay—Diane Keaton—hadn't been in the first scene of *The Godfather,* that would have been a problem?

M: Yes—you discover right away who she is. She's obviously the naive outsider: "Who's that? . . . Look at that person over there! Michael, my God!" You quickly get a sense first of all that she's not Italian, and second that this is all unbelievably outrageous to her. And then Michael says to her, "It's my family, Kay. It's not me." And we know fate will grab him.

The opposite approach is *convergent*: two or three stories that start separately and then flow together. *The English Patient* is a good example. It starts out with two mysterious figures in a plane, flying across the desert. The plane gets shot down by the Germans and then—*cut*—you're on a train, with a young

Ron Howard, Candy Clark, and Charles Martin Smith from *American Graffiti.*

woman, a nurse, in a completely different situation: bantering with wounded soldiers. The two stories appear to have nothing to do with each other, but the audience trusts that these two rivers are going to come together. You follow Hana and her story, then you cut back to the Patient, going through the desert on the back of a camel; then you cut to Hana again. And you reach a point where almost accidentally these two stories fuse—it just happens that when the Patient is being interrogated as a possible spy, Hana is the nurse who gives him a glass of water. Later their stories merge even more closely: she takes him out

of the convoy into the monastery, and they spend the rest of the film together.

O: What about Caravaggio?

M: Hmm . . . He comes into the film after perhaps half an hour. But he doesn't have any scenes to himself, he is always tied to Hana or the Patient. It's not that you can't introduce new characters into the body of the work—though it might be risky to do so past the halfway point. It's just that they shouldn't have scenes to themselves, where we have to see things from their point of view.

O: What about the scene where Caravaggio loses his thumbs?

M: . . . You're right. *And* it's a flashback. Hmm . . . Well, rules are there to be broken. (*Laughs*)

Godfather II is probably the most extreme form of convergent structure. The point of convergence, the eventual confluence of the "story rivers," happens at the very end—actually lies *outside* the body of the film.

O: That last scene, with the Don, where they sit down to a meal—

M: *Without* the Don, actually. It seems like he is there, but he isn't.

At the beginning you're following the story of how the young Vito Corleone came to America at the turn of the century. And then you cut to his son, Michael, at the height of his powers in 1958. And the film alternates between

Breaking the rules: Willem Dafoe, *above left,* as Caravaggio in *The English Patient* being tortured—minor characters don't normally have their own flashbacks. Convergent structure: the end of *Godfather II*—it's Christmas after Pearl Harbor—Michael Corleone, *above,* has been left alone at the table.

the two stories seven times during its course. You enjoy thematic parallels between the lives of Vito and Michael, but they're in completely different time frames. The only place their two stories come together is Christmas 1941. And the character who unites them—Don Vito—arrives at the house, but you never see him: he remains off screen. "Dad's here!" says Connie, and everyone runs off and leaves Michael sitting alone at the table. And you just hear the group sing: Hey! He's a jolly good fellow!

Francis had wanted Brando—as Don Vito—in that scene. But Brando wouldn't do it, for whatever reason. Because Francis's plan was to unite the two *Godfather* films, he had wanted the point of juncture within the film itself. Instead, the two stories in *Godfather II* are like two parallel lines that go just off the table. So what Francis did—which was brilliant—was to focus on Michael, and leave Michael sitting alone at the table, thinking about his destiny: it's Christmas right after Pearl Harbor and he has just told Sonny that he has joined the Marines.

At the end of *Godfather II*, we know what his destiny is. But this was the point at which he made his first strike away from the family: I've joined the Marines. Inexplicable, as far as the rest of the family is concerned.

O: The Mafia chief Hyman Roth—who eventually gets shot in the airport—*his* arrival is very late in the film, and then he plays such an important part. Talk about convergence—his arrival comes totally out of the blue and then snakes into the film.

M: You're right. But he is foreshadowed quite early. His messenger, Johnny Ola, comes to the party at Lake Tahoe, and starts to talk about a deal. Physically, it's true, he does come late. But after the assassination attempt, the immediate suspicion is that Hyman Roth was responsible. In that sense, he's a little like Marlon Brando in *Apocalypse Now,* a character who is foreshadowed by events quite early on, but who doesn't appear until near the end.

O: Foreshadowing is such a central device in literature to build up the worth or the danger of a character who hasn't arrived yet. Kurtz in *Heart of Darkness,* of course. Or even Othello in the first act of the play, before we see him.

M: In film characters can be introduced later in a story, but it's unusual to give them their own point of view—scenes that feature them separate from the established main characters. Hyman Roth, for instance, does not have a separate scene with his wife, talking about Michael Corleone after Michael has left. The one scene Roth has to himself is when he's killed at the airport.

When I talk about divergence and convergence as being rules, they are really rules of approximation. You can change them or break them, but it's good to know the rules you're breaking. And breaking them is always somewhat problematic. It can be interesting—like Caravaggio's thumbs scene—but it throws the audience a curve, and to pull it off successfully you have to be fully aware of what you're doing. Probably the most extreme, and the most successful, film to shift points of view unexpectedly is Hitchcock's *Psycho.* Janet Leigh, the heroine, is killed dramatically and unexpectedly twenty-five minutes into the story, and then the point of view switches—for the rest of the film—to a new character, the detective, played by Martin Balsam.

THE DISAPPEARING BROTHER

0: You eventually edited the *Godfather* films into a trilogy. And in a way the divergent/convergent structure of the individual films now lies perhaps a bit awkwardly in this larger structure. I prefer them as individual projects rather than as a unified whole. How do you feel they hold together as a trilogy?

M: I prefer them as separate films myself, though there are many who prefer the story in chronological order.

Even as a triptych, as three separate panels, there is an imbalance with the third film, which is weaker than the other two. It should be said that the first two films are a tremendously hard act to follow—they are regularly at the top of those "greatest films of all time" lists.

I think there was a fundamental problem that surfaced during preproduction. Francis's original intention was to make the story revolve around the death of the fourth Corleone brother, Tom Hagen—Robert Duvall's part. He got the script to a certain stage and in this preliminary form sent it to Duvall with words to the effect: "I'm still working on it, but they've only given me six weeks to get to this point. I ask you to have faith in me and come along for the ride." And Duvall agreed. But he wanted financial parity with Al Pacino, who played Michael, and Paramount wouldn't go along. It became a real battleground, which Francis wasn't able to solve so Duvall was not in the film.

It kind of knocked the legs out from what Francis wanted to accomplish, which was to make each of the three *Godfather* films about the death of a brother: Sonny in the first, Fredo in the second, and Tom in the third—a beautiful symmetry, like a fairy tale. Once upon a time there were four brothers . . . and the one who didn't want to be part of the family at the beginning is the one who survives in the end. And yet at what cost.

It meant that in *Godfather III*, Al Pacino—Michael—had to carry the entire film on his shoulders, both as an actor and as a character: King Lear. Because there was no actor or character in the film who could stare him down from the same level. He was so much bigger than everybody else.

So Tom Hagen just disappeared somewhere between *Godfather II* and *Godfather III*. It was one of those missed opportunities. And it meant that the balance Francis wanted to achieve for the trilogy could not be achieved. It's back to our Negative Twenty Questions: the character who would satisfy all the logical and emotional requirements lay outside the "room" of the film.

PRELUDES

0: You said once, talking about the prelude to *Touch of Evil*, that it settles you into your chair and presents you, in miniature, with all the themes and ideas that the rest of the piece is going to investigate. And the prelude to the new version of *Touch of Evil* really does suggest everything that follows. Are there other examples where you've restructured and built the beginning of a film in order to keep that directional sense you desire in a prelude?

M: The obvious example is *Apocalypse Now.* That opening eight minutes or so where Willard is alone in his room, with his demons, waiting to be given his mission. And you, the audience, are learning about him and the world he's in.

O: And where he's been.

M: And the demons that are pushing him into a very uncertain future.

O: In *The Godfather*—that opening prelude, the long, slow, dark sequence in Vito Corleone's office—is that pacing something that Coppola imagined, or was it something that was discovered in the performance, or in the editing? To decide to pace it in that very low-key, quiet way?

M: That was something Francis decided in the writing of the screenplay. That's how he saw it. That particular technique of starting with a slow zoom back, while a character has a kind of aria in which he states his position . . . this is very similar to what Francis did at the beginning of *Patton,* where George C. Scott stands in front of the American flag and says, This is what I believe. It's a very bold thing to do.

O: He does the same thing at the start of *The Godfather.*

M: The difference is that in *Godfather,* Bonasera, the undertaker, is an anonymous person, unlike Patton. We don't know who he is. Francis starts him out in limbo—just a head, in darkness, saying, "I believe in America." A very strong thing to say at the beginning: "I believe in America" . . . and yet there's a problem. What you want is the audience to say, Yes, I too believe in America, and I too am frustrated by this problem, either I have experienced it or I know people who have experienced it. As we're feeling this, the context in which this speech is being given is revealed, and eventually the shoulder of the man who

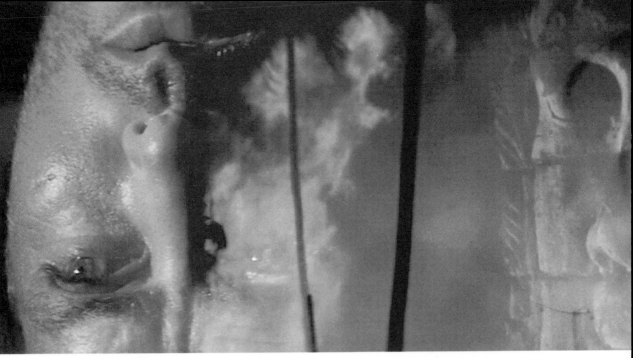

The opening of *Apocalypse Now:* not a zoom back but a rotation so that Willard is eventually right side up.

will solve the problem comes into frame. We're pretty sure it's Marlon Brando, and we're waiting for the moment he'll be asked the question, and have to give an answer, revealing himself.

The Conversation begins in an inverse way. That long, wide shot that slowly zooms in on Gene Hackman as Harry Caul, electronically stalking the lovers. We get the context of the world, and then we focus in on the individual. In *Godfather*, we focus in on the individual, and then we're given the particular context in which the story will work itself out.

Remarkable to think that those three films—*Patton, Godfather, Conversation*—were made within three years.

O: Even *Apocalypse Now* begins and pulls back from Willard's upside-down head.

M: Yes. It's not quite the same, but it is something similar. The camera doesn't zoom back, but it rotates around so that the upside-down Willard eventually becomes right side up. We're given fragments—jungle, explosion, upside-down head, Cambodian sculpture, flames, helicopter—disjointed things. Then the disjointedness begins to congeal into a world. So, yes, that achieves, by editorial superimposition, a version of what's achieved by zooming in or zooming out, as in *The Godfather* or *The Conversation,* by showing us fragments and then puzzling us with the context in which those fragments could exist—eventually, in *Apocalypse Now,* giving us at least enough context to proceed with the story, at the point where Willard, standing at the window, says, "Saigon, shit, I'm still only in Saigon."

■

O: Obviously there are various forms of introduction, so how strict is this rule about preludes? When I was at Zoetrope a few months ago, they told me that *Godfather III* had a different beginning at one point.

M: Yes.

O: And that you persuaded them to have another beginning. What happened there?

M: I felt that the original beginning of *Godfather III,* in the script, was a duplication, in religious terms, of the beginning of *Godfather I.*

O: It had the cardinal smoking a cigarette. It was comic, almost a parody of that first opening.

M: And the camera pulled back from the cardinal and there was Michael, and they're talking about the deal that he wants to make with the Church—he wants a participation in Immobiliare, the Church's real estate arm, the business arm. This was followed by the scene at the church where Michael is being invested with the Knighthood of Saint Sebastian. And then there was a celebration party.

I'd come into the project at a late date, to help them meet their deadline. So I was new to it, and that has its disadvantages—you don't yet know the ropes.

On the other hand, you can see something clearly, sometimes, that other people who've been buried in the project can't see.

What was clear to me was that the scene didn't take into consideration Michael's state of being at the end of *Godfather II,* which was extremely compromised. He's a little like Harry Caul at the end of *The Conversation.* He's sitting alone in a chair by the lake, but he's empty. So now we're picking him up many years later, and he's full again. The question is, What happened? How did he get so full after being so empty? I felt that a more interesting place to begin would be at the church, with all its associations with sin and redemption and confession.

In that scene in the church, where Michael is being knighted—as we hear how wonderful a person he is—we could reintroduce the images of the death of his brother Fredo. Here is this person who is being given the Church's highest honour, who is in fact the murderer of his brother, Cain to Fredo's Abel. Here is somebody being knighted by the Church who committed the first sin there ever was—to kill your own brother.

There's a tension in that, which I thought would be an interesting provocation for the rest of the film. Yes, Michael, you are now financially successful— but you're going to have to deal with this ancient, primal sin. I was also envisioning the moment that the three films would be played together so that each one would have to pick up, in a way, where the other left off—even if we didn't get around to doing that for twenty-five years.

So the sequence now goes: church, party, and then the meeting at the Vatican, where the deal is consummated.

■

O: I'm particularly fond of the prelude to *The Conversation.* That opening shot where the camera comes down through several stratospheres—a slow zoom shot—right down into Union Square, to the mime artist, and then as you get close to him you start to pick up the specific sound of his footsteps, something very intimate even though you've practically travelled from outer space. The use of that guy is brilliant: the way he follows on Gene Hackman's heels through the square in that first shot lets you feel the paranoia that is in Hackman. He *knows* he's being followed, being drawn attention to, but he's trying not to make much out of it.

M: It's funny—to watch how it's easy for the mime to mimic or mock other people, but he's stymied with Hackman. Harry Caul is so anonymous that even the mime doesn't know how to make a character of him, except by imitating the hold he has on his paper coffee cup. It's a wonderfully orchestrated shot because it's a long, automated zoom that moves very smoothly over a period probably about the same length as the opening of *Touch of Evil*. It just has the titles over it, three minutes or so.

O: I realized only much later that although the whole film is singularly and fiercely made from Harry's point of view, in all the later scenes where Harry is playing and replaying the tape, we're *watching*—and rewatching—that opening scene, being given this extra visual narrative that doesn't actually exist in Harry's vision.

Coppola talking to the mime from *The Conversation*.

```
FADE IN: .

EXT   UNION SQUARE    DAY

MEDIUM VIEW
A band of street musicians have just set up in the park: Clarinet,
trombone, banjo, saxophone and trumpet.  They wear fragments of
velvet and silk, pieces of old uniforms and odd-ball hats.  They
haven't yet attracted a crowd.  One of them takes a top hat from
his head on the ground, and throws a few coins and bills into it.
They break into a jazz ▨▨▨▨▨▨▨ " RED, RED Robin".

HIGH FULL VIEW
December in San Francisco.  The Downtown area, centering around
Union Square.  Christmas decorations are already up, the electricity
turned on in the middle of the afternoon.  The crowds of shoppers
have swelled with office workers out for their lunch hour.

THE  CREDIT TITLES ARE  PRESENTED IN SIMPLE LETTERS

A young Mime dressed as a Drum-Major has a slight crowd drawn
around him as he imitates certain unsuspecting people as they
come down a park walkway.  He is very good, and usually gets a
round of applause for his imitations.

CLOSE VIEW ON THE MUSICIANS
One of them puts down his instrument and does a rollicking tap
dance, his ruby-red tap-shoes out of another period than his long
hair and youthful beard.

CLOSER VIEW
The tap-shoes step out rhythms near the top hat.

VIEW ON THE MIME
Imitating a middle-aged, slow, bobbing walk.  But precise and
purposeful.  He sips coffee out of an imaginary cup.

THE  VIEW ALTERS revealing the subject: a chubby near-balding man
in his middle forties, dressed immaculately in an out of fashion
suit, with a slow, bobbing walk.  He sips coffee from a steaming
cardboard cup wrapped in a paper bag.  THIS IS HARRY CAUL.

THE MUSICIANS
The saxophonist blares into a raspy solo to everyone's delight,
especially Harry's.  He stops for a moment, appreciatively, as ,,
they go into the last chorus of ▨▨▨▨▨▨ " RED, RED Robin".
```

The screenplay from *The Conversation*.

M: That's true.

O: All Harry has got is sound.

M: I guess the device works as well as it does because it implies that Harry feels
himself getting so close to those two people that he can imagine the details of

their walk around the square—going over those details again and again in his mind, just as we see them.

O: Is it true that there was a problem with the sound in Union Square and that it had to be re-recorded?

M: The film was begun in 1972, which was early in the evolution of radio mikes—which is what we use in film when we're very far away from characters who have to be speaking. We hide a little microphone about the size of a peanut somewhere on their clothes, and a radio transmitter in their pocket. It's the same technique that Vargas uses at the end of *Touch of Evil*: he plants a radio mike on Menzies.

But the radio mikes we had back then were not that good, and they picked up miscellaneous static and the microwave transmissions that swamp a city like San Francisco. That meant that the actual soundtrack we were getting at the time of filming was about as imperfect as the track that Harry himself records in Union Square! Everything would be fine, and then suddenly there'd be the sweep of a microwave pulse across the track. You'd hear distortion and some garbled tonality that would obliterate everything else.

I used some of that noise in the finished film: as noise, it's very good. But I had to have—as a resource—a complete recording of the conversation itself, without any interference. One day, while something else was being filmed, I took Cindy Williams, who played Ann, the director's young wife, and Fred Forrest, who played her lover, Mark, off to a quiet residential area of San Francisco. I didn't use radio mikes. I just had a Nagra tape recorder with a handheld microphone—like a "man on the street" interview. Cindy and Fred walked around a park—there was nobody else about, just some birds—and I walked in front of them with a microphone and recorded what they said. If you can get actors soon enough after they've done a scene, their rhythms will still be what they were in the scene. There's a little variation, but actually much less than you would think.

I recorded that conversation three times. So the final soundtrack for the opening sequence is a mixture of the real conversation, filmed on location in

Union Square with radio mikes, and this secondary conversation, which was recorded under acoustically more controlled conditions.

The side benefit was that on the third take, Fred Forrest accidentally said, "He'd kill *us* if he got the chance." Which I mentally filed away as being the wrong reading of the line, and only came back to eight months later, when I had the intuition that, if we used that inflection as the last reading in the film, it might help the audience understand that these two young people were actually the murderers, and that the Director, the man the audience may have thought was the murderer, was actually the victim.

O: So that line wasn't planned to be said a different way at the end of the film, with that emphasis on "us"?

M: No, that was purely fortuitous—one of those things that came out of our relentless search to make the film convey information about what was going on yet not violate the single point of view of the film, which belongs to Harry.

The question is this: Harry Caul is a man on the fringe, who doesn't know—who initially says he doesn't even *want* to know—what's going on, so how do you convey, at the end, what actually took place? It was stylistically inconceivable to have a Perry Mason wrap-up, where somebody says, Well, Stan, this is what really happened! But we still had to get an audience to the point where they understood what had happened, and who the murderer was.

It took some time to get there! We were trying out possible solutions, and inserting that particular reading of the line at the end was just one of many. It came very late in the process: when the idea occurred to me, I was mixing the film in San Francisco and Francis was already shooting *Godfather II* in New York. When I was finished, I took the mix to New York, and ran it for Francis. He liked the idea of the shift in inflection, so it stayed in the film.

It was a risky thing to do, because it contradicted the basic premise of the film, which was to repeat the identical conversation over and over again. Because of the different contexts, the audience is supposed to hear different shadings of meaning in it each time. Even though the conversation itself remains identical.

Then, at the very end, we tweak the conversation itself, and the emphasis of the line-reading shifts.

Sometimes you can get away with violating your basic premise, which has the effect of throwing the premise into greater relief.

A GREASE PENCIL AND REAL TIME

And the threshing floor for the dance? Is it anything but the line? And when the line has, is, a deadness, is it not a heart which has gone lazy?

Charles Olson

O: Can you tell me more about how you cut film in real time?

M: When you're putting a scene together, the three key things you are deciding, over and over again, are: What shot shall I use? Where shall I begin it? Where shall I end it? An average film may have a thousand edits in it, so: three thousand decisions. But if you can answer those questions in the most interesting, complex, musical, dramatic way, then the film will be as alive as it can be.

For me, the most rhythmically important decision of the three is the last: Where do you end the shot? You end it at the exact moment in which it has revealed everything that it's going to reveal, in its fullness, without being overripe. If you end the shot too soon, you have the equivalent of youth cut off in its bloom. Its potential is unrealized. If you hold a shot too long, things tend to putrefy.

O: You get Polonius.

M: Indeed! For every shot, there is one specific place to end, and no other. A specific frame, and not the one before or after. So the question is, How do you decide which frame that is?

A trap you can fall into—as I did in my very early editing jobs on Encyclopaedia Britannica films—is to scan back and forth across the shot, looking for the frame where, for instance, the door closes. You mark that frame and cut at that point. It works. But it doesn't work particularly well, and it doesn't help the film to do it that way.

You remember you told me how much you liked the line breaks in my translations of Malaparte? The decision where to cut film is very similar to the decision, in writing poetry, of where to end each line. On which word? That end point has little if anything to do with the grammar of the sentence. It's just that the line is full and ripe at that point, full of meaning and ripe with rhythm. By ending it where he does, the poet exposes that last word to the blankness of the page, which is a way of emphasizing the word. If he adds two words after it, he immerses that word within the line, and it has less visibility, less significance. We do very much the same in film: the end of a shot gives the image of that last frame an added significance, which we exploit.

In film, at the moment of the cut you are juxtaposing one image with another, and that's the equivalent of rhyme. It's how rhyme and alliteration work in poetry, or how we juxtapose two words or two images, and what that juxtaposition implies. Either by emphasizing the theme or by countering it, modulating it, like an invisible Greek chorus. What's being stated may be one thing, but by juxtaposing two different images at the moment of the cut, and making them as striking as possible, we can say, Yes, but there's something else going on here.

The trick is to make that flow an organic part of the process. Editing is a construction, a mosaic in three dimensions, two of space and one of time. It's a miniature version of the way films are made, which is an artificial, piece-by-piece process.

To determine that end frame, I look at the shot intently. It's running along, and then at a certain point I flinch—it's almost an involuntary flinch, an equivalent of the blink. That flinch point is where the shot will end.

0: So you hit the button. Or do you use a grease pencil?

M: In the early days I marked the frame with a grease pencil when I was working on a Moviola. But on *The Conversation,* I reset a counter to 0 at that moment. Then I repeated the process. I would back up to some arbitrary start point and run the whole thing again and flinch again. Today, with the Avid, I hit a key. That's it. Cut.

O: So your response then is: Enough! Let's look away.

M: Exactly. Every shot is a thought or a series of thoughts, expressed visually. When a thought begins to run out of steam, that's the point at which you cut. You want that to be the moment at which the impulse to go to the next shot is at its strongest, so you are propelled into it. If you hold the shot too long, the impulse is deadened, and when you do go to the next shot, it lacks a certain energy. I'm always trying to find that balance point between fruition of the internal dynamics of the thought and the rhythm of the shot.

The key, on an operational level, is that I have to be able to duplicate that flinch point, *exactly,* at least two times in a row. So I run the shot once and hit a mark. Then run it back, look at it, and flinch again. Now I'm able to compare: Where did I stop the first time, and where did I stop the second? If I hit exactly the same frame both times, that's proof to me that there is something organically true about that moment. It's absolutely impossible to do that by any conscious decision. Imagine—there are twenty-four targets going by every second and with your gun you have to hit one of them, out of the twenty-four, every second.

O: And that happens.

M: Yes. If it doesn't happen, I don't make the cut at that point. I have to be able to hit that mark each time. That's the proof to me that I'm responding to something that is beyond my control, that has to do purely with thought and emotion, with rhythm and musicality.

O: So if you flinch in frame 17 the first time, and then flinch in frame 19—

M: Then I don't cut. That tells me something's off. If I can hit 17 twice, that's good. At least it certifies something. If I hit frame 17 first and then frame 19 the next time, that means something in my approach is wrong. I'm thinking the wrong way about the shot. So I'll ask, What's wrong? Maybe we need more time: I'm not giving enough time to absorb the fact that the actress in the scene is also taking off her coat. She says the line but she's taking off her coat. The line is a thought, but so is "taking off coat."

It takes time for an audience to understand and appreciate both the line of dialogue and the idea of coat-taking-off. I have to allow for that. I now realize I was thinking about only the line of dialogue and not the coat. All right, I will think now about the line *and* the coat, and cut at frame 26. That's where it happens this time. All right. Let me try it again. *Zut!* 26. Okay, good. That's the cut point. And so it goes.

This is the most significant thing that I think I do. If I had to abstract one element from the way I work, I'd say that no matter how you work as an editor, this is a good thing to do. You can have completely different approaches to everything else, but do this.

The wonderful advantage—and it is miraculous to me—is that by doing it you quickly develop instructive feedback. Not only about this particular shot, or film, but about your own talents as an editor. When choosing a cut point, an editor is like somebody playing a violin. . . . There is a bowing technique that you have, that you want to develop and have mastery over, whatever kind of music you're playing. You want to have a touch or a tone.

When I mark frame 17 and the next time frame 19, I have a feeling that goes with each. When I mark frame 19, I feel, Oh, it was a little longer that time—I can feel it. Then, looking at the counter, I realize, That was two frames. In this context, that's what two frames feels like: one-twelfth of a second. But I now have an emotional feeling in my gut about what a twelfth of a second feels like, with these shots in this context, and that's teaching me something.

Throughout all this, you're working with the rhythms of the actors, and the rhythms of the camera moves. You are internalizing everything—the rate of the speech of the actors, how they deliver their lines, how they are physically moving in the space, how the camera is or is not moving in the space. You are taking all this into consideration, and that is what, over a period of time, allows you to begin to assimilate and learn the particular language of this film. What's the rhythmic signature of this scene? And then, of the whole film?

Every time conductors confront a piece of music with a new orchestra, they have to determine the rhythmic signature. An editor is doing that with the film.

O: If you've cut the film at this rhythm, and then you go into the mix, doesn't the work you do in the mix alter the pacing of the scene—if you add, say, a musical touch or the sound of rain, during the mix?

M: Yes. And that's one of the peculiarities of the way I work. When I assemble a scene for the first time, I turn off the sound. Even if it's a dialogue scene. I look at the people's faces and imagine what they're saying and read their body language. Significantly, this envelope of silence allows me to imagine the mix the way it will finally be. I'm allowing the space for these sounds in advance. Even though I'm not sure exactly what they will be.

I find this method essential, because the only sound that's recorded at the time of filming is dialogue and it's sometimes quite rough. You can become mesmerized by the particularities of that sound, which is not the way it's going to be when it's all cleaned up and it has music and sound effects running along with it. It's important for me, when I first assemble a scene, to imagine the music and the sound and the dialogue working together in some ideal dynamic form.

O: So this editing by hitting the seventeenth frame is done in silence?

M: I look at it solely as a piece of silent film, imagining the music and the sound as much as I can. I construct the whole scene silent, run it back silent, and make revisions in silence. Does it work? I turn on the soundtrack and confront the reality of what is now added by the dialogue. Sometimes it's exactly the way I imagined it. Other times, fortuitous things have happened that are much more interesting than what I could have ever achieved intentionally had I been listening to the sound.

Of course, there can be mistakes. I might select a take that is good visually, but without knowing it I was imagining the reading from another take, which is smoother. So I make a correction: I'll use the good sound from that other take and superimpose it over the good visual, so the actor is saying one thing, visually, but the sound is coming from another take. Because that's what I heard in my head when I was putting the scene together. Jean Renoir would have had me burned at the stake! But you try to seize these opportunities, which sometimes come by chance and sometimes from an impression you've gleaned that's deeper than the reality actually in front of you.

This method allows you to superimpose the rhythmic signature of the film on shots that have no internal dynamic at all, which are simply held for length.

In *The Talented Mr. Ripley,* for example, Ripley is sitting on the beach and looks out to sea. There's a shot of the sea. How long do you hold it? You hold it for as long as the thoughts you imagine Ripley is thinking can be held while you are looking at that shot. As I run the sea shot, we're looking at his point of view and we're thinking what Ripley is thinking. When those thoughts have danced in my head, with the image, to this point of fruition, I mark the frame. And then go back and do it all over and hope to hit the same frame. It's still amazing to me that this happens, even though I've been doing it for thirty years. But because the thoughts have their own internal dynamic, which is miraculously invariable, the shot can last for fifteen seconds or more—360 frames—and you can still repeatedly hit exactly the same frame, the 361st.

O: And this mental decision has been set up by your prior knowledge of the way Ripley has been thinking before?

M: Yes. I have internalized the rhythms that the actor has given me, and internalized the rhythms that the camera operator has given me. The camera operator has been internalizing the rhythms that the actor is giving him and the rhythms that the director is giving the camera operator. So all of that is coming into play, and I am now metabolizing all those things and getting to the point where I can superimpose those rhythms even on shots that have no internal dynamics at all—no dialogue, no camera movement, no actors moving.

O: Like the learned habit of a guy who shoots clay pigeons—knowing how long the target needs to be in the air before he raises his gun and points . . .

M: It's very similar to gunslinging. That's the reason I stand when I edit—I'm fully engaged in my body. It's possible but hard to imagine somebody shooting clay pigeons while sitting down. There's something about the engagement of the entire body in the rhythmic motion that allows you to hit the clay pigeon. Similarly, when gunslingers faced one another on D Street in Kansas City, they stood, they didn't sit on chairs and shoot at each other.

From *The Talented Mr. Ripley:* How long do you hold the shot of Ripley looking out to sea— "as long as the thoughts you imagine he is thinking can be held."

"Waiting for Provocation"
by Anthony Minghella

Walter has become inextricably bound up with my ideas about film, with my plans as a filmmaker. His rigour in the cutting room; the standards he has set for himself and expects of his collaborators; the tacit understanding that he is a fellow filmmaker, a peer, not a servant of the director; his profound grasp of every aspect of the filmmaking process—these make him a partner, and an exhilarating one. He has been a writer, he has been a director, he has done pioneering work on the way films sound, and the way they look. Among the many things Walter has taught me is the necessity for every element in the film to work, and to be working in concert. His technique of lining the cutting room with stills extracted from each of the movie's setups is a constant reminder that each cut affects the entire movie, that each sequence lives inside a gestalt, that internal rhymes in a scene have to relate to the larger rhymes.

He has an extraordinary grasp of how music works in a movie, and unusually for Walter, it is not a theoretical strategy. He seems to throw music at the film, carving up cues, subverting their intended placement: a savant with the score. Watching him at work with Gabriel Yared's painstakingly choreographed sketches is, for someone who prides himself on being a musician and possessing a musician's ear, entirely destabilizing. I remember having devised with Gabriel a series of rules to organize the composition of the *English Patient* score, with a particular orchestration delineating scenes at the monastery and in the desert. Walter listened to these cues with a certain detachment, while I explained their intended destinations. He then stood, as he always does, at his editing lectern and laid in cues, apparently randomly, using the Avid to stretch and contract lengths, often not listening to the entire piece, and certainly paying no attention to the map I had out-lined. The results were often startling, always provocative.

This was one of several occasions where one or both of us have left the cutting room with emotions running at danger point. And yet the finished version of the movie reflects as much of Walter's sense of how the score should sound as it does mine or Gabriel's.

And I've learned to relax into this, to wait for these provocations, just as I expect them with the picture. I have no interest, watching dailies, to indicate to Walter how I've imagined a scene will cut, even though I have always planned a cutting sequence. I've come to understand that the joy of film is in letting everybody play and empowering the play. Walter knows who the director is; the director knows he's got an enormous resource and should exploit it.

Ripley has an opening title treatment where "talented" evolves as the final adjective in a rosary of descriptions that have preceded Ripley's name: mysterious, unhappy, fragile, and so so. An attempt to identify the contradictions surrounding this complex character. So: The brilliant, baffling, brittle, loyal, tender, curmudgeonly, impenetrable, wise, wonderful, cheerful, stern, obsessive, loving, abrupt, professorial, encyclopedic, patient, impatient, and essential Mr. Murch.

O: What about the other crucial consideration in editing—where to *begin* a shot?

M: I'd discovered very early, during *The Conversation,* that I was allergic to a certain style of editing, which is called "matching action." That's the standard kind of Hollywood editing, where you cut from one shot to another in the middle of a character's movement. It was considered significant when it was invented, because it seemed to mask the moment of the cut. Somehow the audience was supposed to think this was all continuous action.

When I started out, I obediently tried to work that way, and discovered that I didn't like it. I wound up instead finding places where the movement of the incoming shot was just beginning, like a flower opening up. So my cuts generally are made not at the midpoint but at the beginning of the gesture.

I prefer to initiate the motion in the incoming shot. I'll take a shot right to the point where a character is about to move his head, then cut and initiate that motion in the next shot. There are times when I do not do this, mainly in fight scenes, action scenes.

But on the whole, I'm taking into consideration, at the point of the cut, where the audience's eye is and in what direction it's moving, and with what speed. The editor has to imagine the audience's point of attention when the film is projected, and has to be able to predict where ninety-nine percent of the audience is looking at any moment. You've said you always look at the person typing—the court stenographer in courtroom scenes. You may be the one percent I can't account for. . . ! But by and large I have to be able to say with some certainty that at such-and-such a moment ninety-nine percent of the audience will be looking at this point on the screen, and in the next second they will be looking *here.* That means that their eye is travelling, say, left to right, to the upper corner of the frame, at a certain speed. If I choose to cut at this point—at frame 17—I know that at that moment their eye is right here, in the Cartesian grid of the screen.

That's a very valuable piece of information. When I select the next shot, I choose a frame that has an interesting visual at exactly that point, where the audience's eye is at the moment of the cut, to catch and redirect their attention somewhere else. Every shot has its own dynamic. One of the editor's obligations is to carry, like a sacred vessel, the focus of attention of the audience and move it in interesting ways around the surface of the screen.

However, in the middle of a fight scene, you want to abuse an audience's expectations. You want to send their eye off in one direction, then cut with something that is going completely in the opposite direction, somewhere else. That induces in the audience the sense of visual disorientation you get when you're really physically in a fight with somebody. You don't know where the next punch is coming from. We try to duplicate that feeling visually.

O: And also probably in a love scene.

M: Yes. There is no stage line to love. In a passionate love scene there's actually an advantage to be gained by crossing the stage line as many times as possible. If you look at the dance scene in *Ghost,* after Sam and Molly have been playing with clay and start to dance to the music on the jukebox . . . that's full of cuts that cross the stage line. Each cut, once the dancing gets passionate, puts the characters on the "wrong" side of the frame.

Visually, I'm taking care of the eye, it's rhythmically and sensuously done but— Wait a minute! Isn't she supposed to be on the left and he's supposed to be on the right? No, no, it's the opposite! What that does is put you in the state of mind of making passionate love to somebody—disorientation, spacelessness. You are physical beings, but you have gotten to a spaceless place. By fracturing the grammar of film, in that way, you induce in the audience a little of that same mentality.

If I cut it the way it *should* be cut—according to classical film grammar—it feels kind of flatfooted: these people are doing passionate things and we're just standing outside them, watching them. So we're not as fully involved. But by breaking the rules, you can bring the audience into the madness that is passionate love.

L A S T

C O N V E R S A T I O N

T O R O N T O

In 1928, Walter's father left Toronto to move to the United States. Now, more than seventy years later, Walter was back in the city, accompanied by his son (also named Walter, and himself an assistant editor), to work for several months on the editing of *K-19: The Widowmaker,* a film starring Harrison Ford and Liam Neeson, about a hidden piece of Soviet history—the Chernobyl-type meltdown of Russia's first nuclear submarine. So our final conversation took place in Toronto, in June of 2001.

On his last Sunday we met at my house. In a few days he would be returning to California to finish the editing. Walter, relaxed, spoke about his experiences as a director and scriptwriter. He reminisced about his childhood love for the Oz books; and about his use of the cult book *Wisconsin Death Trip* as a historical source for his *Return to Oz.*

He went on to speculate whether one could perhaps design a notational system for film the way there is one for music, and as our conversations drew to a close, he ended by returning once more to the subject of dreams.

Murch directing Fairuza Balk, who played Dorothy in his film *Return to Oz,* 1985.

BLESSED UNREST

O: I wanted to talk to you about working as a director on *Return to Oz*. Since then—1985—you've continued as an editor but have not gone back to directing. Do you want to direct again? Was that something you felt at ease and comfortable with?

M: I learned something during the process, which is that I'm not temperamentally interested in directing for the sake of directing. *Return to Oz* was a project that was dear to my heart. I initiated it and I am very glad to have made the film, which I think is wonderful and strange in a way that is true to the spirit of the original Oz books. There are some people who love the process of directing for its own sake, of mobilizing large groups of people. Francis is a classic example of that. I'm just not—I'm a more solitary person.

On a moment-by-moment basis, the state of mind that you're in when you're editing is probably very similar to the state of mind the writer is in when reorganizing material he's already written, and deciding what order to put it in and what to truncate.

The advantage of writing and editing is that at any time you can stop what you're doing and walk around the block, or have lunch, or take a phone call, or go dig in the garden and think. At any particular moment, the editor has the freedom to interact or not interact with the material. You can always step away and let the subconscious do some work.

In directing, once the rails have been laid down, you have to pretty much stick to them. If you're shooting a scene, you have to keep shooting it even if it's not working as well as you hoped, and you have to make the best of it no matter what the variables are. I'm exaggerating to make the point. If something *really* isn't working, then of course the director has to stop and rethink. But you're stopping a huge machine when you do that, and there are very large knock-on costs, which reverberate for a long time afterwards.

That leads me to another point. You, as a director, are the audience for whom the actors and the technicians are performing. They're looking to you to see how it's going. Emotionally, you are the litmus test. This is exacerbated by shooting out of sequence—which means an actor is sometimes asked, in a single day, to go from carefree exuberance to crushing grief. And to repeat that exuberance thirty times, then have lunch, and then do crushing grief.

The usual "keel" of continuity that keeps a theatre actor's performance on track is gone. There is no natural keel, because of the fragmentary nature of the filming process. So the director becomes the keel. He has to have the whole film in his head and be able to respond, Yes, this grief is all very well, the actor is right to be grieving, but the grief I'm seeing is too blue, it needs to be a redder grief—whatever that means—because of where the scene is in the film. Because the director has a reference point that is not immediately accessible to everyone else, he knows it's the wrong colour grief, and now must ask the actor to change.

So as a director you must be very much in the present, paying attention to all the minute things everyone is doing. At the same time, you're being surprised by what they're doing—usually in some proportion of good and bad. You try, in shepherding the scene through, to emphasize the good and eliminate or deemphasize the bad, either through something the actor does or through where you put the camera. You then have to balance that against the material that's already been shot and against what's going to be shot. Decisions that you make have to meld with what has gone before, and they will affect things in the future. To be truly effective you have to live simultaneously in the past, the present, and the future.

It's a completely unnatural state of being—for me, anyway. The closest is probably what a general goes through in organizing troops in the middle of combat. You as a writer and I as an editor are allowed, in fact obliged, to sometimes step away. It's not an indulgence, it's an absolute necessity. But a director cannot step away.

0: There's that great story about Chaplin shutting down a film to work out an aesthetic problem. . . .

M: He was a master at that kind of force majeure, and probably did that more often than anyone else in the history of film. Because of who he was, he had unprecedented control over the process, as writer and director and actor. He wrote as he shot. His scripts were not scripts that we would recognize as such. He would stage things and take a lot of time to figure out what was funniest, then look at it later and say, No, it doesn't work, we're going to do it over again.

He probably, for the first and last time, had the kind of freedom as a director that you and I are used to as writer and editor. Because of how incredibly wealthy he was, in terms of both money and power. There really has been nobody like him, before or since.

O: I think it was *City Lights* where he had to solve the problem of how the blind girl could mistake the tramp for a millionaire. And he eventually worked it out that the tramp would cross a crowded street by comically climbing through the cars, in one side and out the other, until he reached the other pavement. The last car he goes through is a limousine, and the blind girl hears that door-slam and misinterprets the tramp's status. So everything hinges on a sound. And yet the film is silent!

M: Even though it's a silent film, it's asking you to listen to how the blind girl would hear it and what the implications are. It was a masterstroke.

O: For me the idea of directing seems like hell: composing, in finite time, on Wimbledon's Centre Court!

M: I remember, in London in 1984, when we'd finished principal photography on *Return to Oz,* Jim Henson threw a July Fourth party in Regent's Park for Americans working on films in the city. While we were eating our hot dogs and watching baseball, Jim asked, Are you happy? I was momentarily taken aback. I thought it was an odd question for one director to ask another. Of course I understood that what he meant was, How are you doing? He didn't mean *happy* in the deeper, literal sense of the word. So I answered, Oh yeah, I'm very happy. Things are great! But later that evening I kept mulling over that question, thinking, What I said was the right social response, but what's the real response to that question—from one director to another? The closest I came was, No, I'm not happy, but I would be absolutely miserable if I were prevented from doing what I'm doing now. Don't stop me—I'm miserable, but don't stop me. I'm miserable in the amazing, cosmic way that a director is miserable.

There's a phrase from something Martha Graham once said about that process. She calls it "blessed unrest." If I were back at that party now, I would say to Jim, Hmm, yes, I'm experiencing blessed unrest.

WRITING
RETURN TO OZ

O: Let's talk about you as a writer!—and writing for film. You wrote *THX 1138* with George Lucas, the sampan scene in *Apocalypse Now,* and *Return to Oz* with Gill Dennis.

M: I've always collaborated on what I've written. *THX* with George, and then the original *Black Stallion* screenplay with Carroll Ballard and Gill Dennis. Then *Return to Oz,* with Gill. Then he and I wrote a screenplay called "Intrusive Burials," which has never been made. We just enjoy working together.

O: I was talking to him the other day, and he said the process of *Return to Oz* was very long. Writing it took about three or four years. Is that right?

M: We wrote the treatment in 1981 and the screenplay a number of months after that. Then, as you know, you go through several drafts. Preproduction started in the spring of 1983 and filming began in the spring of 1984. We were writing throughout that period.

O: Was this a project that you two dreamed up and then approached a studio with? Or did they approach you and say, Are you interested—

M: No. It was a call out of the blue from Tom Wilhite, who was then an executive at Disney. The studio had received a number of shocks to the system, in the mid-to-late 1970s. Mainly in the form of *Star Wars* and *The Black Stallion.* The studio recognized these were exactly the kinds of films they should be making,

but were not. Disney was an almost hermetically sealed studio at that time. You could forget that it was part of Hollywood. If you worked at Disney, you worked only there. And vice versa—they didn't bring people in from the outside. I think that was part of Walt's character, vis-à-vis Hollywood—something that he had fostered and that continued even after his death.

So they looked at *Star Wars* and *Black Stallion* and thought, Hmm, there's something happening out there. It's time to open the doors of the monastery and bring in other people. I was on a list that a film critic for the *L.A. Times* had compiled at Wilhite's behest—a list of people who were not directors now but who might soon be. I guess the Disney people worked their way down to the M's, and I got a call.

They asked what kind of film I'd be interested in that they would also be interested in. And I said, right away, a sequel to *The Wizard of Oz.* For three reasons. I had loved L. Frank Baum's Oz series when I was a child. I also loved the daring of trying to make a sequel. A little like saying, Let's make a sequel to *Gone With the Wind.* It's a classic film. In fact, when *Return to Oz* came out, one of the sticks it was beaten with was, How dare you make a sequel to *The Wizard of Oz?* And how dare you make it in the way you made it? I knew in advance that it was risky.

O: I remember David Cronenberg mentioning—when he was remaking *The Fly*—that everyone cried, Oh my God! How can you do that to such a well-known movie! And he replied, Listen, it's *The Fly,* it's not *Citizen Kane.* But in a way you *were* dealing with a *Citizen Kane.*

M: Certainly as a cultural artifact. *The Wizard of Oz* has a huge cultural sophistication, and there are innumerable points of reference between that film and American society. So I was taking on something pretty heavy-duty.

And the third reason was that after my son, Walter, was born I began watching *Sesame Street,* with the Muppets. I recognized in the Muppets a sensibility and a technical simplicity and sophistication that reminded me of Oz.

Dorothy, Billina, and Tik-Tok from *Return to Oz.*

O: Do you remember when you first read the Oz books?

M: *Ozma of Oz* and *The Land of Oz*—the books that *Return to Oz* were based on—were the very first books I read. I was five years old and I said, I'm going to read a grown-up book all by myself! Meaning a book that had many more words than pictures. My mother had already read me some of the other Oz books. As a girl growing up in Ceylon at the turn of the century, she had been overwhelmed by them. They were the cultural equivalent of Harry Potter now.

My mother was the daughter of two Canadian missionary doctors who had gone to Ceylon in the 1880s to establish a clinic. Her parents would talk about "going home to Canada," and she knew that one day she would go there. And so the Oz books struck a particular nerve, with their journeys back and forth between ordinary and exotic worlds, and their strong but ambiguous evocation

of "home." It was as if my mother was a Dorothy who had been born in Oz and knew she had to go someday to Kansas.

O: Frank Baum was very much a social radical, wasn't he? His books were banned from public libraries in Kansas, I believe.

M: And they still are removed from certain libraries, because they deal with witches—the existence of witches being seen as anti-Christian—not an idea children should deal with. But how many witches are there in the Grimm stories? And they aren't removed. There is something about Baum being quintessentially American, and yet dealing with witches, that unnerves people. Witches are not American. They're European. In Europe, in the Land of Toads and Goblins, that's okay. But don't mix Americana with witches. There's a wonderful dissonance there. It even appealed to me as a four-year-old, when my mother

In an illustration by John R. Neill, Mombi, *far left,* turns the boy Tip back into Princess Ozma, who was supposed to rule the Emerald City. Jean Marsh as Mombi in *Return to Oz.*

read the books to me. Also, Baum deals with marvellous metaphysical questions. He doesn't wink at you from behind these things, or think they are too much for children.

A good example is in *The Tin Woodman of Oz.* The Tin Woodman began as a real human being, who kept losing parts of his body by accident. He chopped off an arm and replaced it with a tin one. Then he chopped off the other arm, again by accident, and replaced that with another tin arm. Then a leg, then the other leg—and he replaced each with a tin version. And finally his head got chopped off, and he put a tin one on. So he ended up being all tin.

The metaphysical question is: Where is the Self? Can the Self survive the dismemberment of the body? A profound question, which people have been debating for many years. If I lose the tip of my finger, am I less myself?

But in *The Tin Woodman of Oz,* Baum adds a twist to the question: The Tin Woodman, in the course of the story, meets his old head, which has been kept in a box, and they have a conversation. The head is understandably angry and complains, You're out there running around, and I'm here in a box! Take me back! And the Tin Woodman replies that he's perfectly happy being all tin. He has to watch out for rust, but he has none of the troubles of the flesh. He doesn't have to eat anything. Clearly what Baum is dealing with is all the bedevilments that the flesh is heir to but the Tin Woodman is now liberated from. In *The Wizard of Oz,* the one human thing he wanted was a heart. He regretted only lacking the ability to feel. In this book, however, the Tin Woodman shuts the box on his old head and walks away. But you have to think, Where is the Self?

There's an ambivalence about the fact that in Oz nothing ever dies. That's

Murch with the Tin Woodman and Jack Pumpkinhead on location in England for *Return to Oz.*

why the Tin Woodman's head can survive in a box. It's a world in which there is dismemberment but no death. Yet think of living forever as a conscious head locked in a box. Hellish! Young as I was the point was not lost on me when I first read that book.

So from a certain point of view—what you might call a traditional, American, optimistic, Christian, hierarchical point of view—Baum's message is anarchic. It's also feminist. All the really creative, interesting people in his books are women. The men, for the most part, are charlatans and fools—the soldiers, the Wizard himself, the demons, the Nome King. The really intelligent, benevolent people are Ozma and Dorothy and Glinda the Good, those wonderful beings who are sensible, and see the truth.

The men who are *real* men, and caring, are artificial creations: Jack Pumpkinhead, the Tin Woodman, Scarecrow, Tik-Tok. They're all metaphors for wounded people who have dismembered and re-created themselves, or people like Jack Pumpkinhead, whose head is always rotting and needing replacement. Think about the metaphysical implications of that! He's a creature brought to life by a magical powder, but every two weeks he has to carve himself a new head and put it on.

For all these reasons, Baum's books have had their adherents and their violent opponents. Because *Return to Oz* was trying to explore those same issues head on—without the relief of songs and the more openly artificial, vaudevillian approach of the 1939 *Wizard*—I think it suffered at the box office. I was tapping into the same kind of opposition Baum himself had encountered. Popular as certain books were, they absolutely were not popular with a part of the American public.

O: Gill Dennis said I should ask you about *Wisconsin Death Trip*. That's a remarkable book, but how does it link up with this?

M: I think it's another reason *Return to Oz* was disturbing to people. Gill had a copy of the book, which was written by Michael Lesy. It's a collage of photographs and newspaper stories from Wisconsin, around 1890, and occasionally a poem from *Spoon River Anthology*. It's a realistic look at what life was like

in that part of the world, just before the turn of the century, very much the world into which a hypothetically real Dorothy would have been born. Once things have passed and become irretrievable, we tend to see them with a hazy, golden glow. If only life could be simple, like it was in the old days! Or, If only people could live on farms and grow their own food!

Above: "There is a beautiful picture I have from *Wisconsin Death Trip* of a girl standing by a river, with her back to us. I always thought of her as the real Dorothy."—Walter Murch

The reality was very different. There was a lot of insanity, disease, barn-burning, and revenge. The human condition at the time. It made me ask: What if the first story, *The Wizard of Oz*, had really happened, reported by a local newspaper? That a tornado came and blew an old couple's house away, destroyed it—which happened all the time—and a girl, the niece of the couple, survived and when she was finally found, miraculously alive, she had a story to tell about where she'd been. What would her aunt and uncle think? What would be the real conditions for that family? What if they had to build a new house, take out a second mortgage? And the uncle had broken his leg in the tornado, and was trying to survive as a farmer? And their niece kept talking about this magical place she'd been. They'd say, Don't talk like that, there isn't a place like that! What should she do? Should she deny that it had happened to her? That's Dorothy's dilemma at the beginning of our film. *Return to Oz* is a fusion of the reality of *Wisconsin Death Trip* and the fantasy of *Ozma of Oz*.

And another big influence was Willa Cather's *My Antonia*. I even went to visit her house in Red Cloud, Nebraska. . . .

O: When you and Gill wrote the script together, did you work on it as a pair constantly, or separately?

M: Separately. We'd develop the outline together then divide it in half and write each half separately. Then we'd meet, read it together and give each other notes, and switch. I would rewrite his part and he would rewrite mine. It was literary musical chairs. We're very congenial to each other's sensibilities.

O: The claymation in the film was wonderful.

M: At the time I was wondering how I was going to cope with the Nome King and his army of Nomes—in the book, they're all two-foot-high round creatures who run around in grey costumes, with little beards and pickaxes. I was horrified at the thought of finding myself on the shooting stage with a hundred dwarves—I didn't want to do that, I wanted something else, something more magical. Luckily I saw Will Vinton's claymation at a film festival. I sent him a copy of the script, along with my idea that the Nomes were spirits living in rock, should *be* rock, and capable of emerging from it in sometimes human form. He thought it was a great idea. His studio had been struggling with the nature of clay—trying to make it seem like flesh. And here was a chance for them to let it be what it really is: a malleable form of rock.

O: What about characters like Tik-Tok and Jack Pumpkinhead? Did you use the illustrations in Baum's book as a model?

M: I tried to make all the art direction and the characters—with the exception of the Nomes—as close to the original illustrations as possible. My mother had especially loved the sequel books, which were illustrated by John Rea Neill. He had a very different style from that of W. W. Denslow, the illustrator of the original *Wizard of Oz.* Baum and Denslow had a creative and financial falling out, so Baum hired Neill, a young illustrator from Philadelphia. From the beginning, my association with the world of Oz was inspired by Neill.

Clockwise: The Nome king from *Return to Oz,* whose army of Nomes were created as claymation by Will Vinton; a scene with the Gump from the film. Dorothy, Tik-Tok, the Scarecrow, Jack Pumpkinhead, and the Tin Woodman fly in the Gump in an original illustration by John R. Neill.

O: The talent to edit and the talent to conceive or write a film, how distinct are they?

M: Pretty distinct. Everyone creative has elements of both. The editorial part of me is fairly muscular, but the other part—the generative part—is weaker, more undernourished. Or becomes frightened of the muscularity of the editorial part.

So when I'm writing I have to find a way to let these two parts work safely with each other. Born writers—well, they're people who, by some fluke, have those two aspects of their mind in perfect harmony. Without even being conscious of it, they are generating and editing at the same time, in perfect modulation. It's like those double-barrelled tubes of epoxy glue, which dole out the resin and the hardener in equal amounts.

In my case, I realized the danger was that I would come up with an idea and then, immediately, the editorial part of me would begin to attack it. And you never get anywhere that way. On the other hand, if the generative part of you is very strong and the editorial part weak, you wind up with lots of words but a lack of structure and precision to the ideas.

When I write a script, I lie down—because that's the opposite of standing up. I stand up to edit, so I lie down to write. I take a little tape recorder and, without being aware of it, go into a light hypnotic trance. I pretend the film is finished and I'm simply describing what was happening. I start out chronologically but then skip around. Anything that occurs to me, I say into the recorder. Because I'm lying down, because my eyes are closed, because I'm not looking at anything, and the ideas are being captured only by this silent scribe—the tape recorder—there's nothing for me to criticize. It's just coming out.

That is my way of disarming the editorial side. Putting myself in a situation that is as opposite as possible to how I edit—both physically and mentally. To encourage those ideas to come out of the woods like little animals and drink at the pool safely, without feeling that the falcon is going to come down and tear them apart.

O: It's a bloodthirsty profession!

O: I know you're interested in the idea of a theory of notation for the staging of scenes in film.

M: Well, I've a hunch that some systematic approach to cinematic notation is possible but has yet to be developed.

As we discussed earlier, I think filmmakers are somewhat like those cathedral builders in the Middle Ages, who had a hands-on yet mystically intuitive sense of the dynamics and physics of supporting such a vast structure on such slender columns. The buildings are still standing. But if they'd been asked to write down the rules for doing it, I don't know that they *could* have done so.

Music was in that state in the tenth century—there was no modern system of notation. The music somehow evolved and then it was passed on by imitation. Somebody would sing it, and then everyone would imitate that, and it would progress. Then, early in the eleventh century, Guido d'Arezzo had this fabulous insight that you could actually write down the music.

The fact that these sounds, which were ethereal, religious tones, could somehow be captured by dots is remarkable. It's just as remarkable as the invention of writing words or of recording sound.

The ability to write music clearly began to influence the kind of music that was written, just as the invention of writing changed the nature of the stories that were told.

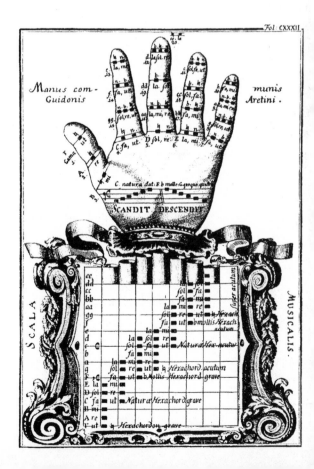

The eleventh-century Benedictine monk Guido d'Arezzo (990–1050) devised a system of musical notation using the Guidonian hand.

O: And what was told or recited originally depended on how much you could remember. When it's written, you can splinter that tale much more, refer back or leap forwards. . . .

M: Right. It becomes much more synaptic. There are more detailed connections that can be made. That's what happened to music. Before notation, there was no polyphony. People didn't sing two or three different harmonic lines at the same time. It was just too much for the mind to deal with—aside from the fact that it was considered irreligious. Nonetheless, once it was on the page, you could write another line that would be harmonic with the first and have somebody else sing that line. Then have the other instrument do something else. They would all flow together in a complex pattern. Western music of the last eight hundred years is a continuous elaboration of Guido's insight.

So here we are, making films for a hundred years, and we haven't got our Guido d'Arezzo yet. But perhaps one way to imagine a notational system for film is to look at something like the I Ching, the ancient Chinese system for forecasting the future.

O: How would the I Ching relate to film?

M: Well, more profoundly, the I Ching is an attempt to grapple with the complexity of the human condition by breaking it down to sixty-four different states, symbolized by patterns called hexagrams. (Sixty-four being a significant number, by the way—large, but not overwhelmingly so. Think of the chessboard with its optimal sixty-four squares. Or the fact that the DNA code of life is written in sixty-four possible three-letter words.) The relevant hexagram is chosen by chance, by six tosses of three coins. Each hexagram has a name corresponding to a state of being: The Creative, The Receptive, Difficulty at the Beginning, Youthful Folly, et cetera. And with each name there's an accompanying Judgement and explanation.

Despite its surface, film drama is also an attempt to deal with the complexity of the human condition in a fundamentally structured way. A number of years ago, I began to wonder if there was a connection, as unlikely as it might seem, between the structure of the I Ching's hexagrams and the staging of scenes in motion pictures. The film that triggered this question was *Absence of Malice*, directed by Sydney Pollack, and the scene in particular was a secret meeting between a businessman under investigation, played by Paul Newman, and the district attorney of Miami.

Newman was momentarily the weaker character—he wanted something that the DA was reluctant to give—and the camera put him on the right side of the frame, looking off screen left at the DA.

But the DA, surprisingly, was placed on the same side of the frame as Newman, so at the point of the cut his image landed on Newman's with a thump, as if to say "*No!*" To intensify the rejection implicit in the framing, the DA was mostly facing away and his body was turned away from Newman who was thus being triply rejected.

The scene ran around in my head for a couple of days and then it suddenly came together into a system of organization. A kind of miniature Guido d'Arezzo idea, that you could write down the staging of a scene in a very simple code, a code based on two binary triads: for each character there are three questions, and each question has a Yes or No answer.

For Newman the three questions were: (1) Is he looking at the DA? (2) Is his body facing the DA? And (3) Does the way he is framed accommodate or reject the DA? For Newman the answers are: Yes, Yes, Yes.

The equivalent three questions about the publisher would be answered: No, No, No.

I suddenly made the connection with the I Ching: that's exactly how it's organized—two Yes/No trigrams. The I Ching has Yin and Yang where I had Yes and No, and writes Yin with a broken line and Yang with a solid line.

In any film scene there's a petitioner and a grantor, a weaker character and a stronger. Otherwise you don't have a scene. It may be obvious what the power relationship is, or it may be hidden from one or even both of the characters themselves. So at each moment in every scene there is a dynamic between two people that can be expressed in many ways.

In *Absence of Malice* we have the powerful DA as grantor and Newman, the hero, as petitioner. The DA's three lines are: No, No, No.

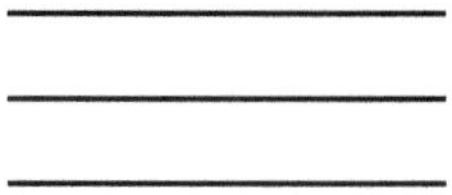

―――――――――
―――――――――
―――――――――

And Newman's three lines are: Yes, Yes, Yes.

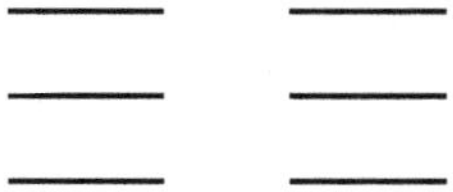

―――   ―――
―――   ―――
―――   ―――

In the I Ching the more powerful trigram is placed on top, and the weaker trigram on the bottom, so in its complete form, the scene in *Absence of Malice* would look like this—the twelfth hexagram, Standstill:

―――――――――
―――――――――
―――――――――
―――   ―――
―――   ―――
―――   ―――

The judgement for the hexagram Standstill reads: *The evil will not prosper. Through perseverance, the superior person will attain his goals. The strong depart; the weak approach.*

There are obviously many shadings to something as oracular as this, but it might be interpreted: *The DA will not prosper, and Newman, through perseverance, will attain his goals.* Which is very close, in fact, to the underlying truth of the scene.

It would be an interesting exercise to take a script, throw the I Ching for every scene, and read what the hexagrams have to suggest about the potential stagings of those scenes and the accompanying human condition. At the very least, it would be provocative!

0: It's interesting in terms of the opening of *The Godfather.* Vito Corleone, Brando's character, at first appears so worried and hesitant, though he holds the power, while the "petitioner" pleads clearly and efficiently.

M: Exactly. Sometimes the objectively weaker character appears stronger, and vice versa—then as the scene progresses there is a surprising reversal. There are many examples of the creative manipulation of these fundamental staging elements in both *Godfather I* and *Godfather II.* There's that scene in *Godfather I* between Kay and Michael, at the hotel.

O: With Kay at the left edge of the frame and Michael having all the space behind him to the right.

M: In that scene Kay is a petitioner—she's asking to be allowed to go with Michael when he visits his father in the hospital, and Michael is reluctant to let her. He is trying to be nice and not hurt her feelings, particularly in the first half of the scene. He is looking at her, facing her, and the framing of his shots accommodates her. Yes, Yes, Yes. She is also Yes, Yes, Yes to him.

But she keeps asking to tag along, until he has to take a more definite position. He gets up for his coat—he's still nice to her, still facing her, but when he sits down, his framing has changed: it is now short-sided. He is still looking at her, still facing her, but his framing is rejecting her: Yes, Yes, No. When the two shots are cut together, his image lands right on top of her, and there is a big empty space to the right of frame, the space into which Michael is going to turn when he leaves the room to go see his father. With that empty space, the family has made an invisible entrance into the room and is making its presence felt.

The wonderful thing is that as far as Kay is concerned, Michael is still looking at her and facing her. Nothing has changed, apparently. Deeper down, though, invisible but more powerful, something *has* changed. We all know the feeling. The use and orchestration of this kind of framing gives filmmakers a powerful tool to comment on, undercut, or amplify what is being said or communicated overtly between the characters.

O: It's a chess game.

M: It's exactly that. One of the greatest practitioners of this is Sidney Lumet. If you look at his breakthrough film, *12 Angry Men,* it's all about orchestrating the

staging of twelve people—twelve jurors—in a room, and having that staging reflect what is being said on the surface and the hidden meanings and tensions just below the surface.

O: Twelve men in a room, unable to leave, could at first suggest very limited dramatic possibilities.

M: It would obviously be unwatchable if everyone simply sat around the table, facing each other, and said their lines of dialogue. But what makes it a fascinating, classic film is that you see Lumet fully developing the relationship between the people and then the relationship between the people and the camera. The task of the camera in his films is not only to record but to reveal the hidden agenda, the hidden psychology—psychology that may even be hidden from the characters themselves, but which he's revealing to us.

Henry Fonda in, *far left*, *12 Angry Men*: director Sidney Lumet had to stage the twelve jurors in the room to reflect barely disguised tensions. Kristin Scott Thomas as Katharine and Ralph Fiennes as Almásy have their first dance in *The English Patient*. Garbo, *center*, dancing the Chica-choca in George Cukor's *Two-Faced Woman*, 1941.

O: What about something like the seemingly formal dance sequence in *The English Patient*—with Kristin Scott Thomas and Ralph Fiennes? These two people are hanging on to each other . . . but there's a continual battle and change in the relationship happening there.

M: Formal dance is a wonderfully special case. The custom of the dance forces you to move in a certain way—social convention forces your body to face the other person. That's the nature of it, even if you don't like your dancing partner. But your head—and specifically your eyes—can avoid or confront. And the framing also—how people are framed within the context of the larger dance—can reveal a great deal.

O: When Anthony filmed that dance sequence, was it one shot? It felt like one intense shot.

M: No, it was four or five.

O: So what were the subliminal issues in that scene when you cut it? How did you read it?

M: We wonder why Katharine would dance with Almásy—she could have said, No, I'm tired, but she accepted. She's obviously attracted to him, but afraid of that attraction. So she spends a certain amount of time during the dance not looking at him. She's talking to him but not looking at him. Then, since her body is forced to face him, the moment that she *does* look at him becomes very powerful. The only freedom of movement she has is either to avert her eyes or to gaze at him.

O: But what she *says* is argumentative. Even though the intimate dance continues.

M: That's the great thing about all of this! Katharine's words can be, I hate you—but I'm not looking at you, which means I'm actually saying I love you.

And my body is facing you, so I really do love you. Then again, this can be framed in an unreceptive way to say, I really don't love you after all.

Thus you add harmonic richness to the scene. Because we want film mostly to be interestingly argumentative, through the words that are being said and the emotions that are being expressed.

We've taken the line of development from the screenplay, and now it's being orchestrated into visual, spatial, rhythmic, and sonic terms. What makes it appealing is to show and to develop the ambiguities, and then, by the end of the scene or the film, to resolve them in some way.

O: It would be fun to take this kind of frame structuring and apply it to screwball comedies, which are so sedate sexually but so anarchic in their physical slapstick that somehow it all leads to bonding. A film like *The Lady Eve*—where you've got a passive Henry Fonda and a quick-witted, high-strung Barbara Stanwyck going after him—results in a lot of physical leaping around, with lovers locked in a small cabin with a possibly dangerous snake, et cetera. . . .

In something like the love scene between Katharine and Almásy at the Christmas party in *The English Patient,* where there are moral and social forces

Two madcap scenes from *The Lady Eve:* a high-strung Barbara Stanwyck, *far left* and *center,* in pursuit of a rather passive Henry Fonda; *The English Patient:* "The love scene at the Christmas party is dangerous."

surrounding the two of them, did you play any part in choreographing all those dramatic angles when you cut the scene?

M: A lot of those elements are of course largely determined by what I'm given. By how the director, the cameramen, and the actors have shot the scene. Sometimes, as an editor, you can change the staging. But only in a limited way. Whereas when the director is arranging the actors relative to each other and to the camera, that's when you're really grappling with those elements. But on the other hand, some things happen accidentally, and the editor can take advantage of that.

The love scene at the Christmas party is dangerous, because of what's happening. It's Christmas, after all, and Almásy and Katharine are an adulterous couple making love in a semi-public place. If somebody came around the corner at the wrong time, it would be a disaster. The sexual charge of the scene is enhanced, complicated by the danger. Not only is there complexity in the physical geography of the party—how they meet, what he says to her, and where they go—the *soundscape* of that scene is very complex. There is Arabic music and there are people singing Christmas carols, improbably, in Cairo. A very English party. Then there is the love theme, the orchestral music. All three are going on at the same time.

O: And sometimes one is more powerful than the other, so we *hear* the shift in the power structure of the various emotions.

M: Right! I would say that in that particular scene the collision of emotions, the contradictory mess of emotions, is being amplified more by the soundtrack than by anything I am doing in the picture editing.

You can achieve the same kind of thing with, for example, costume. The costume designer can say, This character Tom Ripley wants to be a certain kind of person, but he really is another kind of person. So I'm going to dress him in a way that reveals, profoundly but subtly, the contradiction in him. Everything is perfect, except his shoes. . . . When you look at his shoes, you realize he's not the person he has presented himself to be. The director and the cameraman and the actor can take advantage of that by having him cross his legs and unconsciously reveal to the world that his shoes are wrong. Or is he aware of the fact that his shoes are wrong, and does he try to hide them?

You can achieve this kind of thing also with art direction—how the set of a person's room can reveal and amplify the desires and contradictions of that character. What we're discussing here really should be developed at every level, from the staging, the casting, the photography, the sound, the music, the editing, the costuming, the art design, the props. . . .

In making a film you're trying to get the most interesting orchestration of all these elements, which, like music, need to be harmonic yet contradictory. If they're completely contradictory, then there's chaos. It's like when instruments are tuning up before a performance, you can't make anything coherent out of it. It's a fascinating, evocative sound, but only for about fifteen seconds. If, on the other hand, all the instruments play the same notes—if they're too harmonic, in other words—yes, there's coherence, but I'm bored after a few minutes. Just as bored as with the chaos of tuning up.

A symphony can last for an hour or more because the composer and the performers have developed a harmonic argument, musical questions and answers and contradictions, affirmations and resolutions, all tumbling together in a continually surprising and yet ultimately self-evident way.

A film is really trying to do the same thing, by bringing together all the different cinematic crafts, *including* music.

O: I'm remembering your early edited versions of that Christmas scene in *The English Patient*. In the last stages, just before the mix, there was a huge leap—there was now a sort of upheaval of sounds: romantic music, singing, then the cupboard banging behind Katharine. A huge landscape or soundscape being choreographed. As editor, you at that point are the orchestra leader, deciding how long to hold the cut of Almásy's arm on her thigh, how brief the look on her face will be—

M: And what music will be played at that moment. That's something I would at least sketch out. When the sound editor, Pat Jackson, and I discussed it, I said that it would be great to have the sound of a cupboard banging. That provides a rhythmic element, it accentuates the rhythm of the lovemaking, but also adds an element of danger—they're making a sound that can be heard. If everyone stopped singing, people would hear it, and Katharine and Almásy would be discovered. They're able to make love in a passionate, noisy way, and Ralph Fiennes and Kristin Scott Thomas really give themselves over completely to that moment. That's the essential foundation on which everything else is built.

O: I remember Anthony Minghella talking about how as the director he had to choreograph the lovemaking scene. He gave the actors very specific directions. He charted out each individual movement, which gave them a greater freedom to *act,* so they didn't have to worry about inventing or have to compose the movements themselves. Then in the editing stage you performed another sort of choreography on a three-dimensional level, finessing what you were given.

M: I guess what I'm trying to get at with all this—the I Ching business included—is that films, when they work, are functioning at a complex level of harmonic interaction—of sounds and images and acting and costume and art direction and photography and on and on. At the beginning we have a script which, complex as it may be, is like a simple melodic line, but we don't yet have an orchestrated score. The director—who is the closest we have to the conductor of the piece, visually speaking—doesn't have a way of orchestrating all these things except through talking and instruction by example and sometimes, it seems, through some kind of divine intervention. If every decision that had to be made on the film had to be articulated, spelled out in detail, the film would never get done. . . .

O: But surely on one level, the lack of rules and codes, and the lack of a too premeditated theory is what keeps film alive. Obviously film is an *art* form and it's a *made* form, but what's wonderful about film is how it also catches an uncontrolled reality. There's the chance of the accidental, which then can be selected, chosen, and shaped by the director and the editor. But to begin with something too controlled . . . it's why I cannot stand cartoons, which are a hundred percent premeditated, totally manipulative, and therefore completely artificial.

M: It's true. That's the amazing thing about film. I suspect it's impossible to have a cinematic Guido d'Arezzo, but who knows? In the fifth century, who would have predicted modern musical notation?

When you look at all the things that have to be done, within such a short period of time, and they all have to harmonize in a structured yet wonderfully random way. . . . Filmmakers are dependent on luck to a great degree, even perhaps on Sheldrake's morphic resonance: somehow just being in the same place, thinking about the same things, causes people of very different natures to start to spontaneously align themselves, like iron filings onto a magnet. Otherwise, I just don't know how it's possible to do what we do.

A WONDERFUL LINE FROM RILKE

O: Do you think success and failure can distort the lessons an artist is able to learn?

M: There's that wonderful line of Rilke's, "The point of life is to fail at greater and greater things." Recognizing that all our achievements are doomed, in one sense—the earth will be consumed by the sun in a billion years or so—but in another sense the purpose of our journey is to go farther each time. So you're trying things out in every film you make, with the potential of failure. I think we're always failing, in Rilke's sense—we know there's more potential that we haven't realized. But because we're trying, we develop more and more talent, or muscles, or strategies to improve, each time.

Every film has lessons to teach us—if we receive those lessons in the right way. That's the trick. It's especially tricky, I think, in worlds where there's either complete rejection or complete adoration, inexplicable anonymity or soul-destroying celebrity. How do you deal with that? Those things obviously have an emotional impact that is undeniable.

I could see the danger of great success very clearly when I went to Disney Studios in 1980, when we were talking about doing *Return to Oz*. Walt Disney had been dead for about fifteen years, but he was such a presence that everything he'd said—even the most accidental comment—was the word of God. He had been screening dailies once for a live-action film, and he happened to ask: What was the f-stop on this shot? The f-stop determines the depth of field— how much is in focus. Someone answered 5.6. Disney said, I like that. Enough is in focus, but not too much, it's just right. Somebody took that to heart, and it became an edict. So every film at Disney Studios had to have the exteriors shot at an f-stop of 5.6, to give the Disney depth of field.

Whether Disney himself approved of that, or whether he would be horrified to learn that the answer to an accidental question was copied down by one of his monks and became part of the liturgy of Disney Studios, I don't know. When something is successful, everything that went into it, both the good and the bad, tends to get bundled up as the recipe for how to make a success. It becomes very difficult to separate out what was true and what was untrue, what was good and what was bad, what was superficial and what was profound.

The idea of this kind of success—of people liking his paintings, of getting frozen into a certain mould as a result—so terrified van Gogh that it contributed to his mental imbalance and suicide. What he wanted to do was to investigate. He secretly enjoyed the freedom that poverty and anonymity gave him.

The distortions of failure, of course, are the opposite: instead of having everything unjustly accepted, everything is rejected. Or that's the risk, at any rate. Truly great lessons can be learned from work that fails, but failure is stamped on the product and there's a tendency to think everything you did was wrong, and you vow not to go there again. You have to resist this impulse, just as you have to resist the syrupy entanglements of success. These are, almost, religious issues. What the world thinks is a success, what it rewards, has sometimes very little to do with the essential content of the work and how it relates to the author and his own development.

O: That's probably one reason I don't reread my books after they come out. So that my memory of *Anil's Ghost* or *The English Patient* or *In the Skin of a Lion* is of my emotional relationship to the book just before it came out. You are hanging fire. You don't know if it's going to work or not, but this is the best you can do at this point. After that, as Wordsworth said, it may or may not be pudding. . . .

M: Yeah. It's important to hold fast in this hanging-fire state. That's the only thing, in the long run, that will allow the true lessons to emerge. It may take years for you to recognize them.

O: And there's always something I remember in a previous book that I was not able to get right. That's what I somehow carry with me into the next work—I'll have to deal with that the next time. There was a moment in *In the Skin of a Lion* that I couldn't quite get—to do with the death of Ambrose Small and his strange solitude during his last days. Now I can look back and see that much of Almásy's situation in *The English Patient* came from that "lack" in the earlier book.

DREAMS

O: I'm going to ask you one last question, about dreams. I'm curious whether sound—since you work so much with it in your waking life—is a central part of your mind in the sleep state. Is sound more evident in your dreams than in other people's?

M: I don't think so. Dreams have a funny absence of sound for me. I'm trying to remember—I think I had a dream six months ago in which sound was important.

But a funny thing happens to me, especially in the final stages of making a film. Everything is aiming towards a specific goal and you have to be alive to the moment, creatively, but you also have to pare things down to their essential nature because you have to meet that deadline. Things that earlier you would have investigated, now you can't. In those times, I rarely dream. The film itself so preoccupies the dreaming part of my mind that it's as if terrorists had come and taken control of the airport. All the dreams that are waiting to land can't land.

When I finish a film, there's a blank period of about a week. Then, very quickly, particular kinds of dreams start coming, and for about a month I live in a state where the dreams are so intense and so real that I'm exhausted when I wake up in the morning.

O: Are these dreams anything to do with the film you've done?

M: No.

O: It's all new material?

M: New stuff. What's striking about the dreams, and what's also exhausting about them, is that they don't have the lightness of dreams. They are anti-filmic dreams. Dreams and film share the ability to skip from one place to another with great levity. Suddenly we're in the Grand Canyon! Before, we were walking through the jungle, but here we are in the Grand Canyon. Why? What's the story?

These postfilm dreams have a plodding reality to them. If I'm dreaming that I'm in a room this big, when I cross the room every step is acted out, laboured over. Step, step, step, step. Then I'll talk to you over in that corner. Then we'll get a cup of coffee. Then step, step, step, step, step, step back again. I guess the dreams are compensating in a way for the "lightness" of film, which is that skipping around.

O: Maybe during the edit you have been the Tin Woodman cutting off all those extra limbs of human time.

M: Yes!

O: Now you're back in a slower reality.

M: The dreams become impatient with me. They're waiting to come in, and they can't, because something else—the film—is occupying that space. Only when that space is empty can they come in. And they come in to redress the situation. They are, it seems, relentlessly temporal. . . .

THE END

MISCELLANY

The Rain People (1969), sound montage and re-recording mixer. American Zoetrope/ Warner Bros. Written and directed by Francis Ford Coppola; starring James Caan, Shirley Knight, Robert Duvall, Marya Zimmet, Tom Aldredge

Gimme Shelter (1970), camera. Maysles Films/Cinema 5. Directed by Albert Maysles, David Maysles, and Charlotte Zwerin; starring the Rolling Stones, Ike and Tina Turner, Jefferson Airplane, the Flying Burrito Brothers, The Grateful Dead

THX 1138 (1970), co-writer, sound montage, and re-recording mixer. American Zoetrope/ Warner Bros. Written by George Lucas and Walter Murch; directed by George Lucas; starring Robert Duvall, Donald Pleasence, Maggie McOmie, Don Pedro Colley, Ian Wolfe

The Godfather (1972), supervising sound editor. American Zoetrope/Paramount. Written by Francis Ford Coppola and Mario Puzo, from the book by Mario Puzo; directed by Francis Ford Coppola; starring Marlon Brando, Al Pacino, James Caan, Richard Castellano, John Cazale, Diane Keaton, Talia Shire, Robert Duvall, Richard Conte, Sterling Hayden, John Marley

American Graffiti (1973), sound montage and re-recording mixer. Lucasfilm/The Coppola Company/Universal. Written by George Lucas, Willard Huyck, and Gloria Katz, and directed by George Lucas; starring Richard Dreyfuss, Ronny Howard, Paul LeMat, Charlie Martin Smith, Cindy Williams, Candy Clark, Mackenzie Phillips

The Conversation (1974), film editor, sound montage and re-recording mixer. American Zoetrope/The Coppola Company and The Directors Company/Paramount. Written and directed by Francis Ford Coppola; starring Gene Hackman, John Cazale, Allen Garfield, Frederic Forrest, Cindy Williams

The Godfather, Part II (1974), sound montage and re-recording mixer. American Zoetrope/The Coppola Company/Paramount. Written by Francis Ford Coppola and Mario Puzo, from the book by Mario Puzo; directed by Francis Ford Coppola; starring Al Pacino, Robert Duvall, Diane Keaton, Robert De Niro, John Cazale, Talia Shire, Lee Strasberg, Michael V. Gazzo, Troy Donahue

Julia (1977), film editor. Twentieth Century–Fox. Written by Alvin Sargent, from the book *Pentimento* by Lillian Hellman; directed by Fred Zinnemann; starring Jane Fonda, Vanessa Redgrave, Jason Robards, Maximilian Schell, Hal Holbrook, Rosemary Murphy, Meryl Streep, Cathleen Nesbitt, Maurice Denham

Apocalypse Now (1979), film editor, sound design and re-recording mixer. Omni/American Zoetrope/Paramount. Written by John Milius and Francis Ford Coppola; directed by Francis Ford Coppola; starring Marlon Brando, Robert Duvall, Martin Sheen, Frederic Forrest, Albert Hall, Laurence Fishburne, Sam Bottoms, Dennis Hopper

Dragonslayer (1981), re-recording mixer. Walt Disney/Paramount. Written by Hal Barwood and Matthew Robbins; directed by Matthew Robbins; starring Peter MacNicol, Caitlin Clarke, Ralph Richardson, John Hallam, Peter Eyre, Albert Salmi

Return to Oz (1985), co-writer and director. Walt Disney/Silver Screen Partners. Written by Gill Dennis and Walter Murch, from the books *Land of Oz* and *Ozma of Oz* by L. Frank Baum; directed by Walter Murch; starring Fairuza Balk, Jean Marsh, Nicol Williamson, Piper Laurie, Matt Clark

Captain Eo. (1986), editor. LucasFilm/Disney. Written and directed by Francis Ford Coppola. Starring Michael Jackson, Anjelica Huston, Dick Shawn

The Unbearable Lightness of Being (1987), supervising film editor. Saul Zaentz/Orion. Written by Jean-Claude Carrière and Philip Kaufman, from the book by Milan Kundera; directed by Philip Kaufman; starring Daniel Day-Lewis, Juliette Binoche, Lena Olin, Derek de Lint, Erland Josephson, Daniel Olbrychski

Call from Space (1989), film editor. A Showscan Co. film. Written by Chris Langham and Sarah Paris; directed by Richard Fleischer; starring Bill Campbell, James Coburn, Charlton Heston

Ghost (1990), film editor and re-recording mixer. IP/Paramount/Howard W. Koch. Written by Bruce Joel Rubin; directed by Jerry Zucker; starring Patrick Swayze, Demi Moore, Whoopi Goldberg, Tony Goldwyn, Stanley Lawrence, Christopher J. Keene, Susan Breslau, Martina Degnan

The Godfather, Part III (1990), film editor and re-recording mixer. Paramount/Zoetrope. Written by Francis Ford Coppola and Mario Puzo, from the book by Mario Puzo; directed by Francis Ford Coppola; starring Al Pacino, Diane Keaton, Talia Shire, Andy Garcia, Eli Wallach, Joe Mantegna, George Hamilton, Bridget Fonda, Sofia Coppola, Raf Vallone, Franc D'Ambrosio, Donal Donnelly, Richard Bright, Helmut Berger, Don Novello

The Godfather Trilogy: 1901–1980, editor. Paramount Pictures. Re-edit of *The Godfather* (1972); *The Godfather, Part II* (1974); *and The Godfather, Part III* (1990) into one film. Written by Francis Ford Coppola and Mario Puzo; directed by Francis Ford Coppola

House of Cards (1993), film editor and re-recording mixer. A&M Films/Penta. Written and directed by Michael Lessac and Robert Jay Litz; starring Kathleen Turner, Tommy Lee Jones, Park Overall, Shiloh Strong, Asha Menina, Esther Rolle, Michael Horse, Anne Pitoniak

Romeo Is Bleeding (1994), film editor and re-recording mixer. Working Title/Polygram. Written by Hilary Henkin; directed by Peter Medak; starring Gary Oldman, Lena Olin, Annabella Sciorra, Juliette Lewis, Roy Scheider, David Proval, Will Patton

I Love Trouble (1994), co–film editor. Caravan/Touchstone/Buena Vista. Written by Nancy Meyers and Charles Shyer; directed by Charles Shyer; starring Julie Roberts, Nick Nolte, Saul Rubinek, James Rebhorn, Robert Loggia, Kelly Rutherford, Olympia Dukakis, Marsha Mason, Charles Martin Smith

Crumb (1994), re-recording mixer. Artificial Eye/Superior. Directed by Terry Zwigoff; starring Robert Crumb, Aline Kominsky, Charles Crumb, Maxon Crumb, Dana Crumb, Beatrice Crumb

First Knight (1995), film editor and re-recording mixer. Columbia/Zucker Brothers. Written by William Nicholson; directed by Jerry Zucker; starring Sean Connery, Richard Gere, Julia Ormond, Ben Cross, Liam Cunningham, Christopher Villiers, Valentine Pelka, John Gielgud

The English Patient (1996), film editor and re-recording mixer. Saul Zaentz/Miramax/Tiger Moth/Miramax. Written by Anthony Minghella, from the book by Michael Ondaatje; directed by Anthony Minghella; starring Ralph Fiennes, Juliette Binoche, Willem Dafoe, Kristin Scott Thomas, Naveen Andrews, Colin Firth, Julian Wadham, Jürgen Prochnow

Touch of Evil (1998), restoration film editing and sound. Universal International. Restoration of 1958 film written and directed by Orson Welles, from the book by Whit Masterson; starring Charlton Heston, Janet Leigh, Orson Welles, Akim Tamiroff, Ray Collins, Dennis Weaver, Marlene Dietrich, Joseph Calleia

The Talented Mr. Ripley (1999), editor and re-recording mixer. Mirage/Miramax/Paramount. Written and directed by Anthony Minghella, from the book by Patricia Highsmith; starring Matt Damon, Gwyneth Paltrow, Jude Law, Cate Blanchett, Philip Seymour Hoffman, Jack Davenport, James Rebhorn, Sergio Rubini, Philip Baker Hall, Rosario Fiorello, Stefania Rocca

Apocalypse Now Redux (2001), film editor and re-recording mixer. American Zoetrope/Miramax

K-19: The Widowmaker (2002), film editor and re-recording mixer. First Light/Intermedia/Paramount. Written by Christopher Kyle and Louis Nowra; directed by Kathryn Bigelow; starring Harrison Ford, Liam Neeson, Peter Sarsgaard, Joss Ackland, Ravil Issyanov

ACKNOWLEDGEMENTS

I would like to thank Shelley Wanger and Louise Dennys who worked with me on this book almost from the start, and also Aggie Murch who inspired me with that first three-way interview, and who later helped find and clarify many of the personal photographs in this book. Thank you to George Lucas, Francis Coppola, Rick Schmidlin, and Anthony Minghella for their personal thoughts about Walter Murch. The remarks by George Lucas and Rick Schmidlin are drawn from their comments made at a tribute to Walter at the Academy of Motion Pictures in Los Angeles, in October 2000. The statement by Francis Coppola is made up partly from comments at that event and partly from an interview he gave me. Anthony Minghella's remarks were written especially for this book.

I would like to thank all at Knopf in New York and Vintage Canada in Toronto, especially Kathy Hourigan, Susan Roxborough, Carol Carson, Kapo Ng, and Deirdre Molina. Also Rick Simon, Darren Wershler-Henry, and Stan Bevington at Coach House Press in Toronto. For transcribing the many hours of taped conversations, thank you to Donya Peroff. For photo research, thank you to Ann Schneider; also to Fantasy Films, to Miramax, and to Phil Bray for the photographs from the set of *The English Patient.* Thank you also to Walter Murch, Jr., for his work on obtaining "pulls" from various films, and also Sean Cullen.

Thank you to John Berger, to Donald E. Westlake, to Dai Vaughan for the use of quotes from *The Invisible Man* (BFA), to Sharon Thesen, Atom Egoyan, Alexandra Rockingham, Gill Dennis, Davia Nelson, Kim Aubrey at Zoetrope, Ellen Harrington, The Directors Guild of Canada, and Ellen Levine and Tulin Valeri.

Finally thanks to the following who helped me with the manuscript at various times during the early drafts: Esta Spalding, Griffin Ondaatje, Linda Spalding, Liz Calder, and Sonny Mehta.

And to Saul Zaentz.

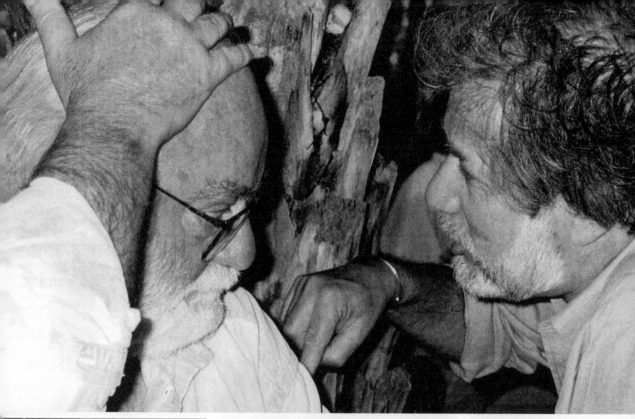

181A-G 5/7

181A-G 6/7

181J 1/3

181J 2/3

PHOTO CREDITS

Frontmatter by Phil Bray © 1996 The Saul
Zaentz Company. All rights reserved/
© Miramax Films

Half-title page by Phil Bray © Miramax Films/
MPTV

Title page left by Kim Aubry © American
Zoetrope; right from The Murch Family
Collection

Copyright page: right page © Warner Brothers

vi from The Everett Collection

viii–ix all © American Zoetrope

x by Phil Bray © 1996 The Saul Zaentz
Company. All rights reserved/
© Miramax Films

xxii–xxiii © American Zoetrope

First Conversation

2 by Kim Aubry © American Zoetrope

7 © American Movie Classics

8 © Robert Doisneau/RAPHO

11 from Photofest

12 from Photofest

13 from Photofest

14 by Matthew Robbins/The Murch Family
Collection

16–17 © American Zoetrope

18 from Photofest

21 from The Murch Family Collection

22 left from The Murch Family Collection;
right from MPTV

23 left from The Murch Family Collection;
right by Francis Ford Coppola

24 from Culver pictures

25 © Films du Carrosse/SEDIF

28–29 left to right, courtesy Dede Allen; from
Photofest; The Ronald Grant Archive

30 courtesy of The Academy of Motion
Picture Arts and Sciences

31 by Richard Biggs © American Zoetrope

35 from Movie Still Archives

40 courtesy of Michael Ondaatje

42 both © American Zoetrope/Paramount

44 courtesy Walter Murch

48 by Phil Bray © 1996 The Saul Zaentz
Company. All rights reserved/
© Miramax Films

52 from Photofest

55 by Wayne Miller/Magnum Photos

56 from The Ronald Grant Archives

57 by Mary Ellen Mark

60–61 all © American Zoetrope/Paramount

62 from Photofest

67 both © American Zoetrope/Miramax

71 © American Zoetrope/Paramount

72 by Jacqueline Lopez

75 © American Zoetrope/Miramax Films

314 by Susan Sterner/A.P. Wide World
Photos
317 by Susan Sterner/A.P. Wide World
Photos
318 top from The Everett Collection; bottom
by Phil Bray © 1998 The Saul Zaentz
Company. All rights reserved
320 top by Annette Carducci; bottom courtesy of Walter Murch
340–341 by Phil Bray © 1996 The Saul Zaentz
Company. All rights reserved/
© Miramax Films
342 by Phil Bray/Globe Photos/Rangefinders
343 courtesy of Walter Murch

Front Cover

Top row left © Metro Tartan/Block 2/Par-
adis/Jet Tone, right from The Neal Peters
Collection; center row left to right, from
The Everett Collection, The Neal Peters
Collection, the Ronald Grant Archives;
bottom row left from Photofest, right the
Neal Peters Collection

Back Cover

Top from the Neal Peters Collection;
center row left from Photofest,
right The Murch Family Collection;
bottom row left from Photofest, right
© Metro Tartan/Block 2/Paradis/Jet
Tone

Spine

Left © Miramax Films, right top from Globe
Photos, center The Lester Glassner
Collection/Neal Peters, bottom by
Annette Carducci

I N D E X

Page numbers in *italic* refer to illustrations.

English Patient, The (film), xii, xiv, xvii,
    xviii, 34, 44, *48,* 160, 166, *205,* 236,
    303, 316
    Almásy and Katharine's love scene at
        Christmas party in, xvii, *303,* 303–4,
        305–6
    Almásy's final confession in, 131–34, *135*
    bedridden central character in, 176, 178
    Caravaggio's interrogation in, xix–xxi,
        254, 255, 257
    convergent structure in, 253–55
    editing notes from, *44*
    experience of reading book vs. viewing
        film and, 47
    formal dance sequence in, *301,* 301–3
    Hana after her good-bye to Kip in, *x,* 134
    Hiroshima sequence cut from, 213
    multiple points of view in, 251, 253–55
    Murch's research for, 204
    music in, 171–72, *172,* 274
    photo board for, *237*
    screenplay for, 127, 129, 156
    sound of desert in, 117–18
    sound of distant bell in, xv–xvi, 244–45
    time transitions in, xv–xvi, xix, 124–25,
        129, 130, 156–57, 251
English Patient, The (Ondaatje), 47, 111,
    127, 165, 248, 308, 309
Eraserhead, 117
Erin Brockovich, 26
Étant donnés . . . (Duchamp), 48
Evans, Bob, 97, 99–100, 102
even-tempered scale, 51
Exorcist, The, 113
eye blinks, cuts and, 141–42

failure, success and, 307–8
family life, blending of artistic pursuits
    and, 232

Faulkner, William, 176
Fellini, Federico, 22
Fiennes, Ralph, *48,* 301, *301, 303,* 306
Figgis, Mike, 214
fight scenes, 41–42, 91, 276, 277
film adaptations, 25, 126–30, 144
film history, xiii
    early influences in, 88–94
    early technological achievements and,
        88, 89, 93–96, *94–95*
    Eastern vs. Western traditions and, 107–9
    societal changes and, 92–93
film libraries, 20, 97
Film Quarterly, 181
Finian's Rainbow, 14
Finney, Albert, *56,* 59
first drafts:
    of books, 37, 38, 45–46, 219
    of films (assemblies), 31, 36–38, 45, 49,
        238–39, 271–72
    of poems, 136, *138*
First Knight, 316
Fishburne, Larry, 77–78
Fitzgerald, F. Scott, 208
Fitzgerald, Zelda, 208
Flaherty, Robert, 226
flashbacks:
    more than one person having, 251
    time transitions and, xv–xvi, xix,
        124–25, 128–30, 156–57
Flaubert, Gustave, 88, 89, 127
Fly, The, 285
Follett, Ken, 165
Fonda, Henry, *300, 302–3,* 303
Fonda, Jane, 225, 227, *228*
Ford, Ford Madox, 149
Ford, Harrison, 69–70, 163, 279
Ford, John, 164, 208
foreign languages, without subtitles,
    121–22

Heston, Charlton, *177,* 188, *194–95, 195–96*
history of film, *see* film history
Hitchcock, Alfred, 114–15, 164, 190, 216,
 216, 217, *218,* 257
Hodgson, Les, 64
Hollywood studio system, 12, 15, 97, 99
Hopper, Dennis, 3
House of Cards, 316
Housing Problems, 96
Howard, Ron, *253*
Huppert, Isabelle, 127
Hustler, The, 25
Huston, John, 64–65, 142
hybridization, 235

I Ching, 296–98, 306
I Love Trouble, 316
Informer, The, 136
In the Blink of an Eye (Murch), xiv, xvi, 141
In the Mood for Love, 160, *161*
In the Skin of a Lion (Ondaatje), 308, 309
intimacy, 47, 48
 in narration, 64–65
"Intrusive Burials," 283

James, Henry, 235
Japanese film, 23, 107, 109
Job, 134
Joyce, James, 205
Julia, xiv, 32, 127, 129–30, *200, 223,*
 223–29, *224,* 315
 faulty shots in, 225–26, 227–29
 narration in, 63, 64
 shooting of rehearsals for, 225, 229

Kant, Immanuel, 108
Kaputt (Malaparte), 144, 148–49

Kastner, Peter, *97*
Kaufman, Philip, 129, *129,* 130, 131
Keaton, Diane, *252,* 253
Keitel, Harvey, 57–59
Keller, Harry, 184
Kelly, Grace, *161,* 222
Kershner, Irvin, 152
Key to Rebecca, The (Follett), 165
Kinetoscopes, 48
King Kong, 112, *113,* 206
Kirchberger, Michael, 82
Knight, Shirley, *12,* 243–44
K-19: The Widowmaker, 279, 317
Kubrick, Stanley, 22–23, 171, 224,
 229
Kundera, Milan, 128
Kurosawa, Akira, 22, 23–24, 27, 107,
 108

Lady Eve, The, 302–3, 303
Lady Vanishes, The, 114
Land of Oz, The (Baum), 286
Lang, Fritz, 112
Lawrence of Arabia, 26, *56,* 59
Lean, David, 27, *28–29,* 164
"leaping poetry" style, 34, 248
Leigh, Janet, *177,* 188, *188,* 189, *195,*
 195–96, *218,* 257
Leinsdorf, Erich, 247
length of film:
 single point of view and, 33–34
 two approaches to shortening of,
  136–40
lens choice, 197–99
Lesy, Michael, 291
Leung, Tony, *161*
Library of Congress, 94–95
Life, 152
light, sound compared to, 116–17

Wilder, Billy, 164, 165, 224
Wilhite, Tom, 283–85
Williams, Cindy, *249,* 265–66
Williams, William Carlos, 149
"Wind, The" (Malaparte), 147
Wisconsin Death Trip (Lesy), 290–91, *291,*
    292
Witherspoon, Reese, 251
Wizard of Oz, The (Baum), 292, 293
Wizard of Oz, The (film), xiv, 100, 112, 285,
    290
Wolfman Jack, 119
women, as editors, 26–27
Wong Kar-Wai, 160, *161*
Woodstock, 29
Wordsworth, William, 308
"worldizing," 119
Wright, Frank Lloyd, 217

writing:
    as discovery process, 128
    editing phase in, 38–41, 236, 294
    invention of, 295–96
    see also books; notation systems

Yared, Gabriel, 171, 274
Yeats, William Butler, 206
You're a Big Boy Now, 97, 162, 163, *220,*
    220–21

Zaentz, Saul, xvii, 87
Zinnemann, Fred, 63, 64, 104, *223,* 223–29,
    224, 228, 230, 239
    randomness sought by, 225–29
    rehearsals shot by, 225, 229

ABOUT THE AUTHOR

La Jetée by Chris Marker, edited by Jean Ravel (1963); *The Life and Death of Colonel Blimp* by Michael Powell, edited by John Seabourne (1943); *The Lady Eve* by Preston Sturgess, edited by Stuart Gilmore (1941); *Les Enfants du Paradis* by Marcel Carné, edited by Madeleine Bonin and Henri Rust; *The Searchers* by John Ford, edited by Jack Murray (1956); *The Hustler* by Robert Rossen, edited by Dede Allen (1961); *Edvard Munch* directed and edited by Peter Watkins (1974); *The Tree of Wooden Clogs*, directed and edited by Ermanno Olmi (1978); *Yeelen* (*Brightness*) by Souleymane Cisse, edited by Dounamba Coulibaly (1987); *The Grifters* by Stephen Frears, edited by Mick Audsley (1990); *Raise the Red Lantern* by Yang Ymou, edited by Yuan Du (1992); and *Ekti Jiban*, directed and edited by Raja Mitra (1988), about the man who spent his life compiling the Bengali dictionary.

A N O T E O N T H E T Y P E

This book was set in Minion, a typeface produced by the Adobe Corporation specifically for the Macintosh personal computer, and released in 1990. Designed by Robert Slimbach, Minion combines the classic characteristics of old style faces with the full complement of weights required for modern typesetting.

Composed by North Market Street Graphics, Lancaster, Pennsylvania

Printed and bound by R. R. Donnelley & Sons, Harrisonburg, Virginia

Designed by Kapo Ng